Cognitive-behaviour therapy for people with learning disabilities

Cognitive-behaviour therapy is a well known and widely used means of help-ing people overcome problems such as depression, anxiety and anger. *Cognitive-Behaviour Therapy for People with Learning Disabilities* marks an important new development in the care of people with learning disabilities by showing how cognitive-behavioural interventions can be applied to this much neglected client group.

The book contains contributions from highly experienced practitioner-researchers, who offer an informed approach to cognitively based treatments for a wide range of clinical problems. They also address clinical issues such as the use of self-instructional approaches, social problem-solving groups and working with carers of people with learning disabilities.

Since cognitive therapy is usually understood to be language based, the com-munication difficulties and challenging behaviours associated with this popu-lation make cognitive-behaviour therapy for people with learning disabilities a fascinating topic.

Cognitive-Behaviour Therapy for People with Learning Disabilities provides a wealth of practical examples for training and will be invaluable to clinical psychologists, psychiatrists and all researchers and practitioners who work with people with learning disabilities.

Biza Stenfert Kroese is Senior Lecturer in Clinical Psychology at the Uni-versity of Birmingham and Head of Clinical Psychology Services for People with Learning Disabilities in the Dudley Priority Health NHS Trust. **Dave Dagnan** is Lecturer in Clinical Psychology at the University of Birmingham, and **Konstantinos Loumidis** is a Clinical Psychologist at North Manchester General Hospital.

Cognitive-behaviour therapy for people with learning disabilities

Edited by Biza Stenfert Kroese,
Dave Dagnan and Konstantinos Loumidis

London and New York

First published 1997
by Routledge
11 New Fetter Lane, London EC4P 4EE

Simultaneously published in the USA and Canada
by Routledge
29 West 35th Street, New York, NY 10001

Typeset in Times by RefineCatch Limited, Bungay, Suffolk
Printed and bound in Great Britain by
Mackays of Chatham PLC, Chatham, Kent

British Library Cataloguing in Publication Data
A catalogue record for this book is available from the British Library.

Library of Congress Cataloguing in Publication Data
Cognitive-behaviour therapy for people with learning disabilities /
    edited by Biza Stenfert Kroese, Dave Dagnan, and Konstantinos Loumidis.
        p.   cm.
    Includes bibliographical references and index.
    1. Cognitive therapy. 2. Behavior therapy. 3. Learning disabilities –
Treatment. I. Stenfert Kroese, Biza, 1954– . II. Dagnan, Dave, 1960– .
III. Loumidis, Konstantinos, 1966– .
    RC489.C63C628 1997
    616.85′8890651–dc20   96–29129

ISBN 0-415-12750-5
    0-415-12751-3 (pbk)

Contents

Illustrations

Contributors

Laura Black, Forensic Clinical Psychologist, State Hospital, Carstairs, Lanarkshire.

Paul Chadwick, Honorary Senior Lecturer, Department of Psychology, University of Southampton, and Clinical Psychologist, Royal South Hants Hospital.

John Clements, Clinical Psychologist, Applied Psychology Services, Warlingham, Surrey.

Chris Cullen, Professor of Psychology of Learning Disabilities, Psychology Department, Keele University, and Consultant Clinical Psychologist, North Staffordshire Combined Health Care Trust.

Dave Dagnan, Lecturer in Clinical Psychology, University of Birmingham, and Clinical Psychologist, Solihull Health Care NHS Trust.

Jacqui Goldthorp, Research Assistant, School of Psychology, University of Wales, Bangor.

Andrew Hill, Clinical Psychologist and former Lecturer, Department of Psychology, University of Keele.

Robert S.P. Jones, Senior Lecturer in Clinical Psychology, School of Psychology, University of Wales, Bangor.

Albert Kushlick, Consultant Psychiatrist in Learning Disability, North Downs Community Health Trust, Greenlaws Resource Centre, Guildford.

Helen Lawrenson, Clinical Psychologist, Strathmartine Hospital, Dundee.

William Lindsay, Head of Clinical Psychology Learning Disabilities and Child Health, Dundee Health Care NHS Trust, and Professor of Learning Disabilities, University of Abertay, Dundee.

Konstantinos Loumidis, Clinical Psychologist, Department of Clinical Psychology, North Manchester General Hospital.

Beth Miller, Teaching Fellow, School of Psychology, University of Wales, Bangor.

Clare Neilson, Trainee Clinical Psychologist on the Doctorate Course in Clinical Psychology, Strathmartine Hospital, Dundee.

Raymond W. Novaco, Professor of Social Ecology, University of Irvine, California.

Julie Reed, Consultant Clinical Psychologist, Birmingham Children's Hospital NHS Trust, Birmingham.

Biza Stenfert Kroese, Senior Lecturer in Clinical Psychology, University of Birmingham, and Clinical Psychologist, Dudley Priority Health NHS Trust.

Peter Trower, Senior Lecturer in Clinical Psychology, School of Psychology, University of Birmingham.

Huw Williams, Clinical Psychologist, Oliver Zangwill Centre for Neuropsychological Rehabilitation, The Princess of Wales Hospital, Ely, Cambridgeshire, and Visiting Scientist, Cambridge University.

Preface

Raymond W. Novaco

It is certainly fitting, at a time of world-wide concern for the enhancement of well-being and a general enthusiasm for health promotion, that clinical scholars are here responding to the challenge to provide higher quality services to people with learning disabilities. Biza Stenfert Kroese, Dave Dagnan and Konstantinos Loumidis have composed an exciting volume of contributed writings that imparts important knowledge about the application of cognitive-behavioural interventions for this much neglected clinical population. This thoughtful book will stimulate innovations in both research and practice.

My own interest in the human and clinical needs of persons with learning disabilities is actually long standing. My very first research project, done as an undergraduate student in 1968 at the University of Notre Dame, concerned the development of curiosity and exploratory behaviour with children having 'moderate mental retardation', as was then the terminology in the States. The project was a behaviour modification study that was conducted with my faculty mentor, Bobby J. Farrow, in which we used lively music and rousing visual and audio effects as reinforcing stimuli for the children's manipulation of colourful cranks, plungers and levers operating as switches that activated the reinforcers. This training condition also involved learning to discriminate the active versus the non-active switches, all mounted on colourful wooden boxes inside a research trailer.

Before the multi-session training condition, we had put the children in a testing room that had many toys and seemingly interesting objects. The children did very little to examine them visually or by touch. Observed through a one-way window, they behaved much as had been expected of them – without curiosity or exploratory behaviour.

The training sessions consisted of a simple modelling of a switch operation and then leaving the child alone in the room for about 15 minutes to experience the effects of his or her own exploratory manipulations of the colourful devices. In contrast to the pre-test lethargy and self-containment, the post-training visit to the trailer's testing room produced dramatically different results in curiosity and exploration. Moreover, in a subsequent session in the training room, we reversed the active and non-active switches, and the children learned the reversal. We never got around to publishing that study, but Bob Farrow had already taught me psychology and inspired me for a lifetime before he helped me to see how foolish it is to underestimate what institutionalized children could do.

The application of cognitively based treatments to people with learning disabilities has been too often not attempted because it is assumed, tacitly if not explicitly, that the mental capacity is lacking. Reliance on externally controlled contingency management procedures has also proceeded with the belief that people with learning disabilities lack the capacity to self-regulate. Such an assumptive framework has been less than wise. Coincidentally, I have found to my delight that many of the contributors to this volume have been stimulated by another of my University of Notre Dame professors, Tom Whitman, whose article on self-regulation and mental retardation has prompted considerable discussion. Tom taught me behaviour modification when I was an undergraduate and served on my Collegiate Scholar honours committee.

Stenfert Kroese, Dagnan, Loumidis and the book's contributors here offer an informed approach to cognitively based treatments for a wide range of clinical problems affecting persons with learning disabilities, who often have dual diagnoses. The book is rich in practical and academic material. It offers insightful analyses of the needs of the focal population and clear ideas of the extension of cognitive approaches to assessment and treatment, showing the use of creative modifications of standard protocols to fit the cognitive capacity of the clients.

Should one wonder about what gains can be expected from applying cognitive-behavioural, self-regulatory therapies to persons with mental deficiencies, it would be wise to ask also about what affordances are normally provided to enable them to engage in such treatment. Preordained beliefs about the lack of fit between clients and this treatment mode will surely hinder client engagement and the development of innovative applications by clinicians and institutions. The learning of self-control coping skills is intrinsic to cognitive-behavioural interventions, and cognitive therapy is predicated on the human tendency to behave as guided by symbols, to seek meaning and to formulate strategies to optimize quality of life. It is very much about self-determination. As many contributors to this book make clear, people with learning disabilities are as much disabled by externally imposed impediments as they are by their own limitations.

Learning disabled persons, especially those who are institutionalised, unfortunately reside in environments that are inherently constraining and are too often peppered with aversive events. It takes little experience in care environments to recognise that distressed emotions are often part of the clinical picture. While there is now much discussion of 'challenging behaviour' regarding this client population, attention must also focus on the emotional antecedents and sequelae of such behaviour. Much of psychology has not only 'gone cognitive', it has also 'gone affective', and this book splendidly gives attention to the distressed emotional conditions of learning disabled people. It shows how cognitive approaches to the assessment and treatment of anxiety, anger and depression can be efficaciously extended to this client group.

One of the most pleasing aspects of this volume is that several contributions urge that care providers do not fix their focus on the individual but instead give consideration to the treatment context. Clinicians ought to think contextually about the target problems that they seek to remediate. Our clients' problems are embedded or nested within physical and social environments that are dynamically connected to problem manifestation and resolution. While traditional behaviour therapy has a tendency to neglect attention to environmental fields by focusing primarily on contingencies, cognitive therapy has a tendency to omit consideration of the external environments by thinking that they are all in the head. Because clinicians cannot easily 'import' the physical and social environment into the therapy room, ambient conditions that have recurrent impact on a client's well-being too easily pass from consideration. However, cognitive restructuring and self-regulation will not get very far in a life domain that lacks opportunities for self-fulfilment. People need motivation for self-regulatory control efforts. Beyond the adding on of new office-bound treatment techniques, we must continue to look towards clients' immersion in a therapeutic environment that envelopes their day-to-day functioning and allows them to view themselves, metacognitively, as agents and architects of their activity systems.

This book marks an important new development in providing care for people with learning disabilities. It invites you to enlist your clients in a collaborative treatment enterprise that is designed to foster self-efficacy and will prospectively facilitate better transfer of therapeutic gains. Moreover, as dedicated clinicians work diligently to apply cognitively based treatments to this population, we may learn a great deal more about cognitive deficiencies and thereby be stimulated to further innovations in treatment.

Acknowledgements

We are very grateful to Mrs Lena Stretton for her co-ordinating role and for preparing the manuscript. We also thank Guy, Sandie, Jacob and Emily for their personal and practical support and patience.

1 Cognitive-behaviour therapy for people with learning disabilities

Conceptual and contextual issues

Biza Stenfert Kroese

This chapter will provide a brief overview in order to put the application of cognitive-behaviour therapy* for people with learning disabilities into a historical, clinical and political context. The development of cognitive-behaviour therapy will first be briefly described, after which the application of one-to-one psychotherapy in learning disabilities services will be discussed. I will attempt to provide: (1) some background as to why people with learning disabilities rarely receive therapeutic services which allow them (and their therapists) to explore personal meaning; and (2) some information on how the potential barriers due to clients' cognitive deficits have been overcome in order to enable cognitive change and ultimately an increase in psychological well-being.

The chapter aims to be a 'taster' to this volume as a whole. Most of the issues discussed here will be presented in much greater depth in further chapters.

THE DEVELOPMENT AND PRINCIPLES OF COGNITIVE-BEHAVIOUR THERAPY

In the 1970s the application of behaviour therapy had become the preferred treatment for many psychological disorders, and the rejection of introspection pronounced over half a century ago (Watson and Rayner, 1920) continued to have a powerful influence over researchers and therapists with a behavioural orientation (Hawton *et al.*, 1989). However, some reservations started to be voiced regarding the exclusive use of learning theory as an underlying framework. Particularly, the research by Bandura (e.g. 1977) on observational learning indicated that cognitive mediation takes place during learning. In the clinical field, Kanfer and Karoly (1972) described a model of *self-control* consisting of self-monitoring, self-evaluation and self-reinforcement, and Meichenbaum (1975) convinced many that the concept of *mental* operant behaviour (coverants) is not only acceptable, but essential

---

* The term 'cognitive-behaviour therapy' is used predominantly throughout this volume as most approaches described combine cognitive and behavioural components. The term 'cognitive therapy' will refer specifically to Beck's (1976) treatment approach.

in explaining behaviour change. Other authors introduced the concept of *metacognition*, that is, 'knowing about knowing' and 'knowing how to know' (Brown, 1975) and specific *problem-solving techniques* (e.g. D'Zurilla and Goldfried, 1971).

Since then, cognitive-behavioural principles have been introduced into clinical practice on a large scale. There now exists a substantial body of evidence which indicates that cognitive-behaviour therapies can be effective for a wide range of psychological problems (see Hawton *et al.*, 1989). The underlying assumptions that these cognitive-behavioural approaches have in common can be summarised as follows:

- thoughts, images, perceptions and other cognitive mediating events affect overt behaviour as well as emotion or affect;
- focusing on these mediating cognitions in a systematic, structured manner can be an effective way of changing behaviour, emotion or affect;
- people are active learners, not just passive recipients of environmental influence. To some extent they create their own learning environment. Sometimes their specific learning histories result in cognitive dysfunctions;
- treatment goals centre around creating new adaptive learning opportunities to overcome cognitive dysfunctions and to produce positive changes for the client, which can be generalised and maintained outside the clinical setting;
- the client has an understanding of the intervention strategies and goals, and participates in planning and defining these.

Thus a cognitive-behaviour therapist makes the assumption that the psychological problems with which clients present are at least in part caused by cognitive dysfunction, and that clients' psychological well-being can be improved by teaching new and more adaptive ways of thinking.

COGNITIVE PROCESS AND COGNITIVE CONTENT

Kendall (1985) made the important distinction between two types of cognitive dysfunction – *cognitive deficits* and *cognitive distortions*. The former refer largely to problems in the cognitive *processing* whereas the latter are concerned with cognitive *content*.

The earlier cognitive-behaviour therapies were based on a *deficit* model and emphasised cognition as a process: that is, they addressed the deficits in the manner in which (1) people collect information about and interpret the world, and (2) they resolve problems. The aim of self-instructional training (Meichenbaum, 1975), for example, is to rote-learn and internalise a set of explicit self-instructions which are to replace or override maladaptive thoughts.

A number of more recent cognitive-behavioural approaches are more focused on identifying the actual *content* of thoughts and assumptions. Beck's (1976) cognitive therapy and Ellis' (1973) rational-emotive therapy are the two most influential of these approaches. Both assume that the content of *distorted* cognitions must be made explicit by the client and questioned by the therapist before 'guided discovery' (Young and Beck, 1982) can take place. That is, awareness and evaluation of the cognitive content are necessary in order to 'learn to view thoughts and beliefs as hypotheses whose validity is open to the test' (Beck *et al.*, 1979). Dagnan and Chadwick (in this volume) have adopted the distinction introduced by Ellis (1977) to discuss the origins and aspects of these *elegant* cognitive therapies and contrast them with more *simple* approaches. Also in this volume, Williams and Jones describe cognitive-behaviour therapies in terms of those which require *metacognition* and those which merely involve *rote-learning* of self instructions. Roberts and Dick (1982) previously made a related but nevertheless independent distinction. They identified that self-control can be either achieved through *contingency management* or through *cognitive change*. Similarly, Whitman (1990a and 1990b) talks of *passive* and *active* self-control methods and postulates that active self-control methods are more likely to produce lasting and generalised changes in behaviour.

Whether we describe certain cognitive-behavioural therapies as elegant, active, involving understanding or requiring cognitive change, they appear to have two aspects in common – a search for *personal meaning* and an assumption of *self-determination*. The question posed here is: Why do people with learning disabilities so rarely receive therapy (be it cognitive-behavioural or not) which contains both these ingredients?

PERSONAL MEANING

The meaning of people's overt behaviour is discussed at length by Lovett (1985) in his book *Cognitive Counselling and Persons with Special Needs*, which is a critique of traditional behavioural approaches to people with learning disabilities. He observes that carers and professionals who work with people with learning disabilities sometimes describe the behaviours of their clients in a seemingly objective but meaningless way (e.g. attention-seeking) rather than specifying the possible motivation or emotion driving that behaviour (e.g. wanting to make more friends or feeling bored or lonely), thus ignoring the meaning of the behaviour and labelling a person's wish for human contact in a negative way.

Some data reported by Harper and Wadsworth (1993) illustrate this point. A group of adults with learning disabilities who had recently experienced a significant loss were asked how they expressed grief and dealt with their loss. A group of carers and professionals were also asked their views of how people with learning disabilities cope and respond during grief. The participants with learning disabilities reported mainly *emotions* such as loneliness, anxiety, sadness, depression, dislike of the new residential place, worry about not being able to locate the grave or inadequate income. Only a small percentage of responses concerned *behaviour* (decrease in activities and behaviour problems). The carers and professionals, on the other hand, reported largely on *behaviours* or somatic symptoms such as crying, sleep problems, hostility towards others, passivity and poor hygiene, and very few responses concerned *emotions*. Thus, the personal experience and meaning of grief reactions were largely ignored by carers, although clearly reported by the participants with learning disabilities.

SELF-DETERMINATION

Lovett (1985, p. 33) also stressed the importance of self-determination, especially through creating a collaborative relationship rather than an authoritarian one between the therapist and the client:

> I think that the relationship between the person helping and the person helped is often a critical variable. I think it is more than just 'playing with words' to say that when we 'treat' a person, we are putting ourselves in a relationship that is very different (and for me, less desirable) than when we work with a person on a challenging situation.

Working *with* a person on a challenging situation means that the client is centrally involved in determining therapy goals and the methods by which these will be achieved. The literature that describes the application of cognitive-behaviour therapy for people with learning disabilities indicates that this collaborative relationship does not often exist. An overview by Harchik, Sherman and Sheldon (1992) of fifty-nine studies using self-management techniques showed that nine of these studies addressed the reduction of challenging behaviour and fifty aimed to increase social skills or performance (accuracy and speed) in academic or work settings. The authors conclude that self-management procedures are effective for people with learning disabilities but note that 'methods to expand the range of self-management procedures to include those that more fully involve the person in the design of the procedures would be of interest to researchers and practitioners' (p. 222).

Such an initiative would also perhaps be of some interest to the client. Cognitive-behavioural *treatments* applied to people with learning disabilities have been almost exclusively concerned with social control and therapy goals are largely determined by the therapist or instructor. Success has been measured in terms of productivity and/or the eradication of challenging behaviours. The psychological well-being of the client is rarely mentioned as an outcome measure.

WHY THIS THERAPEUTIC DISDAIN?

The lack of reported studies where a collaborative relationship has existed between the client with learning disability and the therapist is not unique to cognitive-behaviour therapy. Bender (1993) talks about 'therapeutic disdain towards people with a learning difficulty'. There is a higher incidence of psychological disturbance in people with learning disabilities (e.g. Reiss, Levitan and McNally, 1982; Lund, 1985) and consequently a greater need for psychotherapeutic services. However, Bender's description of the attitudes of mental health professionals towards clients with learning disabilities strongly suggests a common ethos of pessimism and rejection. Freud (1904) stated that psychoanalysis is not suitable for 'those patients who do not possess a reasonable degree of education and a fairly reliable character' (1953, p. 263). Since then, with very few exceptions, psychoanalysts and other psychotherapists have strictly adhered to the principle that learning disabilities are contra-indicative of successful outcome (Tyson and Sandler, 1971). It is interesting to note that the exceptions, (i.e. those therapists who *did* provide therapy for people with learning disabilities) shared the notion (described by Gunzburg in 1974 and more recently expounded by Sinason, 1992) that learning disabilities are often the *result* of social and psychological distress in early life. Sinason has described the phenomenon of 'becoming stupid' as a mechanism to protect the self from 'unbearable memory of trauma'. Therefore, a possible outcome of effective psychoanalysis or psychotherapy is an increase in intellectual functioning (e.g. O'Connor and Yonge, 1955).

Since Sinason's publications and an edited book by Waitman and Conboy-Hill (1992) entitled *Psychotherapy and Mental Handicap*, more psychotherapists have been inspired to consider the possibility of entering into a therapeutic relationship with people who may have limited verbal skills and be seemingly unresponsive to their environment (see Beail (1995) for a review of this area).

A parallel development has taken place in the cognitive-behavioural field. Other than psychotropic medication, the therapy of choice for people with learning disabilities was behavioural, usually aimed at controlling or changing the individual's behaviour through external contingency management. With the increasing influence of normalisation principles (Wolfsenberger, 1972), the sole use of contingency management programmes (particularly avoidance contingencies) has become less acceptable to practitioners (Chadwick and Stenfert Kroese, 1993). Added to this, positive, non-aversive therapies (e.g. Carr and Durand, 1985; La Vigna and Donnellan, 1986) were found to be effective for people with challenging behaviours and learning disabilities. These methods still employ behavioural principles but they combine the traditional behavioural approach with constructional principles (Goldiamond, 1974) and emphasise the importance of perceived control, real choice and the opportunity to express oneself. This has made professionals more inclined to 'listen' (even if the client is non-verbal) in order to extract personal meaning from the clients' utterances or their overt behaviours, and to create a collaborative relationship (where therapy goals are negotiated) rather than an authoritarian one. However, although the pure Skinnerian 'black box' approach to cognitive processes has been rejected by most, and people with learning disabilities are now credited with thought (be it verbal or non-verbal), cognitive-behaviour therapists have so far failed to show any great interest in welcoming these clients into their clinical practices.

Bender (1993, p. 11) is critical of the widely held view that the existing cognitive-behavioural techniques are inappropriate. He postulates that the most likely explanation for the exclusion of people with learning disabilities is 'that psychotherapy involves intensely relating over quite a long period to another person – a certain kind of intimacy. The giving of this intimacy is more difficult, aversive and more energy consuming when that person is seen as unattractive'. If we agree with Bender that we have a moral obligation to provide the same psychotherapeutic services for people with learning disabilities as we do for the rest of the population, the question remains whether cognitive-behaviour therapies can be adapted to meet the needs of people with limited intellectual functioning. We have already seen that cognitive-behaviour therapies which deal with the *process* level of cognitions are very effective in addressing cognitive deficits (e.g. Harchik *et al.*, 1992). Indeed, it is because cognitive deficits are by definition more prominent in people with learning disabilities that these therapies have been so widely employed. Moreover, cognitive deficits are more easily identified, (task-) analysed and measured as this can be achieved by observing overt behaviour and there is no need for self-report. For example, Thierman and Martin (1989) devised a training package with a self-management component for four adults with severe learning disabilities in order to improve the quality of their household cleaning. They identified four cleaning tasks and used sequential picture cues, self-monitoring (the client placed a marker next to the picture, signifying that the area had been cleaned), feedback on performance and public posting of results. The baseline and follow-up measure consisted of the number of inconspicuously placed markers cleaned from the appropriate surfaces (e.g. toothpaste smears on the bathroom mirror). Thus, an easily quantified, accurate, objective and purely behavioural measure was used to assess the efficacy of a self-management technique.

When attempts are made to access cognitive *content* (i.e. to ask 'what is the person thinking?'), however, some type of self-report is an essential part of the measurement procedure. Cognitive distortions involve complex, abstract concepts, often related to emotional states. To report on these may be problematic for a client who also has cognitive deficits. Morover, the therapist who addresses cognitive distortions with their client may expect complex outcomes where causal links are difficult to make in the absence of valid and reliable self-reports. For this reason, it is much more challenging to be a proper 'scientist-practitioner' who can add to the existing body of scientific knowledge.

I will briefly address a number of questions regarding the adaptability of cognitive-behaviour therapy for this client group by drawing on some of the existing empirical knowledge. They are:

- can people with learning disabilities report on their own cognitions in a valid and reliable manner?;
- can deficits in comprehension and expression of abstract concepts be overcome?;
- can deficits in self-regulation be overcome?

A more comprehensive discussion of these topics is the main purpose of this book as a whole.

CAN PEOPLE WITH LEARNING DISABILITIES SELF-REPORT?

Self-reports of people with learning disabilities have been considered to have only limited use by a number of authors (e.g. Balla and Zigler, 1979) because of the greater likelihood that factors such as social desirability (including acquiescence and dependency), memory problems, recency effects, anxiety and incomprehension threaten their validity. Any self-report instrument is open to such criticisms (Anastasi, 1982) but researchers such as Sigelman *et al.* (1981) found a significant correlation between levels of acquiescence and intelligence. However, it has also been shown that such pronounced effects can be overcome by applying a number of minor modifications in the construction of self-report materials for people with learning disabilities. For example, the use of pictorial materials instead of (or in addition to) auditory presentation of the assessment items can be used to aid understanding and memory (Kabzems, 1985). Open-ended rather than yes/no questions can avoid acquiescence (e.g. Sigelman *et al.*, 1982) and inserting a probe after each assessment item in order to elicit examples or further detail from the client will establish whether the item has been understood and answered in a valid way.

Jahoda, Markova and Cattermole (1988) described an approach which attempts to collect valid and reliable data regarding self-concept and the experience of stigma in people with learning disabilities. The interviewer spent approximately 12 hours in total prior to the interview with each interviewee in order to gain their confidence and presumably to reduce interfering variables such as social desirability, anxiety and incomprehension. They found consistent response patterns which indicated that the participants had awareness of the stigma attached to being 'handicapped' and had developed a 'cognitive-emotional' awareness of themselves in relation to other people.

Lindsay *et al.* (1994, but see also Lindsay, Neilson and Lawrenson in this volume) presented people with mild and moderate learning disabilities with a battery of independent (but related) self-report measures. They found a high degree of convergent validity in the responses, indicating a stable and reliable cognitive system related to emotion.

On a less abstract plain, Voelker *et al.* (1990) used self-report measures in order to establish whether people with mild learning disabilities can reliably report on their own adaptive and maladaptive behaviours. For this purpose, they compared self-report with the reports of care staff. They found high consistency between the two groups for adaptive behaviour scores but the maladaptive behaviours were under-reported by the participants themselves when compared to the reports of the care staff. The authors postulate that the participants with learning disabilities had shown a tendency to response bias in a socially desirable direction when asked about their challenging behaviours. However, an alternative explanation could be that care staff had *over*-reported maladaptive behaviours, possibly because these behaviours induce stress responses in staff (e.g. Lally, 1993) which may bias their judgements regarding the individual and the range, severity and frequency of the individual's challenging behaviours. One would have to introduce a third measure, based on objective, longitudinal and systematic observations, in order to resolve this issue. This also goes for Benson and Ivins' (1992) interpretation of the finding that staff usually rate their clients as 'angrier' than the clients rate themselves. They attribute these results to a response bias (denial, changeability or fatigue) on the part of the clients rather than the members of staff. However, their general conclusion is that people with learning disabilities can self-report on emotional states (anger and depression) when slightly modified questionnaires are used.

CAN DEFICITS IN COMPREHENSION AND EXPRESSION OF ABSTRACT CONCEPTS BE OVERCOME?

There is a wealth of evidence to suggest that people with learning disabilities are often unclear or confused about even basic concepts relevant to the psychotherapeutic setting. It is therefore important to assess people's understanding of concepts related to causes and consequences of cognitions, affect and behaviour before therapy, particularly where cognitive-behaviour therapy is concerned. For example, Reed (in this volume) describes her own (Reed and Clements, 1989) and others' research concerning the problems that people with learning disabilities have with recognising and expressing basic emotions such as 'happy' and 'sad'.

Emotions are not the only area which may pose problems in comprehension and expression. A number of studies have investigated the conceptualisation of death in people with learning disabilities. Emerson (1977) states that emotional disturbance or challenging behaviours are frequently associated with death or loss. This emotional vulnerability has been supported by other studies (e.g. Day, 1985) and it has been suggested that: 'Intellectual impairment and communication deficits can complicate the grieving process because the individual may experience greater difficulties in expressing emotions, adapting to changes in relationships, and understanding the difference between life and death' (Harper and Wadsworth, 1993, p. 315). Indeed these authors found that the cognitive understanding of death (e.g. understanding its irreversibility and universality) was patchy in approximately one fifth of their sample of thirty-seven adults with moderate to severe learning disabilities. Similarly, McEvoy (1989) had previously found that over one-quarter of his sample answered 'yes' to the question 'Can you make dead people come back to life?' and less than three-quarters of the sample answered affirmative to 'Does everybody die?'. Confusion about the irreversibility and universality of death may lead to more severe and prolonged emotional disturbance after the death of a relative or friend because the person with learning disabilities may be waiting for the death 'to cease' or may feel angry and deserted by the deceased if they perceive death as optional rather than inevitable.

Such cognitive confusion regarding irreversibility and subsequent emotional turmoil may also be apparent in the case of other loss events such as parents' divorce or placement into residential care. Frequently, a person with learning disabilities will experience a number of loss events in rapid succession, as a death in, or break up of, the family may result in emergency or long-term admission into residential care (Wadsworth and Harper, 1991). The person with learning disabilities is all too often excluded from discussions or rituals surrounding these significant life events, causing further confusion and mystification. In the worst (but not unlikely) scenario, the person's emotional reactions are then 'treated' through simplistic behavioural or psychopharmacological methods. The resulting cognitive framework may then well and truly be described as *learned helplessness* (Seligman, 1975). If the person is fortunate enough to receive a more sophisticated psychological service, one of the first and most crucial tasks of the therapist will be to assess the conceptual knowledge base of the client and then to provide sufficient factual (and honest) information regarding the past loss events.

Another issue relevant to therapeutic interactions is the client's ability to comprehend and appreciate humour. The therapeutic effectiveness of humour for people with learning disabilities has been described by authors such as Davidson and Brown (1989). However, people with learning disabilities are at greater risk of being subjected to 'abusive humour' (Lally, 1993) and it is important that the therapist, when using humour to create a relaxed atmosphere or to increase positive affect, is confident that the client has the cognitive prerequisites to comprehend the jokes. According to Short, Basili and Schatschneider (1993) the ability to understand humour is determined not only by level of cognitive ability but also by degree of social knowledge, awareness and sensitivity. They found that 10-year-old children with mild learning disabilities showed deficits in humour comprehension ('What is funny about this cartoon?') and in differentiating between funny and neutral cartoons. When jokes are made, people with learning disabilities may laugh in order to respond in a socially desirable way even if they don't understand the humour. Because they are likely to have past experiences of abusive humour, their lack of understanding may make the interaction aversive to them. Any therapist tempted to make jokes whether they be informal asides or carefully planned therapeutic interactions must therefore be aware of their clients' level of humour comprehension.

These examples illustrate the necessity of careful assessment of clients' knowledge and comprehension of, as well as their ability to express, abstract concepts. Some innovative and clinically useful assessment methods are discussed throughout this volume.

CAN DEFICITS IN SELF-REGULATION BE OVERCOME?

Whitman (1990a and 1990b) defines 'mental retardation' (the North American term for learning disabilities) not as the problem of learning *per se*, but a problem in *generalising* acquired skills to new situations and in *discriminating* between appropriate and inappropriate situations in which to execute these learned behaviours. These deficits are, according to Whitman, closely associated with a failure to transfer from an external to an internal locus of control. This transfer in turn is said to be largely dependent on the development of language, as language enables 'inner speech' and therefore allows the individual to develop 'rule-governed' behaviour (Vygotsky, 1962). See Jones *et al.* and Williams and Jones (Chapters 2 and 5, this volume) for a more detailed discussion of the function of language in learning and self-regulation.

In addition, many authors have commented on the lack of self-regulation in people with learning disabilities due to experiential deprivation (e.g. Shapiro, 1981; Zigler and Balla, 1982; Whitman, 1990a). Children and adults with learning disabilities are often exposed for long (and sometimes indefinite) periods to segregated institutional settings where there are few external motivating factors. That is, the physical environment is bereft of stimulation, interactions with carers are brief and inconsistent, and carers' expectations of the person are low. This will result in motivational disorders because the normal developmental process where the individual sets goals and performance standards for her/himself does not occur. Moreover, the experience of a long history of failure will discourage the individual from trusting their own cognitive resources (Zigler and Balla, 1982), resulting in dependency and apathy and negative self-attributions which in turn lead to low self-esteem. The question for the cognitive-behaviour therapist is whether these inherent and acquired motivational disorders can be ameliorated by means of psychotherapeutic sessions alone. Certainly, the difficulties of generalisation and maintenance of therapeutic gain have been discussed widely (e.g. Whitman, 1990a and 1990b) and a number of effective techniques to overcome these problems have been described in the literature. For example, the use of peer-mediated training (e.g. Knapczyk, 1989) has been shown to be successful in generalising and maintaining social skills.

However, this assumes that the client will enter into a 'reasonable' world after therapeutic change has occurred and that newly acquired coping techniques will be acceptable to others and will result in positive outcomes for the client. This may be the most challenging aspect for the therapist who aims to help her/his client to achieve a long-term increase in psychological well-being. Gunzburg's (1974, pp. 722–3) observations still hold today:

The ensuing disappointments, when 'warm' therapeutic sessions which have aroused hope end abruptly and the everyday institution life comes into full force again without any apparent changes, throws some doubt on the value of such isolated experimentation for the patient. It seems that far from being helpful, the lack of concrete results and the disappearance of personal interest may well strengthen the anti- and asocial attitudes of the patients who once again have been 'let down'.

There seems to be little justification for initiating therapy of that type merely in order to learn or to prove that it has value, unless it can be reinforced and followed up by concrete achievements. The therapist must, therefore, have some definite administrative power and some weight in the decisions concerning the future life of his patients.

Recent service developments have improved living conditions and the opportunities for clients to be involved in making choices for themselves. However, despite lengthy policy documents vowing allegiance to O'Brien's (1987) Five Accomplishments (community presence, community participation, choice, respect, competence), people with learning disabilities are still largely passive recipients rather than active consumers of support services (e.g. Simons, 1995). If self-regulation is seen in the light of empowerment and the *opportunity* (as opposed to the *ability*) to practise self-determination, people with learning disabilities are still more disabled by the external, material and political barriers which are put in their way than by their inherent disabilities. Some (e.g. Johnstone, 1995) argue that mental health and learning disabilities support services are not only remarkably ineffectual but are in fact *causing* clients' psychological problems. Johnstone (1995, p. 27) discusses this in the context of psychiatric rehabilitation: 'Most people need rehabilitation not mainly from their "illnesses" but from their "treatment" and this is just as true nowadays as it was in the days of Goffman's asylums.'

It is therefore important, for clinical as well as ethical reasons, to assess the influence of current environmental factors on the psychological distress of the client before cognitive-behaviour therapy is offered. If, after this assessment, the therapist concludes that the client is exposed to unacceptable living conditions, he or she may well need to consider whether in addition to clinical skills and knowledge 'some definite administrative power' (Gunzburg, 1974) is needed to enable long-term positive change to take place.

CONCLUSIONS

From a historical perspective the last decade has seen not only a growing interest in cognitive-behaviour therapies for people with learning disabilities, but also an increase in the application of psychotherapeutic methods in general. In fact, in Britain, some colleagues in psychoanalytic therapy, counselling and more eclectic fields had already discovered that people with learning disabilities are willing and able to enter into a search for personal meaning when cognitive-behaviour therapists started to make tentative moves towards exploring their clients' 'cognitive contents' and to use self-report and a collaborative therapeutic relationship to agree and achieve outcome goals. These recent explorations have shown that:

1 self-report can be a reliable and valid means by which to collect information;
2 people with learning disabilities can deal with abstract concepts, providing their knowledge and understanding are assessed and the therapist is prepared to take on a didactic role;
3 self-regulation (and therefore generalisation and maintenance of therapeutic gain) can be achieved but only if the client lives in a world where individual rights are respected and opportunities to practise self-determination are present.

It is the purpose of this book to present a collection of papers by researchers and clinicians who have all been personally involved in the development of this new and exciting area.

REFERENCES

Anastasi, A. (1982) *Psychological Testing* (5th edn). New York: Macmillan Publishing Co.

Balla, D. and Zigler, E. (1979) Personality development in retarded persons. In N.R. Ellis (ed.), *Handbook of Mental Deficiency: Psychological Theory and Research* (2nd edn), Hillsdale, NY: Laurence Erlbaum.

Bandura, A. (1977) Self-efficacy: towards a unifying theory of behavioral change. *Psychological Review*, **84**, 191–215.

Beail, N. (1995) Outcome of psychoanalysis, psychoanalytic and psychodynamic psychotherapy with people with intellectual disabilities: a review. *Changes*, **13**, 186–91.

Beck, A.T. (1976) *Cognitive Therapy and the Emotional Disorders*. New York: International Universities Press.

Beck, A.T., Rush, A.J., Shaw, B.F. and Emery, G. (1979) *Cognitive Therapy of Depression*. New York: Guilford Press.

Bender, M. (1993) The unoffered chair: the history of therapeutic disdain towards people with a learning difficulty. *Clinical Psychology Forum*, **54**, 7–12.

Benson, B.A. and Ivins, J. (1992) Anger, depression and self-concept in adults with mental retardation. *Journal of Intellectual Disability Research*, **36**, 169–75.

Brown, A.L. (1975) The development of memory: knowing about knowing, and knowing how to know. In H.W. Reese (ed.), *Advances in Child Development and Behavior*, Vol.10. New York: Academic Press.

Carr, E.G. and Durand, V.M. (1985) Reducing behavior problems through functional communication training. *Journal of Applied Behavior Analysis*, **18**, 111–26.

Chadwick, R. and Stenfert Kroese, B. (1993) Do the ends justify the means? Aversive procedures in the treatment of severe challenging behaviours. In I. Fleming and B. Stenfert Kroese (eds), *People with Learning Disability and Severe Challenging Behaviour*. Manchester: Manchester University Press.

Davidson, I.F. and Brown, W.I. (1989) Using humour in counselling mentally retarded clients: a preliminary study. *International Journal for the Advancement of Counselling*, **12**, 93–104.

Day, K. (1985) Psychiatric disorder in middle-aged, elderly mentally handicapped. *British Journal of Psychiatry*, **147**, 665–8.

D'Zurilla, T.J. and Goldfried, M.R. (1971) Problem-solving and behavior modification. *Journal of Abnormal Psychology*, **78**, 107–26.

Ellis, A. (1973) *Rational-Emotive Therapy*. Itaska, It: Peacock.

Ellis, A. (1977) The basic clinical theory of rational-emotive therapy. In A. Ellis and R. Grieger (eds), *Handbook of Rational-Emotive Therapy*. New York: Springer-Verlag.

Emerson, P. (1977) Covert grief reactions in mentally retarded clients. *Mental Retardation*, **15**, 46–7.

Freud, S. (1953) On Psychotherapy (1904). In *The Standard Edition of the Complete Psychological Works of Sigmund Freud*, Vol. XVI, London: Hogarth Press.

Goffman, E. (1961) *Asylums*. Harmondsworth: Penguin.

Goldiamond, I. (1974) Toward a constructional approach to social problems. *Behaviorism*, **2**, 1–84.

Gunzburg, H.C. (1974) Psychotherapy. In A.M. Clarke and D.B. Clarke (eds), *Mental Deficiency. The Changing Outlook* (3rd edn), London: Methuen & Co.

Harchik, A.E., Sherman, J.A. and Sheldon, J.B. (1992) The use of self-management procedures by people with developmental disabilities: a brief review. *Research in Developmental Disabilities*, **13**, 211–27.

Harper, D.C. and Wadsworth, J.S. (1993) Grief in adults with mental retardation: preliminary findings. *Research in Developmental Disabilities*, **14**, 313–30.

Hawton, K., Salkovskis, P.M., Kirk, J and Clark, D.M. (1989). *Cognitive Behaviour Therapy for Psychiatric Problems: A Practical Guide*. Oxford: Oxford University Press.

Jahoda, A., Markova, I. and Cattermole, M. (1988) Stigma and the self-concept of people with mild mental handicap. *Journal of Mental Deficiency Research*, **32**, 103–15.

Johnstone, L. (1995) What clinical psychology trainees will discover about psychiatric rehabilitation. *Clinical Psychology Forum*, **82**, 27–9.

Kabzems, V. (1985) The use of self-report measures with mentally retarded individuals. *The Mental Retardation and Learning Disability Bulletin*, **13**, 106–14.

Kanfer, F.H. and Karoly, P. (1972) Self-control. A behavioristic excursion into the lion's den. *Behavior Therapy*, **3**, 398–416.

Kendall, P.C. (1985) Toward a cognitive-behavioral model of child psychopathology and a critique of related interventions. *Journal of Abnormal Child Psychology*, **13**, 357–72.

Knapczyk, D.R. (1989) Peer-mediated training of co-operative play between special and regular class students in integrated play settings. *Education and Training in Mental Retardation*, September, 255–64.

Lally, J. (1993) Staff issues: training, support and management. In I. Fleming and B. Stenfert Kroese (eds), *People with Learning Disability and Severe Challenging Behaviour*. Manchester: Manchester University Press.

La Vigna, G.W. and Donnellan, A.M. (1986) *Alternatives to Punishment: Solving Behavior Problems with Non-Aversive Strategies*. New York: Irvington Publishers.

Lindsay, W.R., Michie, A.M., Baty, F.J., Smith, A.H.W. and Miller, S. (1994) The consistency of reports about feelings and emotions from people with intellectual disability. *Journal of Intellectual Disability Research*, **38**, 61–6.

Lovett, H. (1985) *Cognitive Counselling and Persons with Special Needs*. New York: Praeger.

Lund, J. (1985) The prevalence of psychiatric morbidity in mentally retarded adults. *Acta Psychiatrica Scandinavica*, **72**, 563–70.

McEvoy, J. (1989) Investigating the concept of death in adults who are mentally handicapped. *The British Journal of Mental Subnormality*, **35**, 115–21.

Meichenbaum, D.H. (1975) Self-instructional methods. In F.H. Kanfer and A.P. Goldstein (eds), *Helping People Change*. New York: Pergamon.

O'Brien, J. (1987) A guide to personal futures planning. In G.T. Bellamy and B. Wilcox (eds), *A Comprehensive Guide to the Activities Catalog: An Alternative Curriculum for Youth and Adults with Severe Disabilities*. Baltimore: Paul H. Brookes.

O'Connor, N. and Yonge, K.A. (1955) Methods of evaluating the group psychotherapy of unstable defective delinquents. *Journal of Genetic Psychology*, **87**, 89–101.

Reed, J. and Clements, J. (1989) Assessing the understanding of emotional states in a population of adolescents and young adults with mental handicaps. *Journal of Mental Deficiency Research*, **33**, 229–33.

Reiss, S., Levitan, G.W. and McNally, R.J. (1982) Emotionally disturbed mentally retarded people: an underserved population. *American Psychologist*, 37, 361–7.

Roberts, R.N. and Dick, M.L. (1982) Self-control in the classroom: theoretical issues and practical applications. In T.R. Kratochwill (ed.), *Advances in School Psychology*, Vol.2. Hillsdale, NJ: Laurence Erlbaum.

Seligman, M.E.P. (1975) *Helplessness – On Depression, Development and Death*. San Francisco: Freeman.

Shapiro, E.S. (1981) Self-control procedures with the mentally retarded. *Progress in Behavior Modification*, **12**, 265–97.

Short, E.J., Basili, L.A. and Schatschneider, C.W. (1993) Analysis of humor skills among elementary school students: comparisons of children with and without intellectual handicaps. *American Journal of Mental Retardation*, **98**, 63–73.

Sigelman, C.K., Budd, E.C., Spanhel, C.L. and Schoenrock, C.J. (1981) When in doubt say yes: acquiescence in interviews with mentally retarded persons. *Mental Retardation*, **19**, 53–8.

Sigelman, C.K., Budd, E.C., Winer, J.L., Schoenrock, C.J. and Martin, P.W. (1982) Evaluating alternative techniques of questioning mentally retarded persons. *American Journal of Mental Deficiency*, **86**, 511–18.

Simons, K. (1995) *My Home, My Life: Innovative Approaches to Housing and Support for People with Learning Difficulties*. Bristol: Norah Fry Research Centre.

Sinason, V. (1992) *Mental Handicap and the Human Condition*. London: Free Association Books.

Thierman, G.J. and Martin, G.L. (1989) Self-management with picture prompts to improve quality of household cleaning by severely mentally handicapped persons. *International Journal of Rehabilitation Research*, **12**, 27–39.

Tyson, R.L. and Sandler, J. (1971) Problems in the selection of patients for psychoanalysis: comments on the application of 'indications', 'suitability' and 'analysability'. *British Journal of Medical Psychology*, **44**, 211–28.

Vygotsky, L.S. (1962) *Thought and Language*. New York: John Wiley.

Voelker, S.L., Shore, D.L., Brown-More, C., Hill, L.C., Miller, L.T. and Perry, J. (1990) Validity of self-report of adaptive behavior skills by adults with mental retardation. *Mental Retardation*, **28**, 305–9.

Wadsworth, J.S. and Harper, D.C. (1991) Grief and bereavement in mental retardation: a need for new understanding. *Death Studies*, **15**, 101–12.

Waitman, A. and Conboy-Hill, S. (1992) *Psychotherapy and Mental Handicap*. London: Sage.

Watson, J.B. and Rayner, R. (1920) Conditioned emotional reactions. *Journal of Experimental Psychology*, **3**, 1–14.

Whitman, T.L. (1990a) Self-regulation and mental retardation. *American Journal of Mental Retardation*, **94**, 347–62.

Whitman, T.L. (1990b) Development of self-regulation in persons with mental retardation. *American Journal of Mental Retardation*, **94**, 373–6.

Wolfsenberger, W. (1972) *The Principle of Normalisation in Human Services*. Toronto: National Institute on Mental Retardation.

Young, J.E. and Beck, A.T. (1982) Cognitive therapy: clinical applications. In A.J. Rush (ed.), *Short-term Psychotherapies for Depression*, New York: Guilford Press.

Zigler, E. and Balla, D. (1982) The developmental approach to mental retardation. In E. Zigler and D. Balla (eds), *Mental Retardation: The Developmental-Difference Controversy*, Hillsdale, NJ: Laurence Erlbaum.

2 Theoretical and practical issues in cognitive-behavioural approaches for people with learning disabilities
A radical behavioural perspective

Robert S.P. Jones, Beth Miller, Huw Williams and Jacqui Goldthorp

There has been a tendency in work with severe learning disabilities for professionals to pursue one particular approach to the exclusion of others. Some have focused exclusively on the right of people with severe disabilities to live a normal life in the community. Others have used the technology of behaviour modification to the exclusion of all other approaches. There is a danger when one approach is pursued single-mindedly that the broad basis of relevant psychological knowledge will be ignored. This has happened to a disturbing extent with severe learning disabilities.

Watts, 1987, p. viii

There is clearly a general desire among practitioners to move beyond some of the more narrow confines of the available options for therapy that exist at present and to explore the relevance of cognitive-behaviour therapy for use with individuals with learning disabilities.

In this chapter we ask a number of basic questions in relation to this aspiration. Some of these concern fundamental issues to do with the nature of learning disability itself. These questions are as follows:

- is the move to cognitive interventions theoretically justified?;
- do existing behavioural interventions contain cognitive components?;
- can cognitive interventions be successfully adapted to a learning disabled population?

IS THE MOVE TO COGNITIVE INTERVENTIONS THEORETICALLY JUSTIFIED?

Evidence from a wide variety of sources suggests that the dominant model within learning disabilities has been that of applied behaviour analysis. There is considerable evidence that this model has been successful in a variety of areas, particularly in the development of new skills and in the reduction of challenging behaviour (Remington and Evans, 1988; Remington, 1991; Jones and Eayrs, 1993).

Since the early optimism of the late 1970s and early 1980s, evidence has consistently emerged that using animal-based principles for the modification of human behaviour is not always valid. In particular, this evidence includes work demonstrating that adult humans and animals respond differently to schedules of reinforcement (Leander, Lippman and Meyer, 1968; Lowe, 1979; Lowe, Harzem and Bagshaw, 1978; Lowe, Harzem and Hughes, 1978), although pre-verbal infants do not demonstrate these differences (Bentall, Lowe and Beasty, 1985; Lowe, 1983). We have argued elsewhere that this evidence suggests that *language* is the determining factor in accounting for these differences (Jones, Williams and Lowe, 1993). In this chapter we will explore in more detail the implications of these findings for the use of cognitive-behaviour therapy with people with learning disabilities.

Another factor of relevance to any discussion of the applicability of cognitive-behaviour therapy to people with a learning disability is that human behaviour is inherently more complex than that of animals and that therefore, to be successful, therapeutic interventions need to reflect this complexity. Criticisms have been voiced that applying interventions directly from the animal laboratory will inevitably fail to take account of this complexity. But is this the case?

It is possible to list the ways in which humans display complexity, which are not seen in other animals. Aspects of behaviour such as creativity, abstract reasoning and symbolic representations are clearly aspects of highly developed behavioural systems, but are they more than just complex behaviours? Put more simply, do these higher order mental processes still obey the basic laws of operant conditioning? Is a cognition merely a behaviour located under the skin which can be shaped, reinforced, brought under stimulus control, etc.? Research from the perspective of radical behaviourism seems to suggest that this may be the case and indeed many of the contributors to this book have shown how these very procedures can be applied to people with learning disabilities.

The importance of internal rules

Writing in the context of the literature on self-control, we have previously alluded to the inadequacy of the traditional behavioural perspective in explaining human choice behaviour (Jones, Williams and Lowe, 1993). This has been particularly evident in relation to traditional matching-to-sample experiments. For example, both humans and animals can learn to respond by touching a blue colour patch when the sample stimulus of the word 'Blue' appears (A–B). Humans simultaneously learn the reversal of this relationship (B–A) and, if they are also taught a second relationship B–C, they will spontaneously acquire not only the reversal C–B but also A–C and C–A (Sidman *et al.*, 1982).

This ability to form an equivalence class would not be possible if all behaviour occurred within the traditional behavioural three-term-contingency framework. It seems possible that humans are capable of internally representing their environment through language and making their own rules about it. It is this ability to formulate rules (rule-governed behaviour) which may underlie the relevance of cognitive-behavioural interventions in people with learning disabilities.

Lowe, Harzem and Hughes (1978) demonstrated that in humans the development of language results in rule-governed behaviour taking over from contingency-governed behaviour. Rule-governed behaviour is when the individual has learnt to describe the reinforcement contingencies operating in the environment (i.e. the behaviour is mediated by verbal behaviour). This verbal rule may well exert more control over the behaviour than the environmental contingencies. Traditional behaviour modification did not account for these abilities as it only focused on overt behaviour and environmental stimuli. As we shall see, however, the radical behavioural perspective of functional analysis has little difficulty in including cognitive factors such as internal rules, attribution, inner speech and meaning in any comprehensive analysis of an individual with learning disabilities. What is less clear, however, is whether thoughts or cognitions should be regarded as playing a causal role in the analysis of an individual's behaviour.

Do cognitions cause behaviour?

The relationship between cognitions and behaviour has been a source of both fascination and frustration to psychologists for many years and acrimonious debates continue. For example, Sheldon (1995, p. 37), demonstrating a clear misunderstanding of radical behaviourism, has recently stated that:

> The trouble with Radical Behaviourism is that it fails to distinguish between the person who sits, head in hands, on a railway platform for ten minutes because his train has been cancelled (again); and the person who sits in exactly the same position for exactly the same time who has recently lost a loved one and who may or may not jump under the next incoming service.

The field of cognitive-behaviour therapy is based on the premise that 'certain undesirable emotions and thoughts . . . cause undesirable patterns of living. On that basis these thoughts or emotions are targeted for change, control, or elimination' (Hayes and Wilson, 1994, p. 289). This assumption has achieved almost the status of a truism in the field of cognitive-behaviour therapy. In the widely burgeoning literature on cognitive-behaviour therapy it is comparatively rare to find authors questioning the basic assumptions behind the approach (but see Slocum and Butterfield, 1994).

Can we therefore assume that the case for the causal basis of cognitive events has been proven and that we can proceed to apply the principles of cognitive-behaviour therapy to people with learning disabilities with a strong degree of confidence in the theoretical basis of this approach? Unfortunately, this does not seem to be the case and the battle between behaviourists and cognitivists as to the ideological correctness of their respective approaches seems set to continue for some time yet.

For example, Lee (1992, p. 266) has argued that cognitive models of human behaviour are 'intrinsically unscientific; they have no explanatory value and limited descriptive ability . . . there is a danger that a focus on the development of cognitive models will distract theorists from behavior, the actual subject matter of psychology'. On the other hand, writers such as Bandura (1995, p. 237) have articulated the opposite position: 'A theory that denies that thoughts can affect motivation and action does not lend itself readily to the explanation of complex human behavior'. Slocum and Butterfield (1994, p. 59) make the important point that often these criticisms are based on a different 'worldview' of the other's position and that in reality: 'Behavior analysts criticize cognitivists for mentalism – in other words, for being cognitive. Cognitive psychologists criticize behavior analysts for explaining behavior only at the level of observation – in other words, for being behavioral.'

Perhaps the way around such tiresome and essentially arid debates is provided by the perspective of functional analysis. It is important to emphasise here that we do not mean the linear and comparatively narrow use of the term 'functional analysis' which has been adopted by some branches of behaviourism in the quest for an experimental analysis of behaviour using, for example, analogue assessment procedures (e.g. Iwata *et al.*, 1982). Rather, we refer to the meaning of the term which is derived from radical behaviourism and which recognises that relationships between variables are by their nature interactive and reciprocally causal (Owens and Ashcroft, 1982; Jones and Owens, 1992). As Spaulding (1995, p. 281) stated: 'Stimulus and response are two parts of a larger pattern of organisms' interaction with their environments. Linear causality becomes illusory or meaningless when the entire pattern is apprehended.'

Functional analysis and the role of cognitions

The functional analytic perspective which derives from radical behaviourism accepts that cognitions should be studied in their own right. The followers of radical behaviourism regard a cognition, like any other behaviour, as a legitimate focus of analysis. What may distinguish a functional perspective from that of a cognitivist, however, is in the assumed causality of a cognitive event. Whereas it is quite legitimate in cognitive terms to regard faulty cognitions as a *cause* of depressed mood, this assumption of linear causality would not be held in a functional analysis. Rather, an attempt would be made to analyse the environmental events which cause (a) the cognitive belief, (b) the depressed mood and (crucially) the relationship between the two (Hayes and Wilson, 1995).

What the perspective of functional analysis adds to the debate about the role of cognitions is this emphasis on the analysis of the way in which cognitive and environmental variables interrelate at a theoretical level (Owens and Ashcroft, 1982). A functional relationship may exist between these variables such that a change in behaviour may lead to a change in cognition, a change in thinking (e.g. cognitive restructuring) may affect the behaviour of the individual or there may be other factors which might influence both the cognitions and the behaviour. The emphasis on identifying and modifying as many of these other factors as possible may characterise the unique contribution of functional analysis.

This process may be illustrated by a discussion of a clinical case which involved the application of a functional analytic perspective to the analysis of persistent aggressive behaviour in a 20-year-old woman with mild learning disabilities.

Initial analysis showed a correlational relationship between aggressive outbursts and attention. A simple linear analysis could have interpreted this as a case of attention-seeking behaviour and sought to manipulate the environmental events surrounding this relationship. For example, the staff who worked with this woman could have been asked not to provide attention for such 'acting out behaviours' or the woman could have been taught to seek attention in more socially appropriate ways.

Further analysis, however, led to the questioning of why this woman seemed to need to engage in such attention-seeking behaviour. (In more analytic terms, rather than assuming a direct causal influence between aggression and attention, we were assessing whether there were any other factors which might have been related to either or both of those variables already identified.)

We discovered a number of important facts which were included in the case formulation:

1 she had extremely low self-esteem;
2 she believed she was responsible for the resignation of a favourite member of staff in the previous year;
3 she had been abandoned by significant others on a number of occasions in her past;
4 her mood rapidly alternated between mania and extreme depression;
5 she was jealous of an older sister who had recently been married.

From this wider perspective, formulating the case in a linear causal path seemed less than satisfactory. Rather than searching for a single factor (e.g. low self-esteem) to explain her aggressive behaviour, the functional analysis revealed a number of potential areas where help could be targeted, and a multi-modal treatment package involving both behavioural and cognitive elements was instigated.

Summary

It seems that from a theoretical perspective there are considerable advantages to including cognitive variables within an analysis of the psychological difficulties of people with learning disabilities. From the perspective of radical behaviourism (although the terminology differs) there are good reasons to regard elements such as thoughts, feelings, emotions, ideas, aspirations, expectations and beliefs as legitimate (and indeed important) aspects of behaviour. The danger lies in assuming causality where evidence for such linear analysis is absent. Cognitive events *may* directly cause behaviour but this will not always be the case. As Spaulding (1995, p. 282) states:

> Both Skinnerian and cognitivist clinicians can make the mistake of looking for 'causal primacy' as a way of selecting a target for treatment. This implicitly accepts a linear view, that there *is* a causally primary factor which, if not directly producing the behavior of interest, at least starts a cascade of determining consequences. We can sometimes find overwhelmingly powerful determinants, or strikingly clear and linear cascades, but this is the exception rather than the rule ... In most clinical problems, there are a number of potentially important 'causal' factors, some inferred but still measurable. Our time is better spent trying to influence as many of them as possible than pondering which is most causal in any particular case.

It may be already obvious that unlike many who adopt the perspective of applied behaviour analysis, we do not regard cognitive-behaviour therapy as theoretically misguided or alien to our basic understanding of human behaviour. From the perspective of radical behaviourism, we tend to agree with Spaulding that both behavioural and cognitive practitioners can make the mistake of adopting a linear view of behaviour and thereby missing much of importance to a case formulation. We also feel that many of the successful interventions which exist at present under the rubric of applied behaviour analysis include elements which, from another perspective, might be regarded as cognitive. We will now examine two of these: verbal self-regulation and functional communication training.

DO EXISTING BEHAVIOURAL INTERVENTIONS CONTAIN COGNITIVE COMPONENTS?

Verbal self-regulation

A therapeutic perspective which shares many elements in common with cognitive interventions but which has remained firmly within the behavioural perspective is known as verbal self-regulation. As discussed in Chapter 5, it has become increasingly popular to include aspects of self-management in behavioural intervention programmes although early development was hampered by overly pessimistic views of the ability of people with learning disabilities to benefit from such interventions.

There are a number of reasons why a move towards self-management has become more popular in recent years. First, by learning self-management skills, people with learning disabilities should be able to exert control over lives which are often characterised by very high degrees of dependency. Smith (1990, p. 103) has defined self-management as 'obtaining the skills involved to change one's own behavior and providing intervention for oneself'. Second, self-management has the potential to be used for extended periods of time in the absence of a treatment provider. Third, these techniques may be easily adapted and employed in a wide variety of settings. Finally, helping individuals to acquire the ability to regulate their own inappropriate behaviour may assist the future development of a range of desirable behaviours in addition to the behaviour targeted for intervention.

As with other interventions from a more explicitly cognitive background, the ability to self-regulate behaviour has, in the past, been widely regarded as being beyond the scope of people with learning disabilities (see Jones, Williams and Lowe, 1993 for a fuller discussion of this issue). There are, however, an increasing number of published case reports which suggest that this is not so. For example, Zegiob, Klukas and Junginger (1978) trained a young woman to self-monitor her own rate of self-injurious behaviour (nose and mouth gouging). Data were also presented on the stereotyped behaviour (head shaking) of a 15-year-old girl. Both individuals significantly reduced their levels of stereotypy while monitoring their own behaviour. When external consequences were added to the monitoring procedure, further reductions were noted.

More recently, Koegel and Koegel (1990) assessed whether four students with autism (aged 9 to 14 years) could learn to use a self-management treatment package to reduce their stereotyped behaviour. In their first study, three students were trained to record their own stereotyped behaviour in a treatment room and a fourth was trained in the same techniques in community settings. The students were able accurately to record instances when they were *not* engaged in stereotyped behaviour but they were inaccurate in their recordings of the presence of stereotypy. Despite this, all students showed decreases in their target behaviour during the intervention. In a second study, two of the students from the first study were observed in community settings and it was found that the self-management procedure was learned rapidly in these new settings and that reductions in stereotyped behaviour occurred for extended periods of time in the new settings without the presence of a treatment provider.

Similar results were found by Pope and Jones (in press) in a study which used self-monitoring to reduce the inappropriate behaviour of five people with a learning disability. Each person was taught to monitor and record the frequency of a specified target behaviour. The self-monitoring procedures led to significant reductions in the inappropriate behaviour of each person even though no extrinsic reinforcement was used throughout the study. Although the effects of the intervention did not maintain over time once a final baseline phase was implemented, the findings support those of Koegel and Koegel (1990) in showing the potential for people to use self-regulatory procedures to control their inappropriate behaviour with a minimum of external intervention and without the addition of external consequences to reinforce the reductions.

Perhaps the most interesting overall finding to emerge from the literature on self-control, however, is that individuals with learning disabilities appear to be able to self-regulate their own behaviour. This may not be that surprising considering the fact that the majority of studies on self-control concern people with mild disabilities. A more interesting question to ask is whether there is any evidence that people with severe learning disabilities are able to use similar strategies to modify their own behaviour. To answer this question we now briefly turn to examine the literature on functional communication training.

Functional communication training

This is an approach which includes many elements of verbal self-control but which also contains a detailed functional analysis. In recent years it has become a popular method of decreasing challenging behaviour and, although commonly reported as a behavioural intervention, it is important here because of the debate concerning the relevance of symbolic communication surrounding its success.

The rationale behind this approach is that inappropriate behaviours may function as verbal communicative acts to request specific reinforcers (positive and negative) that are socially mediated. Therefore if, for example, a particular behaviour is construed as a non-verbal request for attention, the suggested intervention strategy might involve teaching an alternative verbal means of obtaining attention. Success using this approach has been reported by a variety of researchers, primarily with self-injurious behaviour (e.g. Bird *et al.*, 1989; Carr and Durand, 1985; Duker, Jol and Palmen, 1991; Durand and Carr, 1991). Durand and Berotti (1991, p. 39) phrase the central issue in functional communication training as follows:

> This work makes one major (and to some, controversial) assumption; namely, that students with severe/profound mental retardation and multiple sensory impairments can learn a formal symbolic communication system. One basis for this assumption is that these students seem to use their problem behavior to access certain things from the environment (e.g., escape from demands, social attention, food). Our job becomes one of transferring their skills in nonsymbolic communication (i.e., problem behavior) to skills in symbolic communication (i.e., using assistive devices).

Regarding problem behaviour as communication is not new. Plato observed that the crying of infants may be an attempt to prompt a caregiver to fulfil their desires. In clinical interventions, family systems theorists have long relied on the idea that non-verbal behaviour has communicative properties (e.g. Hayley, 1963). Inevitably there can be lengthy debates concerning whether or not the success of functional communication training is due to any form of internal (symbolic) representation or whether the notion of communication is best viewed as a metaphor. Nevertheless, as with the examples of verbal self-regulation discussed earlier, the success of this work provides yet another example of the success of a form of intervention which was previously regarded as beyond the capabilities of people with a significant learning disability.

There are already some indications, therefore, that many individuals with learning disability can potentially benefit from cognitive interventions, even perhaps when these individuals are severely or profoundly disabled. We are not suggesting, however, that the relevance of learning disability *per se* should be ignored. Indeed, it is particularly important to recognise that there may be specific therapeutic techniques which will need considerable adaptation if they are to be successfully applied to this population and it is to this question which we now turn.

CAN COGNITIVE INTERVENTIONS BE SUCCESSFULLY ADAPTED TO A LEARNING DISABLED POPULATION?

There are a number of characteristics of people with learning disabilities which may have relevance to how cognitive-behavioural interventions are implemented in clinical settings. It is important, however, to emphasise that in the past it has been popular to view individuals with a learning disability as something of a homogeneous group. We have argued elsewhere that we do not believe such a global categorisation is particularly helpful in designing intervention packages due to the considerable individual variation found in any group of disabled people (Jones, Williams and Lowe, 1993). However, there are some characteristics which *may* be found more frequently among people with learning disability than among populations who more traditionally have been the recipients of cognitive-behavioural interventions. As such, clinicians will need to be aware of the possibility that these characteristics may influence the course of therapy for specific individuals. We are not suggesting, however, that *any* of the following characteristics will *inevitably* be found in a person labelled 'learning disabled'.

By virtue of being learning disabled there will be an increased probability that a number of cognitive deficits will be displayed by individuals. These may include speed of information processing, problem-solving, concrete thinking and difficulties with memory and language. Although the process of cognitive-behaviour therapy may be made more complicated by these difficulties, this volume attests to the fact that many individual clinicians have found innovative methods of overcoming these problems. In this section, however, we shall look briefly at three other areas of difficulty which are more difficult to overcome. These are motivation, self-esteem and social cognition.

Motivation

Zigler and Hodapp (1986) have pointed out that children with a learning disability often experience frequent failure which leads to low goal-setting, learned helplessness, negative self-image and an unwillingness to try which in turn fosters a dependency on others. Zigler, Balla and Butterfield (1968) suggest that social deprivation and institutionalisation result in a heightened motivation for social reinforcement (they learn to do things to please others) but also leads such children to be less intrinsically motivated. Furthermore, Merighi, Edison and Zigler (1990) suggest that social deprivation appears to result in increased motivation for social reinforcement which in turn seems to interfere with attention to learning tasks and even to decreases in IQ.

Contrary to the traditional belief that children must be motivated to learn, writers such as Vygotsky (1978) have said that children must also learn in order to be motivated (i.e. that there is also an influence of intelligence on the affective process). Vygotsky argues that a number of educational practices play a particularly damaging role in fostering this sense of helplessness and dependency on others. For instance, he strongly argues against grouping people of the same abilities together and against teaching which ignores abstract thought and uses the child's developmental level as a basis for teaching concrete concepts only. He suggests that we need to encourage more intrinsic motivation and emphasise co-operative learning strategies.

Vygotsky also said that the development of abstract thought not only facilitates the enhancement of intellectual skills but that the lack of development of abstraction leads to rigidity in the affective sphere and to the immaturity of motivation. For Vygotsky motivation is social, it is socially produced, socially internalised and socially realised.

Many people with a learning disability will have experienced precisely the kind of educational background which Vygotsky warns against. It is likely that a strong dependency on others and a high sense of personal helplessness will be characteristic of many who present for therapy. Perhaps inevitably there will be an initial dependency on the therapist to fix the problem and a slowness to develop a sense of personal empowerment and assertiveness. While these feelings may be common to many clients who present for cognitive-behaviour therapy, the work of such writers as Vygotsky and Zigler alerts us to the possibility that people with learning disabilities may be particularly prone to such behaviours and attributions and may find it especially difficult to change what for many will have been literally the habits of a lifetime.

Self-esteem

In relation to the above discussion it might seem almost self-evident that many individuals with a learning disability will have very low self-esteem.

For example, in looking at the motivations for challenging behaviour, we have found the following exercise to be useful in working with direct care staff:

> Imagine a world where you are constantly surrounded by individuals who are more skilful than you. You have memories of childhood where siblings, relatives and peers were all able to figure out things more quickly than you were. Imagine being able to remember the points in your upbringing where your younger siblings 'passed you by' in terms of problem-solving skills. Imagine being called names in school and getting used to people referring to you as 'stupid' or 'slow'. If this had been your past, year after year since as far back as you could remember, how would you feel if someone asked you to do something but you weren't quite sure what exactly they were asking of you? How would you feel? What would you do?
>
> (Jones, 1994)

Although, as a teaching aid designed to stimulate discussion, this example is deliberately extreme, it nonetheless raises important issues to do with the self-concept of people with learning disabilities. It is likely that in many cases, individuals with a learning disability will have personal histories replete with failure experiences and beliefs in their own incapability to manage environmental demands. It is very probable that the backgrounds of many people with a learning disability will contain far more negative environmental events than many non-disabled clients who will have developed very negative schemas concerning their own worth. Leaving aside the rather sterile argument about the causal role of self-efficacy discussed earlier, it may be that people with a learning disability will have considerably more unhappy personal experiences on which to base a negative view of 'the self, the world and the future' (Beck *et al.*, 1979) than other client groups. In particular, the experience of repeated failure and social rejection may predispose people with a learning disability to be very resistant to therapeutic change. As such, cognitive restructuring may have to work against personal backgrounds which by their very nature predispose towards the development of poor self-esteem and lowered self-efficacy. In some cases, interventions which specifically target improvements in self-esteem may be necessary as a prerequisite to more in-depth cognitive interventions.

In the past there have been comparatively few attempts either to measure or to increase self-esteem in people with any significant degree of learning disability. Indeed, there was considerable pessimism surrounding the ability of people with intellectual disabilities to give valid expression to their feelings and emotions (See Jones, Walsh and Sturmey, 1995 for a more detailed discussion). More recently, however, it is becoming increasingly clear not only that there exists a clear and full emotional life, even in people regarded as severely disabled, but also that aspects of this emotional life are open to empirical validation.

A particularly impressive example of research in this area was conducted some years ago by Lindsay *et al.* (1994). These authors demonstrated that a group of individuals with mild or moderate learning disabilities could show convincingly high levels of consistency in their reports about their own feelings and emotions. Lindsay *et al.* (1994) assessed a group of sixty-seven adults on a variety of self-report measures and found high levels of agreement across the measures (see also Chapter 8).

Clearly, however, there can be difficulties in attempting to measure self-concept accurately. It can be all to easy too impose a preconceived structure on the self-concept of someone with learning disabilities. Similarly, it is potentially easy to omit areas which may be important to the individual's self-perception. Such difficulties can, however, be overcome using measures specifically adapted to this population (Gowans and Hulbert, 1983). For example, Oliver (1986), showed how repertory grid techniques could be useful in assessing self-concept. He showed how a 14-year-old girl with Down's Syndrome who had an IQ 'in the 40s' could be helped, by the aid of photographs, to construct a grid which showed that she was able to recognise children with intellectual disabilities as being different from others. Of particular interest was the finding that she did not apply these differences to herself. The relationship between her view of herself, her ideal self, and others was clear and a repetition of the ranking task showed a reliability on each construct to be about 0.80 suggesting that 'the girl was able to apply the constructs meaningfully' (p. 25). This type of carefully conducted clinical research argues well for the relevance of measuring cognitive variables in people with learning disabilities.

Social cognition

It is perhaps in the area of social interactions where people with learning disabilities face their most severe challenges. There are many industrial and educational situations in which the degree and nature of any intellectual handicap can be minimised by teaching the individual to predict and plan for any likely difficulties. Interpersonal interactions, however, by their very nature are both unpredictable and highly complex while often containing ambiguous or contradictory social cues. Clements (1987, p. 43) provides a clear account of the complexity of skills that are needed in such situations:

> Cognition in social situations involves analysis of information from other people concerning their thoughts and feelings and use of this analysis to generate expectancies about the inner states and overt behaviour of others. Extracting social meaning involves processing a wide range of information – for example, information about the general physical context, the general nature of the social situation, the speech, body postures and facial expressions of others. From the analysis of presenting information and from knowledge available in memory, inferences are made about the general requirements of the situation and about many essentially unobservable

features of other people (their thoughts, emotions and general dispositions). Into this already complex picture the individual must integrate self-knowledge – the kind of person that he or she is, the 'messages' that are to be presented to others, the goals to be achieved from the specific social interaction. On the basis of all this information expectations will be generated about the behaviour of others and the individual will make plans for his or her own behaviour.

Given the range and complexity of these tasks it is hardly surprising that many people, not only those with learning disabilities, have difficulty with social interactions. This is a particularly important consideration for the disabled, however, because when such difficulties manifest themselves in poor or inappropriate social behaviour, a variety of disadvantages accrue to the individual. The work of Benson *et al.* (1985), for example, has shown an association between depression and poor social skills as perceived by others. Similarly, a host of research studies has shown that socially inappropriate behaviour in community settings almost always leads to negative valuing and rejection of the individuals displaying the behaviour (Jones, Wint and Ellis, 1990; Schalock, Harper and Genung, 1981). In addition to these difficulties, however, a further disadvantage may exist in the context of cognitive-behaviour therapy: simply that an advanced level of understanding of social cognition may be necessary if individuals are to benefit from cognitively based interventions.

A number of studies have highlighted specific deficits in the social cognitive system of some people with a learning disability. Perhaps the best known of these are the studies carried out in the 1980s by Baron-Cohen (e.g. Baron-Cohen, Leslie and Frith, 1985) looking at the concept of 'theory of mind' in people diagnosed as autistic. Other evidence, however, suggests that difficulties with social information processing may characterise a far greater proportion of the learning disabled population than just those who are autistic (Castles and Glass, 1986; Clements, 1987; Fuchs and Benson, 1995). In addition, as was mentioned earlier, there may be specific aspects of the life history of individuals with a learning disability which predispose them to having particular difficulties with motivation and self-concept. In working with non-disabled populations it is not uncommon to find individuals who may fully understand a situation but may not be able to respond appropriately due to disinterest or anxiety. It is also common to find individuals who fail to behave in appropriately assertive ways due to an excessive need to please others or to be accepted by a peer group. Clients with a learning disability may present a uniquely difficult combination of developmental and motivational factors which may require particularly skilled interventions.

Of special relevance to the present discussion, however, is the fact that a large component of cognitive-behaviour therapy requires the client to imagine different personal motivations for the behaviour of other people. Once again, it may be necessary to help clients to develop central prerequisite skills before being able to benefit optimally from cognitive-behaviour therapy. The specific combination of skills will differ from client to client but is likely to include the ability to attend to relevant social stimuli, to control impulsive responding, to be clearly oriented in time and space and to be able to report their feelings, thoughts and emotions verbally. Although this might seem to imply that a comparatively high degree of cognitive development will be necessary to benefit from cognitive-behaviour therapy in its pure form, it has clearly been the experience of many contributors to the present volume that cognitively based procedures can benefit this client group if sufficient modifications are made to the original procedures.

Adapting existing procedures

It seems clear from much of what has been written above that many of the existing cognitive-behaviour techniques will need to be modified if they are to prove of optimum benefit for people with learning disabilities. From a theoretical perspective, there should be little difficulty in achieving this end. There is no gold standard which defines 'pure' cognitive-behaviour therapy and indeed, as we have seen, no single accepted definition of what exactly constitutes cognitive-behaviour therapy (Williams, 1992).

Adaptations to cognitive procedures are, in fact, quite common and much helpful guidance already exists. Scott (1992), for example, has discussed the changes in cognitive therapy techniques needed when working with people with chronic depression suggesting that, while the characteristically structured nature of this approach may help this group, creativity and flexibility on the part of the therapist are also necessary. Similarly, Fowler, Garety and Kuipers (1995) have suggested a number of adaptations to cognitive-behaviour therapy needed when working with people with psychosis and Kendall and Braswell (1985) have discussed changes relevant to work with impulsive children. It seems, therefore, that not only is there a long tradition of adapting cognitive-behavioural interventions, but that many of these suggestions are also appropriate in working with people with learning disabilities. Typical suggestions involve having shorter sessions and abandoning rigid agendas (Scott, 1992), breaking complex emotional information into simple and clear components (Kendall and Braswell, 1985) and carefully controlling the induction of high emotional arousal (Fowler, Garety and Kuipers, 1995).

CONCLUSIONS

At the beginning of this chapter we asked some basic questions regarding the use of cognitive-behaviour strategies for people with learning disabilities. We can conclude by stating that there seems much benefit in applying such strategies and that this population is likely to benefit considerably from their widespread use. In particular, we have tried to show that the assumption that, because of reduced levels of intellectual ability, people will *de facto* be unable to benefit from cognitive interventions is not borne out by the existing literature.

As briefly mentioned earlier, perhaps it is inevitable, given our radical behavioural background, that we will regard the 'cognitive debate' differently from many others. We do not feel there is a theoretical axe to be ground surrounding the incorporation of mentalistic variables into a field previously dominated by applied behaviour analysis. Nor do we feel the need to accept uncritically the causal status of cognitions.

In the past we have not shied away from pointing out the limitations of a narrow behavioural standpoint on the field of learning disabilities and we strongly suspect that the adoption of a narrow cognitive perspective would be equally limiting. From our perspective it does not matter whether we use the term 'private events', 'internal rules' or 'cognitions', as long as the central relevance of the thoughts, emotions and feelings of people with learning disabilities is not forgotten.

REFERENCES

Bandura, A. (1986) The explanatory and predictive scope of self-efficacy theory. *Journal of Clinical and Social Psychology*, **4**, 359–73.

Bandura, A. (1995) Comments on the crusade against the causal efficacy of human thought. *Journal of Behavior Therapy and Experimental Psychiatry*, **26**, 179–90.

Baron-Cohen, S., Leslie, A.M., and Frith, U. (1985) Does the autistic child have a 'theory of mind'? *Cognition*, **7**, 37–46.

Beck, A.T., Rush, A.J., Shaw, B.F., and Emery, G. (1979) *Cognitive Therapy of Depression*. New York: Guilford Press.

Benson, B., Reiss, S., Smith, D.S. and Laman, D.S. (1985) Psychological correlates of depression in mentally retarded adults: II. Poor social skills. *American Journal of Mental Deficiency*, **89**, 657–9.

Bentall, R.P., Lowe, C.F. and Beasty, A. (1985) The role of verbal behavior in human learning: II. Developmental differences. *Journal of the Experimental Analysis of Behavior*, **43**, 165–81.

Bird, F., Dores, P.A., Moniz, D. and Robinson, J. (1989) Reducing severe aggressive and self-injurious behaviors with functional communication training. *American Journal of Mental Retardation*, **94**, 37–48.

Carr, E.G., and Durand, V.M. (1985) Reducing behavior problems through functional communication training. *Journal of Applied Behavior Analysis*, **18**, 111–26.

Castles, E.E. and Glass, C.R. (1986) Training in social and interpersonal problem-solving skills for mildly and moderately retarded adults. *American Journal of Mental Deficiency*, **91**, 35–42.

Clements, J. (1987). *Severe Learning Disability and Psychological Handicap*. Chichester: John Wiley.

Duker, P., Jol, K. and Palmen, A. (1991) The collateral decrease of self-injurious behavior with teaching communicative gestures to individuals who are mentally retarded. *Behavioral Residential Treatment*, **6**, 183–96.

Durand, V.M., and Berotti, D. (1991) Treating behavior problems with communication. *Bulletin of the American Speech-Language-Hearing Association*, November, 37–9.

Durand, V.M. and Carr, E.G. (1987) Social influences on 'self-stimulatory' behavior:

analysis and treatment application. *Journal of Applied Behavior Analysis*, **20**, 119–32.

Durand, V.M. and Carr, E.G. (1991) Functional communication training to reduce challenging behavior: maintenance and application in new settings. *Journal of Applied Behavior Analysis*, **24**, 251–64.

Fowler, D., Garety, P. and Kuipers, E. (1995) *Cognitive Behaviour Therapy for Psychosis: Theory and Practice*. Wiley Series in Clinical Psychology. Chichester: John Wiley.

Fuchs, C. and Benson, B.A. (1995) Social information processing by aggressive and nonaggressive men with mental retardation. *American Journal of Mental Retardation*, **3**, 244–52.

Gowans, F. and Hulbert, C. (1983) Self-concept assessment of mentally handicapped adults: a review. *Mental Handicap*, **11**, 121–3.

Hayes, S.C., and Wilson, K.G. (1994) Acceptance and commitment therapy: altering the verbal support for experiential avoidance. *The Behavior Analyst*, **17**, 289–305.

Hayes, S.C. and Wilson, K.G. (1995) The role of cognition in complex human behavior: a contextualistic perspective. *Journal of Behavior Therapy and Experimental Psychiatry*, **26**, 241–48.

Hayley, J. (1963) *Strategies of Psychotherapy*. New York: Grune & Stratton.

Iwata, B.A., Dorsey, M.F., Slifer, K.J., Bauman, K.E. and Richman, G.S. (1982) Toward a functional analysis of self-injury. *Analysis and Intervention in Developmental Disabilities*, **2**, 3–19.

Jones, R.S.P. (1994) Understanding challenging behaviour: workshop notes. Unpublished paper.

Jones, R.S.P. and Eayrs, C.B. (1993). Challenging behaviour and intellectual disability: an overview. In R.S.P. Jones and C.B. Eayrs (eds), *Challenging Behaviour and Intellectual Disabilities: A Psychological Perspective*. Clevedon: BILD.

Jones, R.S.P. and Owens, R.G. (1992) Applying functional analysis. *Behavioural Psychotherapy*, **20**, 37–40.

Jones, R.S.P., Wint, D. and Ellis, N.C. (1990) The social effects of stereotyped behaviour. *Journal of Mental Deficiency Research*, **34**, 261–8.

Jones, R.S.P., Williams, H. and Lowe, C.F. (1993) Verbal self-regulation. In I. Fleming and B. Stenfert Kroese (eds), *People with Learning Disability and Severe Challenging Behaviour: New Developments in Services and Therapy*. Manchester: Manchester University Press.

Jones, R.S.P., Walsh, P. and Sturmey, P. (1995) *Stereotyped Movement Disorders*. Wiley Series in Clinical Psychology. Chichester: John Wiley .

Kendall, P. C. and Braswell, L. (1985) *Cognitive-Behavioural Therapy for Impulsive Children*. New York: Guilford Press.

Koegel, R.L. and Koegel, L.K. (1990) Extended reductions in stereotypic behavior of students with autism through a self-management treatment package. *Journal of Applied Behavior Analysis*, **23**, 119–27.

Leander, J.D., Lippman, L.G. and Meyer, M.E. (1968) Fixed interval performance as related to subjects' verbalisations of the reinforcement contingency. *Psychological Record*, **18**, 469–74.

Lee, C. (1992) On cognitive theories and causations in human behavior. *Journal of Behavior Therapy and Experimental Psychiatry*, **23**, 257–68.

Lindsay, W.R., Michie, A.M., Baty, F.J., Smith, A.H.W., and Miller, S. (1994) The consistency of reports about feelings and emotions from people with intellectual disability. *Journal of Intellectual Disability Research*, **38**, 61–6.

Lowe, C.F. (1979). Determinants of human operant behavior. In M.D. Zeiler and P. Harzem (eds), *Advances in Analysis of Behaviour*, Vol. 1: *Reinforcement and the Organisation of Behaviour*. Chichester: John Wiley.

Lowe, C.F. (1983) Radical behaviourism and human psychology. In G.L.C. Davey (ed.), *Animal Models and Human Behaviour: Conceptual, Evolutionary and Neurobiological Perspectives.* Chichester: John Wiley.

Lowe, C.F., Harzem, P. and Bagshaw, M. (1978) Species difference in temporal control of behavior: II. Human performance. *Journal of the Experimental Analysis of Behavior*, **29**, 351–61.

Lowe, C.F., Harzem, P. and Hughes, S. (1978) Determinants of operant behaviour in humans: some differences from animals. *Quarterly Journal of Experimental Psychology*, **30**, 373–86.

Merighi, J., Edison, M. and Zigler, E. (1990) The role of motivational factors in the functioning of mentally retarded individuals. In R.M. Hodapp, J.A. Burack and E. Zigler (eds), *Issues in the Developmental Approach to Mental Retardation.* Cambridge: Cambridge University Press.

Oliver, C. (1986) Self-concept assessment: a case study. *Mental Handicap*, **14**, 24–5.

Owens, R.G. and Ashcroft, J.B. (1982) Functional analysis in applied psychology. *British Journal of Clinical Psychology*, **21**, 181–9.

Pope, S.T. and Jones, R.S.P. (in press) The therapeutic effect of reactive self-monitoring on the reduction of inappropriate social and stereotypic behaviour. *British Journal of Clinical Psychology.*

Remington, B. (1991) Behaviour analysis and severe mental handicap: the dialogue between research and application. In B. Remington (ed.), *The Challenge of Severe Mental Handicap: A Behaviour Analytic Approach.* Chichester: John Wiley.

Remington, B. and Evans, J. (1988) Basic learning processes in people with profound mental retardations: review and relevance. *Mental Handicap Research*, **1**, 4–23.

Schalock, R.L., Harper, R.S. and Genung, T. (1981) Community integration of mentally retarded adults: community placement and program success. *American Journal of Mental Deficiency*, **85**, 478–88.

Scott, J. (1992) Chronic depression: can cognitive therapy succeed when other treatments fail? *Behavioural Psychotherapy*, **20**, 25–36.

Sheldon, B. (1995) *Cognitive Behavioural Therapy: Research, Practice and Philosophy.* London: Routledge.

Sidman, M., Rauzin, R., Lazar, R. and Cunningham, S. (1982) A search for symmetry in the conditional discrimination of Rhesus monkeys, baboons and children. *Journal of the Experimental Analysis of Behavior*, **37**, 23–44.

Slocum, T.A. and Butterfield, E.C. (1994) Bridging the schism between behavioral and cognitive analyses. *The Behavior Analyst*, **17**, 59–73.

Smith, M.D. (1990) *Autism and Life in the Community: Successful Interventions for Behavioral Challenges.* Baltimore: Paul H. Brookes.

Spaulding, W.D. (1995). Cognition and causality, fiction and explanation. *Journal of Behavior Therapy and Experimental Psychiatry*, **26**, 279–82.

Vygotsky, L.S. (1978) *Mind in Society: The Development of Higher Psychological Processes.* Cambridge, MA: Harvard.

Watts, F. (1987) Series preface. In J. Clements, *Severe Learning Disability and Psychological Handicap.* Chichester: John Wiley.

Williams, J.M.G. (1992) *The Psychological Treatment of Depression: A Guide to the Theory and Practice of Cognitive Behaviour Therapy.* London: Routledge.

Zegiob, L., Klukas, N. and Junginger, J. (1978) Reactivity of self-monitoring procedures with retarded adolescents. *American Journal of Mental Deficiency*, **83**, 156–63.

Zigler, E., Balla, D. and Butterfield, E.C. (1968) A longitudinal investigation of the relationship between preinstitutional social deprivation and social motivation in institutionalised retardates. *Journal of Personality and Social Psychology*, **10**, 437–45.

Zigler, E. and Hodapp, R.M. (1986) *Understanding Mental Retardation.* Cambridge: Cambridge University Press.

3   Anger assessment for people with mild learning disabilities in secure settings

Laura Black, Chris Cullen and Raymond W. Novaco

Among the core elements of challenging behaviour in people with learning disabilities are psychological deficits regarding anger regulation. Socially inappropriate expression of anger is commonly observed among people with learning disabilities:

> Very few intervention plans actually teach people with learning difficulties socially acceptable ways of expressing anger or frustration and challenging behaviour may be the one way in which people in such circumstances can exert any control over the way in which they live.
>
> (Blunden and Allen, 1987, p. 39)

Indeed, the life circumstances of people with learning disabilities are conducive to the activation of anger. Taking a contextual perspective (Novaco, 1993), the anger experiences of institutionalised people are embedded or nested within physical and social environments that are intrinsically constraining and are limited in satisfaction. The social environment of learning disabilities service settings has been described by Clegg (1993) as being one of 'social emptiness', few social relationships and little time in contact with others. Furthermore, the reciprocities between patient and staff behaviour associated with anger episodes can not only diminish social support that mitigates anger and aggression but also escalate antagonism. Just as supportive relationships can act as stress buffers to moderate anger, coercive behaviour can potentiate the occurrence of aggression. Thus, whereas residents have limited opportunities for recreation, occupation and social activities, staff are often subjected to verbal and physical abuse while struggling to maintain an environment that is both safe and therapeutic. High turnover and burnout among staff have been documented as a result of violence risk exposure (Attwood and Joachim, 1994).

A significant proportion of people with learning disabilities has difficulties with recognising, encoding, regulating and expressing emotion (McAlpine, Kendall and Singh, 1991), particularly strong negative emotions, such as anger. Kiernan's comprehensive survey in North West England found that approximately 20% experienced difficulties managing anger (Kiernan, 1991). Clinical observations of this population note a restricted range of feelings, difficulties in differentiating between emotions, an impoverished emotional vocabulary and difficulties in expressing negatively toned emotions appropriately (Bates, 1992).

Deficits in emotional expression can mean that a person's needs or grievances may be disregarded or exacerbated, which can produce a vicious cycle of antagonistic behaviour (Holt, 1994). Unresolved anger may indicate that staff and residents fail to empathise with each other, negatively impacting the quality of their relationship.

As advances in treatment hinge on proficiencies in assessment, this chapter will focus on assessment methodology. Some clinical material will be presented from a treatment outcome study, the participants of which had serious anger problems and mild learning disabilities. Some were seen in small groups and others individually (Black, 1994). We will begin with an overview of conceptualisations of anger and of anger treatment and then discuss how people with mild learning disabilities can benefit from such cognitive-behavioural approaches. A detailed description and evaluation of one such treatment for a person with learning disabilities is described in Black and Novaco (1993).

ANGER THEORY

Anger is a normal emotion having no 'automatic status' as a clinical problem. Anger can serve a number of positive functions, but it is also implicated in a number of clinical disorders (Novaco, 1986). The definitional differentiation made by Buss (1961) between anger as an emotional state, aggression as a behaviour and hostility as an enduring negative attitude is still maintained by scholars in the violence field, such as Blackburn (1989). Anger is a subjective emotional state defined by the presence of physiological arousal and cognitions of antagonism. Novaco's (1979 and 1994a) cognitive mediational framework for anger emphasises the reciprocal relationships between cognitive, arousal and behavioural factors interfacing with environmental circumstances. As the elements of this model have been elaborated previously (see Howells, 1989), we simply direct attention here to the central domains pertinent to clinical assessment.

External circumstances

The external events that function as provocations are anger triggers. Most commonly, anger-provoking events involve social interactions. Indeed, anger is regarded as 'a social emotion' (Watts, 1992), as 'socially constructed' (Averill, 1982), as 'an intimate phenomenon' (Tulloch, 1991) and as 'predominantly interpersonal' (Howells, 1989). Although clinicians endorse a person-environment interactionalist viewpoint, clinical assessment rarely acknowledges the full contributions of physical and social environment elements. Characteristically, environmental influences that are distal and ambient are neglected, while those that are proximate and acute (and more easily recognised) are given attention. Novaco (1993) has argued for a contextual perspective that gets beyond this 'proximity bias'. Thus, we should seek to map dynamic environmental elements that shape and sustain anger reactions, as well as provide coping resources.

Cognitive factors

Anger is cognitively mediated. Cognitive mediation refers to cognitive processes which occur before a provoking event, during the perception of that event (as an automatic and embedded part of the perceptual process) and after the event. All of these processes are mutually influenced and are linked to behaviour. Briefly stated, expectations brought to a situation gear attention and the course of responding. Characteristically, the expectations of a chronically angry person are unrealistic and inflexible, leading to hyperalertness for situational cues associated with provocation schemas. Perceptual processes such as vigilance, selective attention, and cue salience are influenced by cognitive dispositions and contextual variables. Attentional cueing and perceptual matching as information-processing biases have been discussed by Novaco and Welsh (1989).

Appraisal processes, which establish the personal meaning of events, have been shown to be central to emotion and stress since Lazarus (1966). Regarding anger provocation, the actions of others can be interpreted as threatening to self-image, as antagonistic (assuming malevolence and justifying retaliation) and as having exaggerated personal significance. The attribution of blame to others is a salient feature of anger (Howells, 1989), and ruminating about an event also prolongs arousal (Bandura, 1973). The importance of rumination in affecting the duration and reactivation of anger cannot be overemphasised in understanding the anger experiences of institutionalised people.

Physiological arousal

A defining attribute of anger is the activation of the central and autonomic nervous systems. Physiological arousal, particularly involving cardiovascular, respiratory and muscular functions, is readily observable in anger reactions. Detailed presentations of such physiological aspects can be found in Chesney and Rosenman (1985). Pertinent to understanding chronic anger problems, arousal that is prolonged by rumination can, when not fully dissipated, transfer to subsequent situations of provocation. Zillmann (1983) has shown that arousal residues from previous activation add to the arousal potency of new events, a process that he has called 'excitation transfer'. Hence, when anger arousal decays slowly, it can be expected that new provocation will have more intense effects. The defining attributes of anger as being arousal plus cognitive labelling have been well established experimentally by Konecni (1975).

Behavioural reactions

Implicit in the cognitive labelling of arousal as anger, as opposed to some other emotion, is an inclination to act antagonistically towards the perceived source of the aversive experience. As anger is often the product of interpersonal exchanges, behavioural responses to provocation dynamically shape the anger experience. Episodes of anger and aggressive behaviour frequently involve an escalation of aversive events, whereby the conditional probabilities of anger and aggression are raised by the occurrence of succeeding antagonistic responses (Toch, 1969; Patterson, 1974). Much anger-driven aggressive behaviour is impulsive (Berkowitz, 1983), as heightened arousal and the activation of cognitive scripts can override inhibitory controls. Because anger and aggression have instrumental value in response to aversive events, chronically angry people are often locked into their anger habits and lack alternative behavioural coping skills. Their investment in anger can, therefore, be dislodged by learning socially acceptable ways of dealing with conflict.

In contrast to aggressive behaviour, avoidance and withdrawal responses remove the person from the provocation setting, but like aggressive behaviour, disengagement can fuel anger when there is no effort to resolve the conflict constructively. When avoidance and withdrawal are not accompanied by a strategic plan to reduce the probability of subsequent anger, it is then likely that the person dwells on the provocation, thus prolonging anger, and remains susceptible to reactivation of anger when next encountering the provocation source.

Considering institutional context

Howells (1989) has discussed the complexities of clinical assessment with angry patients. Assessment has typically relied on anger self-report measures, such as the Novaco Provocation Inventory (Novaco, 1983) and the Spielberger State Trait Anger Scale (Spielberger *et al.*, 1983), but multiple forms of measurement should be undertaken. To address shortcomings in existing anger self-report measures, Novaco (1994a) developed a new scale based on his conceptual framework and validated it for use with clinical populations.

The scope of assessment regarding anger needs to be widened. For example, Levey and Howells (1991) outlined features of in-patient settings that contribute to increased stress levels, such as lack of privacy, little personal space, inadequate facilities and placement on a locked ward. Similarly, Novaco has discussed the context relevance for anger of the social climate of psychiatric hospital wards, shaped by many factors including environmental design, patient composition, staffing ratios, staff philosophy and attitudes, treatment programmes, social contact and patient perceptions and behaviour. 'Unregulated anger may transform a treatment setting in ways that seriously impair its capacity to heal' (Novaco, 1994b, p. 215).

Given the established prevalence of violence in institutional settings, it is a special challenge for staff in such facilities to provide an environment that is both safe and therapeutic. Secure psychiatric settings are stressful for both those who live and those who work there, hence both residents and staff may react with anger to stressful events. Patient management efforts by staff are likely to be relevant to patient violence, and staff members are likely to be affected by exposure to verbal and physical abuse. Residents in in-patient settings who have anger control problems tend to be socially isolated and have difficulty maintaining relationships. However, we have anecdotal evidence that such residents cite their relationship with their 'key worker' as being important in diluting stress and preventing anger reactions.

ANGER TREATMENT INTERVENTION

A cognitive-behavioural treatment for anger problems was first developed by Novaco (1975). Over time, it has been progressively modified as a stress-coping skills approach (Novaco, 1994b; Tulloch, 1991). The treatment seeks to develop coping skills that are then applied in an inoculation procedure (i.e. exposure to graduated doses of provocation). It involves a three-stage procedure of cognitive preparation, skill acquisition, and application training first developed by Meichenbaum for problems of anxiety and then extended by Novaco for chronic anger (Novaco, 1977, 1980). The core components of the treatment are (1) cognitive restructuring, (2) arousal reduction and (3) behavioural skills training.

Treatment with angry people can present special challenges as many have a combative style, are impatient and can be hostile, impulsive and irritable. They tend to be hypersensitive to perceived threat and respond antagonistically. Therapists may find it difficult to cope with such heightened emotion and being frequently criticised. Because anger has an externalising quality, it can impede the person accepting personal responsibility for change and dilute motivation for treatment. Nevertheless, the stress inoculation approach to anger treatment builds on a collaborative therapeutic relationship, actively involving the client in building anger control coping skills. It has been found to be effective with a broad range of populations, including adult and adolescent out-patients, adult and youth in-patients, adolescents in residential settings, adults in forensic settings and college students. A review of this literature can be found in Novaco (1994b).

Applications to clients with learning disabilities

Clients with learning disabilities judged to be challenging can benefit from learning to express and resolve feelings of anger and frustration by a cognitive-behavioural approach. Yet, anger difficulties in this population have rarely been addressed (Blunden and Allen, 1987). A group treatment study by Benson, Rice and Miranti (1986) did obtain successful outcomes. Their comparative group analysis, using modifications of the Novaco anger treatment components, resulted in significant reductions in measures of anger and aggression across four conditions (relaxation training, self-instruction, problem-solving and a combined condition), but there were no significant differences between groups. Benson (1994) has now elaborated her treatment procedure to include a component focusing on the identification of emotional states.

Some anger case studies also have been reported. Murphy and Clare (1991) were referred a 19-year-old man following two incidents of violence against a staff member. The in-patient treatment lasted approximately one year and included simplified anger control techniques (Cole, Gardner and Karan, 1985): self-monitoring, social skills training (especially negotiating skills), coping skills for anger arousal and a token programme with a mood-monitoring component. Outcome was measured using a behavioural rating scale, token programme performance and self-monitoring assessments. Resulting reductions in physical aggression and verbal aggression facilitated a community placement.

Black and Novaco (1993) reported the treatment of a man in his late forties, living in a secure setting, who had been both verbally and physically aggressive. The treatment was a modification of the stress inoculation protocol. The cognitive preparation phase was subdivided into a self-monitoring and information phase (four sessions each); the skill acquisition phase was subdivided into arousal reduction and coping strategy sub-phases (ten sessions each); and the application training phase was incorporated throughout treatment and during follow-up. Outcome was measured using rating scales completed by staff, self-report inventories, and self-monitoring assessment. Results indicated that the client achieved greater self-control when angry, which was further demonstrated by his transfer to the community. Similarly, Lindsay *et al.* (1994) described work with four male residents in a unit for seriously challenging behaviour. The treatment, lasting between 6 to 9 months, was also a modification of the Novaco procedure. Ratings were obtained using a fourteen-item provocation inventory, a provocation role-play and a self-monitoring assessment. Two of the four people improved significantly and one person showed some improvement.

Thus, it appears that people with mild learning disability can benefit from the individual components of a cognitive-behavioural treatment, such as self-monitoring, self-instruction, impulse control, relaxation training and social problem-solving. For those with serious anger difficulties, the anger-focused treatment should be embedded within a comprehensive social cognitive curriculum (Clements, 1987). The foundation of clinical intervention is the assessment both of the determinants of the presenting problem and of the treatment outcome. The following section presents a suggested assessment approach.

ASSESSMENT FOR ANGER MANAGEMENT TREATMENT

We will focus on aspects of assessment central to the treatment process, guided by the foregoing conceptual framework.

> Without a formulation, the therapist can be likened to a general engaging in a battle without planned tactics to guide him in the deployment of troops and in the timing of his offensive. Similarly, without a flexible conceptualisation and formulation, the therapist would be dealing piecemeal with problems which present themselves and with no idea about whether he is tackling the main targets or making any progress.
>
> (Blackburn and Davidson, 1990, p. 58)

An excellent case description by Clare *et al.* (1992) includes an elaborate formulation which not only underpinned the treatment for a person with learning disabilities convicted of fire raising, but also served to co-ordinate multi-professional working. We urge practitioners to widen their purview of assessment beyond proximal antecedents of target behaviours to take broader consideration of contexts.

Our assessment scheme for anger involves procedures for intake evaluation, outcome evaluation, and assessment of change. The intake assessment entails a functional analysis of the person's difficulties, establishing the involvement of anger in these difficulties, and the dimensions of the anger problem. Additionally, the motivation to engage in treatment and the capability to participate in treatment should be established. The outcome assessment aims to determine whether treatment has lead to improvement and to specify improvement in terms of everyday behaviours and capabilities. The process assessment involves measures of cognitive and behavioural change integral to treatment. Case material will be presented to illustrate the three designated assessment areas.

The key intake assessment issues are the nature of the anger problem, motivation for treatment and ability to follow treatment protocol.

What is the nature of the person's current anger difficulties?

The functional analysis of anger difficulties, as given in Howells (1989) and Novaco (1994b), can be organised by the model previously described, namely in terms of environmental circumstances, cognitive determinants, somatic arousal and behavioural manifestations.

Environmental circumstances

Consideration should be given to proximal situational triggers and ambient conditions within the institution and distal factors influencing the development of difficulties over time (e.g. early experience, role models for conflict resolution, school exclusions, relationship difficulties, offending behaviours and previous therapeutic interventions).

Cognitive determinants

Assessment should encompass cognitive structures and processes before anger events (schemas, expectations), during the perception of events (vigilance, selective attention, cue salience and appraisals) and after the events (rumination and reflections). It should also ascertain the personal meaning of events and the variables that intensify and diminish that meaning.

Somatic arousal

The client's personal pattern of arousal, cues for arousal and customary strategies for reducing arousal should be determined. The effect of heightened arousal (e.g. sleep difficulties or reduced concern about the consequences of actions) should also be identified. Factors that intensify or diminish arousal should be identified as moderator variables.

Behavioural manifestations

The manifestations of anger in conspicuous action (e.g. confrontation, indirect expression) and in more subtle forms (e.g. suppression, withdrawal or avoidance) should be assessed. The short- and long-term consequences maintaining the inappropriate behaviours must also be identified.

These four components are dynamically interrelated. Howells (1989) and Novaco and Welsh (1989) described ways of collecting the information discussed above, including:

- semi-structured interviews with the client, clinical staff, and significant others;
- case note material to indicate chronicity of the behaviours and previous psychological interventions;
- behavioural observation data to specify the frequency and severity of the target behaviour;
- self-report data from questionnaires, psychometric measures, and self-monitoring assessments;
- role-play assessments of interpersonal interactions;
- physiological measures, such as blood pressure and heart rate.

Is the person motivated to change?

As cognitive-behavioural treatments are collaborative, the person must be motivated to change and engage in treatment. The person must be helped to recognise that their anger patterns have had personal costs to well-being, to personal relationships and to personal goals and that treatment could have a beneficial effect on their lives. This personal cost analysis gives leverage for change (Novaco, 1994b). The degree of investment in anger habits should be explored: what are the positive and negative consequences of change and are there any concerns about participating in treatment? Resistance to change tends to indicate that the behaviour is meeting important personal needs. People who have chronic anger difficulties are mistrustful, suspicious and defensive. They attribute blame to others and believe that their behaviour when angry is justified, thereby externalising responsibility and diluting motivation to change. As disclosures concerning socially disapproved behaviours cause anxiety, there is minimisation and denial. In developing a therapeutic relationship, issues of confidentiality and trust (especially if disclosure could impact on discharge decisions) must be concertedly addressed.

Previous therapeutic interventions have a pivotal bearing on motivation. The person may be in the secure setting as a last resort. They are likely to have undergone a number of failure experiences and feel demoralised, discouraged and hopeless. Overcoming these emotion-laden negative expectations is a critical therapeutic challenge, which is one not easily accomplished in the face of continued anger episodes.

Can the person cope with treatment?

Cognitive-behavioural anger treatment requires a set of basic skills or abilities which should be assessed as prerequisites. These are given below.

1 *Communication skills.*
 Expressive communication can be measured by tasks tapping verbal fluency and descriptive ability (e.g. descriptions of pictorial scenes). Receptive communication can be assessed by the British Picture Vocabulary Test (Dunn and Dunn, 1981), which indicates heard vocabulary expressed as age equivalents.

2 *Cognitive aptitude.*
 Self-monitoring assessments hinge on elementary abilities to understand and represent gradation (i.e. 'more than' and 'less than') and to record provocation events. Deficits in short-term memory, attention and concentration should be screened for. Be mindful that performance can be affected by anxiety, intolerance of frustration, or the side-effects of medication.

3 *Emotional identification.*
 Recognition and labelling of emotions in oneself and others is central to the treatment process. Photographs or videotapes (e.g. popular television soap operas) depicting both positive and negative emotions can be used to identify the range of the person's emotional vocabulary and to facilitate discussion (see also Chapter 4). Differentiating the emotion of anger from

aggressive behaviour is an example of an elementary point, as is the entitlement to experience negative emotions (Benson, 1994)

4 *Social interaction skills.*
Anger is a social emotion with many triggers occurring in interpersonal exchanges. Questionnaires and role-play assessments (Hollin and Trower, 1986) can identify an individual's competencies. Treatment seeks to develop socially appropriate strategies to express anger and resolve conflict, hence social skills may need to be shaped.

Case example

At the time of referral Ms H was a 47-year-old woman, who had been a hospital resident for twenty years. She was transferred from an open ward to a ward which was usually a locked facility. She was referred for anger problems, particularly verbal and physical aggression to others, self-aggression and marked physiological arousal. The latter concern was heightened by generalised cardiac difficulties. Staff were also concerned about her depressed mood and low self-confidence.

At the initial interview, Ms H presented as attractive and neatly dressed. She had a good conversational manner, a sense of humour and a ready smile. She appeared anxious and constantly sought reassurance. Ms H described her childhood as happy, having had a close relationship with her parents and three brothers. Although living a somewhat uneventful and restricted life (having minimal education), she did help her mother care for the family and viewed her circumstances positively. After the death of her parents, when she was 23 years old, the family was taken into care. Two of her three brothers went to a hospital for people who have a learning disability, and Ms H went to a psychiatric hospital. She struggled to cope with her bereavement and did not settle in the hospital nor did she successfully adjust when transferred to be near her brothers. She was resident in a number of different wards and a hostel in the community before being admitted to the locked ward. She had found it difficult to cope in the hostel.

Environmental circumstances

At a day centre in the community, Ms H was more relaxed, co-operative and socially appropriate than in the hospital ward or in the Local Authority hostel. She felt that the day centre was quieter, the building was larger and fewer demands were placed on her; she felt she was liked and accepted there. The centre was near her parents' home. On the bus from the day centre returning to the hospital, she was aware of increasing arousal ('getting worked up') and had negative thoughts about the hospital.

The ward staff are obliged to maintain a safe environment, specifying limits and boundaries. Frequent flash-points occurred when Ms H felt constrained by limits placed on her behaviour. She complained about time constraints on her being outside the ward and being prevented from attending the day centre. She disliked being questioned about her movements, as she did not like staff to know about her 'business'. She was hostile towards the young staff (she didn't like the 'young ones telling her what to do'), as she felt that they tried to 'get her high'.

She was sensitive to noise and overcrowding. She felt anxious witnessing physical aggression by other residents, but she was provoked to be violent herself by aversive behaviour from peers, especially teasing.

Cognitive determinants

Ms H had very low self-esteem and felt worthless. She expected people to view her negatively and judge her to be incompetent ('daft' or 'stupid'). She expected staff to prefer the other residents, who were 'petted up' to her detriment. She had a heightened expectation of equity, stating that she 'played fair' with other residents but they often took advantage of her. She felt that they teased her because she was 'easy to upset', even though she had been 'good to them in the past'. Feeling that her views were disregarded, she believed that to be heard, she would have to raise the intensity of her behaviour.

She was vigilant for critical comments, seeing this as being 'shown up'. She would amplify negative comments, disqualify positive ones and interpret neutral comments as personal slights. Impersonal events were taken personally. For example, a ward door locked to accommodate a restriction order was viewed as a deliberate attempt to restrict her freedom.

When aroused, she tended to assume that staff behaviour was maliciously motivated. When staff tried to negotiate time boundaries, she saw this as 'picking on her' and part of a general strategy to control her. She held these views with considerable rigidity. She ruminated about 'getting back at staff' by refusing or secreting her medication to get them 'into trouble' or by making false allegations of assault. Indeed, she admitted injuring herself deliberately but claiming that staff had injured her. Her ruminations often led to an increase of arousal.

Somatic arousal

Physiological arousal was salient for Ms H. She reported high levels of anxiety and experienced palpitations, breathlessness, being 'red in the face' and heavy perspiration. She would speak with a raised voice. Staff reported that she failed to 'listen to reason'. She could not moderate her arousal when provoked and had low frustration tolerance. She had generalised cardiac difficulties, and there was concern about the impact of heightened arousal on her general health.

Behavioural manifestations

Compared to her peer group, Ms H had good social skills. However, when provoked, she behaved in a confrontational manner, tending to escalate the situation. She was physically and verbally aggressive and had deliberately self-injured by picking at her skin, scratching and slapping herself. She could 'walk off in a huff', leaving the ward without informing staff. She felt that talking to her key worker was helpful.

Summary

Ms H's anger reactions were strongly linked to the environmental context and her cognitions about it. She was resentful of the 'system' that sent her to hospital, a decision she judged to be unfair and uncaring. She found the restrictions of hospital life irksome and viewed them as an attempt to exert unwarranted control over her life. She viewed herself as worthless and powerless to influence decisions about her future. Her failing health increased her feelings of vulnerability and anxiety. Her inability to cope with a hostel placement exacerbated her feelings of hopelessness and anger against the system. Ms H recognised that her anger had unacceptable personal costs, particularly her referral to a locked facility and continued detention in hospital. She was thus motivated to engage in treatment and was judged to have the capability for it.

EVALUATING OUTCOME

Few psychometric measures exist for anger that are suitable for use by those with a learning disability. The utility of self-report scales may have varying levels of reliability (Voelker *et al.*, 1990) and staff rating measures also have certain difficulties. Because staff in secure settings must ensure a safe environment, inappropriate behaviour has a low base rate (Alves, 1985) and because the severity of the clients' difficulties affects treatment length, measures must be collected for extended periods of time. Given these circumstances, as well as the complexity of the anger construct, evaluation of treatment requires a convergence of multiple measures.

Traditionally, improvement has been defined in terms of statistically significant change on the outcome measures, but this is now considered inadequate. Decisions about statistically significant change should be extended by consideration of whether the magnitude of change is sufficient to improve general well-being of the clients. Methodologies to demonstrate clinically significant change have yet to proceed beyond the preliminary stages of development, for both quantitative (Jacobson and Truax, 1991) and descriptive (Mavissakalian, 1986) approaches. As yet, there is no consensus on a standard procedure to demonstrate clinical significance (Shapiro, 1989). Clinical expectations of the magnitude of improvement underlie such methodologies. For clients in secure settings with long-standing difficulties, realistic indications of success will involve lesser degrees of change than for out-patients.

Miller, Morley and Shepherd (1987) advocated a shift from the illness paradigm 'treatment model' to a rehabilitative 'coping' model that aims to enable the individual to function 'as well as is feasible' in important areas of life. Instead of the goal of treatment being the relief of all symptoms, a more realistic objective would be to strengthen coping skills to prevent difficulties from disrupting everyday life. Reviews of the literature on clinical significance can be found in Black (1994) and Jacobson and Truax (1991). Three key guidelines can be summarised as follows.

1 Operationalise the criteria of change or goals of treatment in terms of everyday behaviours and capabilities.

2 Select or design outcome measures, using a variety of assessment modalities. Since target problems are multi-dimensional, there may well be desynchronies between measures (e.g. cognitions, affect and behaviour may change at different rates).

3 Following Jacobson and Truax (1991), indicate the magnitude of change needed by specifying cut-off points against which post-treatment scores can be compared. The following demarcations are suggested:

- *Cut-off point A.* Post-treatment scores fall outside the range of a specific dysfunctional population;
- *Cut-off point B.* Post-treatment scores fall within the range of the well-functioning population;
- *Cut-off point C.* The mean of the values of cut-off points A and B, which is usually closer to the mean of the well-functioning population than the dysfunctional population.

Jacobson and Truax (1991) provide a statistic indexing the magnitude of change and a worked example of the calculations to derive the three cut-off points.

Case example

A comprehensive description of the criteria for change developed for Ms H to organise evidence of pre-treatment deficits and post-treatment gains (that is, whether she had developed strategies to cope with provocation) is not possible here. However, for illustration some pre-treatment data are presented below.

The first criterion for change was concerned with socially inappropriate expression of anger arousal and irritability in everyday life and self-rated anger arousal to provocative situations. Staff completed a behavioural rating scale and a visual analogue scale and Ms H completed a provocation inventory. At baseline, staff observed Ms H to be verbally and physically aggressive, to attribute malevolent motives to the actions of other people and to leave the ward when asked not to. Frequently such incidents exceeded severity levels judged to be acceptable. Ms H was rated as being more irritable than her peers. She rated herself as being highly provoked by a wide range of situations.

The second criterion represented the ability to generate socially acceptable strategies to cope with provocation. Staff completed a semi-structured interview and Ms H completed two self-report measures. Pre-treatment Ms H had articulated some socially appropriate strategies, but staff judged that heightened arousal compromised her ability to put such strategies into practice, she 'ceased to act rationally or listen to reason' when anxious.

As triggers to anger often occur in interpersonal exchanges and inappropriate responding can both escalate provocation and distance potentially supportive others, the third criterion reflected the ability to relate to others. Data came from a semi-structured interview and three visual analogue scales. Ms H was not particularly tolerant or sensitive to other people's needs and found it difficult to compromise. She was selective in her social relationships preferring to socialise with staff rather than her peers.

Process assessment

Work on the assessment of cognitive change is sparse, although notable progress has been made on measures of problem-solving skills by Castles and Glass (1986). Given the cognitive mediational framework for anger (Novaco, 1979) that underpins cognitive-behaviour anger therapy, cognitive change processes merit assessment.

Unrealistic expectations, antagonistic appraisals and hostile attributions are intrinsic to anger reactions and violent behaviour (Copello and Tata, 1990: Howells, 1989). For example, chronically angry people, when faced with an aversive situation, tend to assume that non-benign motivations underlie the behaviour of others. These attributions function as 'permission' (Firth, 1993) to act in socially inappropriate ways and allow the angry person to view their aggressive behaviour as justified. These strong interpretive biases can also impact on the therapeutic relationship. Aiming for therapeutic change in cognitive structures, the clinician ought to identify expectations, appraisals and attributions linked to anger at the start of treatment. We illustrate this for clients with learning disabilities with findings from Black (1994). Staff recordings provided details of antecedents and consequences for anger incidents. The staff noted various cognitive constructions voiced by patients during angry incidents. Examples are given below.

Perceived unfairness
- I do not get properly looked after.
- X is spoilt rotten, she is wasted.

- Nurses are always on her side and not mine.

Not being liked
- Nobody likes me.
- I'm the most hated person on the ward.

Being picked on
- Staff get on to me.
- Staff are always on my back.
- I've been victimised.

Being blamed unfairly
- I get the blame for too much.
- I get the heavy end of it and others get off with it.

Belief that the motives of others are malevolent
- People are just trying to get me high.
- Staff are trying to get me into trouble.
- Staff are just here to get the residents high.

One instrument for assessing cognitive change that has utility for a population with learning disability is a modification of the Social Problem Solving Test (SPST) procedure, developed by Castles and Glass (1986), later modified by Black (1994). The advantage of the SPST is that it is not time-consuming to administer, the vignettes can be recalled by those with a limited attention span and the questions can be verbally presented. There is a standardised format but there is flexibility to include individualised elements, such as idiosyncratic provocations. Vignettes are derived from everyday life situations with which the participants have had prior experience. Black (1994) found that the participants had difficulty trying to estimate coping with situations they had not previously experienced.

The assessment used by Black (1994) established whether the participants could articulate coping strategies for three sets of situations:

1 *difficult interpersonal situations* taken from Castles and Glass (1986) – asking for information or favours, refusing unreasonable requests, dealing with legitimate criticism, handling disagreements, meeting new people, coping with unreasonable behaviour from others;
2 *provocative situations*, taken from the Novaco (1983) Provocation Inventory – humiliation/verbal insult, annoying behaviour of other people, personal unfairness, frustration, physical assault, personal clumsiness;
3 *personally provocative situations* identified by intake assessment.

The assessment also included ways of describing problem-solving skills. Problem-solving skills are defined as: *consequential thinking* (predicting the effect of one's behaviour on the outcome of an event), *socio-causal thinking* (inferring attributions or intentions to other people) and *interpersonal perspective taking* (anticipating the effect of one's behaviour on other people).

Case example

Ms H was presented with a number of short vignettes in which she was given a problem situation and a resolution. She was asked to repeat the vignette to ensure accurate recall. She was then asked how she would feel if the situation actually happened to her. A series of questions was then posed requiring her to articulate a coping strategy, which was scored for each of the three problem-solving skills. To elicit her inferences about the hypothetical motivation of the person in the vignette she was asked 'Why did the person act in that way?'. For illustration, examples from pre-treatment measures are given below.

> *Vignette*
> You are walking along the street and you trip up and fall over and hurt your leg. Some young lads start to laugh at you and call you names. In the end it turns out OK.
>
> *Response*
> Maybe the boys don't like me.
> Maybe they think I'm daft.
> Maybe they think I'm stupid.

> *Vignette*
> A resident is playing a radio far too loud. You ask them to turn it down, but they won't. In the end it turns out OK.
>
> *Response*
> Just to annoy you.
> They are wicked.
> They might be angry.
> They might be in a bad mood.

> *Vignette*
> You and another resident are arguing. The nurse thinks you started it and gives you a row. You didn't start it; the other person did. In the end it turns out OK.
>
> *Response*
> If you do the wrong thing they give you a row.

Although this assessment is at an early stage of development, it provides information about the client's cognitions which is the target of treatment. While the verbal responses of a person with a learning disability may not be sophisticated, Lindsay and Kasprowicz (1987) argue that negative automatic thoughts may be no less incapacitating for being linguistically simple.

CONCLUSIONS

The study of emotional disorders has been largely neglected in the field of learning disabilities, yet an inability to regulate emotional arousal, particularly anger, is an important determinant of challenging behaviour. Those who exhibit such behaviour must be helped to express anger appropriately. The literature suggests the utility of cognitive-behavioural methods to help people with a learning disability cope with anger, but systematically conducted outcome studies are needed, especially for those with severe difficulties.

At the foundation of treatment is a comprehensive assessment of deficits associated with the target problem. In this chapter, we have described an approach to anger assessment with this clinical population. Case illustrations were given for a client with mild learning disabilities and anger difficulties. As the client was relatively skilled, it remains to be determined whether those with more severe learning disabilities can participate in such an assessment.

Anger assessment should be seen in the context of seeking clinically significant change. The importance of realistic expectations of improvement was emphasised, and we have suggested that indicators of progress must be specified in terms of everyday behaviours and capabilities.

Secure settings can be stressful for those who live in them and those who work in them. Unregulated anger emerges in physical and social environments that are constraining and that offer limited satisfaction. Obviously, environmental factors must be addressed to ensure that clients' rights and dignity are respected. However, if the treatment setting fails to provide for effective remediation of anger problems, it thereby neglects residents' needs. When anger episodes are exacerbated, both residents and staff can become trapped in a vicious cycle. While anger treatment for people with learning disabilities is at an early stage, we hope that this formulation sharpens the focus of treatment objectives and stimulates further work on evaluation methodologies.

REFERENCES

Alves, E.A. (1985) The control of anger in the mentally abnormal offender. In E. Karas (ed.), *Current Issues in Clinical Psychology.* New York: Plenum Press.

Attwood, T. and Joachim, R. (1994) The prevention and management of seriously disruptive behaviour in Australia. In N. Bouras (ed.), *Mental Health in Mental Retardation: Recent Advances and Practices.* Cambridge: Cambridge University Press.

Averill, J. R. (1982) *Anger and Aggression: An Essay on Emotion.* New York: Springer-Verlag.

Bandura, A.(1973) *Aggression: A Social Learning Analysis.* Englewood Cliffs, NJ: Prentice Hall.

Bates, R. (1992) Psychotherapy with people with learning difficulties. In A. Waitman and S. Conboy-Hill (eds), *Psychotherapy and Mental Handicap.* London: Sage.

Benson, B.A. (1994) Anger management training: a self control programme for persons with mild mental retardation. In N. Bouras (ed.), *Mental Health in Mental Retardation: Recent Advances and Practices.* Cambridge: Cambridge University Press.

Benson, B.A., Rice, C.J. and Miranti, S.V. (1986) Effects of anger management training with mentally retarded adults in group treatment. *Journal of Consulting and Clinical Psychology,* **54**, 5, 728–9.

Berkowitz, L. (1983) The experience of anger as a parallel process in the display of impulsive, 'angry' aggression. In R.G. Geen and E.I. Donnerstein (eds), *Aggression: Theoretical and Empirical Reviews*, Vol. 1. New York: Academic Press.

Black, L. (1994) Helping people with learning difficulty express anger arousal in socially acceptable ways: the development of a treatment intervention and outcome measures. Unpublished PhD thesis, St Andrews: University of St Andrews.

Black, L. and Novaco, R.W. (1993) Treatment of anger with a developmentally handicapped man. In R.A. Wells and V.J. Giannetti (eds), *Casebook of the Brief Psychotherapies*. New York: Plenum Press.

Blackburn, I. and Davidson, K. (1990) *Cognitive Therapy for Depression and Anxiety: A Practitioner's Guide*. Oxford: Blackwell Scientific Publications.

Blackburn, R. (1989) Psychopathy and personality disorder in relation to violence. In K. Howells and C.R. Hollin (eds), *Clinical Approaches to Violence*. Chichester: John Wiley.

Blunden, R. and Allen, D. (eds) (1987) *Facing the Challenge: An Ordinary Life for People with Learning Difficulties and Challenging Behaviour*. London: King's Fund Project Paper, Number 74.

Buss, A. (1961) *The Psychology of Aggression*. New York: John Wiley.

Castles, E.E. and Glass, C.R. (1986) Training in social and interpersonal problem solving skills for mildly and moderately mentally retarded adults. *American Journal of Mental Deficiency*, **91**, 1, 35–42.

Chesney, M.A. and Rosenman, R. (eds) (1985) *Anger and Hostility in Cardiovascular and Behavioural Disorders*. New York: Hemisphere.

Clare, I.C.H., Murphy, G.H., Cox, D. and Chaplin E.H. (1992) Assessment and treatment of fire setting: a single case investigation using a cognitive-behavioural model. *Criminal Behaviour and Mental Health*, **2**, 53–268.

Clegg, J.A. (1993) Putting people first: a social constructionalist approach to learning disability. *British Journal of Clinical Psychology*, **32**, 389–406.

Clements, J. (1987) *Severe Learning Disability and Psychological Handicap*. Chichester: John Wiley.

Clements, J. (1992) I can't explain . . . 'challenging behaviour'. Towards a shared conceptual framework. *Clinical Psychology Forum*, **39**, 29–37.

Cole, C.L., Gardner, W.I. and Karan, O.C. (1985) Self management training of mentally retarded adults presenting severe conduct difficulties. *Applied Research in Mental Retardation*, **6**, 337–47.

Copello, A.G. and Tata, P.R. (1990) Violent behaviour and interpretative bias: an experimental study of the resolution of ambiguity in violent offenders. *British Journal of Psychology*, **29**, 417–28.

Dunn, L.M. and Dunn, L.M. (1981) *Peabody Picture Vocabulary Test – Revised*. Circle Pines, MN: American Guidance Service.

Firth, H. (1993) Self control of aggression: some beliefs about treatment. *Clinical Psychology Forum*, **51**, 20–1.

Hollin, C.R. and Trower, P. (eds) (1986) *Handbook of Social Skills Training*. Oxford: Pergamon.

Holt, G. (1994) Challenging behaviour. In N. Bouras (ed.), *Mental Health in Mental Retardation: Recent Advances and Practices*. Cambridge: Cambridge University Press.

Howells, K. (1989) Anger management methods in relation to the prevention of violent behaviour. In J. Archer and K. Browne (eds), *Human Aggression: Naturalistic Approaches*. London and New York: Routledge.

Jacobson, N.S. and Truax, P. (1991) Clinical significance: a statistical approach to defining meaningful change in psychotherapy research. *Journal of Consulting and Clinical Psychology*, **59**, 12–19.

Kiernan, C. (1991) Services for people with mental handicap and challenging behaviour in the North West. In J. Harris (ed.), *Service Responses to People with*

Learning Difficulties and Challenging Behaviour. BIMH Seminar Papers No. 1, British Institute of Mental Handicap.

Konecni, V.J. (1975) The mediation of aggressive behaviour: arousal levels versus anger and cognitive labelling. *Journal of Personality and Social Psychology*, **32**, 706–12.

Lazarus, R.S. (1966) *Psychological Stress and the Coping Process*. New York: McGraw-Hill.

Levey, S. and Howells, K. (1991) Anger and its management. *Journal of Forensic Psychiatry*, **1**, 3, 305–27.

Lindsay, W.R. and Kasprowicz, M. (1987) Challenging negative cognitions. *Mental Handicap*, **15**, 159–62.

Lindsay, W.R., Neilson, C., Pitcaithly, D., Heap, I., Allen, R., Smith, A.H.W. and Black. L. (1994) Responses to anger management training in clients with intellectual disability. Unpublished manuscript.

McAlpine, C., Kendall, K.A., Singh, N.N. (1991) Recognition of facial expressions of emotion by persons with mental retardation. *American Journal of Mental Retardation*, **96**, 1, 29–36.

Mavissakalian, M. (1986) Clinically significant improvement in agoraphobia research. *Behaviour Research and Therapy*, **24**, 3, 369–70.

Meichenbaum, D. (1975) Self Instructional Methods. In F.H. Kanfer and A.P. Goldstein (eds), *Helping People Change: A Text Book of Methods*. New York: Pergamon.

Miller, E., Morley, F. and Shepherd, G. (1987) Editorial. The trouble with treatment. *British Journal of Clinical Psychology*, **26**, 241–2.

Murphy, G. and Clare, I. (1991) MIETS: a service option for people with mild mental handicaps and challenging behaviour or psychiatric problems. 2. Assessment, treatment, and outcome for service users and service effectiveness. *Mental Handicap Research*, **4**, 2, 180–206.

Novaco, R.W. (1975) *Anger Control: The Development and Evaluation of an Experimental Treatment*. Lexington, MA: D.C. Heath.

Novaco, R.W. (1977) A stress inoculation approach to anger management in the training of law enforcement officers. *American Journal of Community Psychology*, **5**, 327–46.

Novaco, R.W. (1979) The cognitive regulation of anger and stress. In P.C. Kendall and S.D. Hollon (eds), *Cognitive-Behavioural Interventions*. New York: Academic Press.

Novaco, R.W (1980) The training of probation counsellors for anger problems. *Journal of Counselling Psychology*, **27**, 385–90.

Novaco, R.W. (1983) *Stress Inoculation Therapy for Anger Control. A Manual for Therapists*. Unpublished manual. Irvine: University of California.

Novaco, R.W. (1986) Anger as a clinical and social problem. In R. Blanchard and C. Blanchard (eds), *Advances in the Study of Aggression*, Vol. 2. New York: Academic Press.

Novaco, R.W. (1993) Clinicians ought to view anger contextually. *Behaviour Change*, **10**, 4, 208–18.

Novaco, R.W. (1994a) Anger as a risk factor for violence among the mentally disordered. In J. Monahan and H. Steadman (eds), *Violence and Mental Disorder: Developments in Risk Assessment*. Chicago: University of Chicago Press.

Novaco, R.W. (1994b) Clinical problems of anger and its assessment and regulation through a stress coping skills approach. In W. O'Donohue and L. Krasner (eds), *Handbook of Psychological Skills Training: Clinical Techniques and Applications*. Boston: Allyn & Bacon.

Novaco, R.W. and Welsh, W.N. (1989) Anger disturbances: cognitive mediation and clinical prescriptions. In K. Howells and C. Hollin (eds), *Clinical Approaches to Violence*. Chichester: John Wiley.

Patterson, G.R. (1974) Intervention for boys with conduct problems: multiple settings, treatments and criteria. *Journal of Consulting and Clinical Psychology*, **42**, 471–81.

Shapiro, D.A. (1989) Outcome research. In G. Parry and F.N. Watts (eds), *Behavioural and Mental Health Research: A Handbook of Skills and Methods*. Hove: Lawrence Erlbaum.

Spielberger, C.D., Jacobs, G., Russell, S. and Crane, R. (1983) Assessment of anger: the State-Trait Anger Scale. In J.D. Butcher and C.D. Spielberger (eds), *Advances in Personality Assessment*, Vol. 2. Hillsdale, NJ: Lawrence Erlbaum.

Toch, H. (1969) *Violent Men: An Inquiry into the Psychology of Violence*. Chicago: Aldine.

Tulloch, R. (1991) Anger and violence. In W. Dryden and R. Rentoul (eds), *Adult Clinical Problems: A Cognitive Behavioural Approach*. London: Routledge.

Voelker, S.L., Shore, D.L., Brown-More, C., Hill, L.C., Miller, L.T. and Perry, J. (1990) Validity of self-report of adaptive behavior skills by adults with mental retardation, *Mental Retardation*, **28**, 305–9.

Watts, F.N. (1992). Applications of current cognitive theories of the emotions to the conceptualisations of emotional disorders. *British Journal of Clinical Psychology*, **31**, 153–67.

Zillmann, D. (1983). Arousal and aggression. In R.G. Geen and E.I. Donnerstein (eds), *Aggression: Theoretical and Empirical Reviews*. New York: Academic Press.

4 Understanding and assessing depression in people with learning disabilities

A cognitive-behavioural approach

Julie Reed

INTRODUCTION

Depression is one of the most prevalent forms of psychopathology (Seligman, 1975). It can seriously interfere with an individual's personal competence and daily functioning. A large body of recent research has resulted in a strong empirical knowledge base which indicates the efficacy of a wide range of pharmacological and psychological interventions for this disorder. Furthermore, our present understanding of depression is such that we are able to use information about client variables and disorder variables to guide our choice of intervention in order to optimise therapeutic outcome. However, this state of affairs does not hold for people with learning disabilities as this client group has been one of the most ignored populations in terms of receiving mental health services. Fortunately, this situation is changing. In conjunction with the advent of resettlement programmes aimed at facilitating a move from hospital-based accommodation to supported housing in the community, there has been a reappraisal of mental health needs.

This chapter will draw on the relevant research literature to provide an up-to-date account of our understanding of this area. Case studies will be used to illustrate applications of our current knowledge base to psychological therapy. The chapter describes how the life situations and experiences of many people with learning disabilities incorporate known risk factors for depression. It discusses the lack of psychological research into therapeutic techniques to enable individuals to minimise the influence of these phenomena on their lives. It then reports on the current conceptual frameworks for understanding depression in clients with mild, moderate, severe and profound intellectual impairments. The chapter then reviews the research literature on the development of emotional understanding and expression together with information about the self-reporting of internal emotional states by clients with learning disabilities. It concludes with a section which describes and evaluates a number of measurement tools. These are aimed at assessing the presence and severity of depression in this client group. Finally there is a discussion of the emerging issues from this area of research.

RISK FACTORS FOR DEPRESSION IN THE LIVES OF PEOPLE WITH LEARNING DISABILITIES

It seems surprising that the identification and treatment of depression among people with learning disabilities have received so little attention from psychologists and psychiatrists. This is curious when we consider some of the risk factors (e.g. lack of social support, unemployment) which we know to be associated with these disorders in the general population.

It could be argued that people with learning disabilities are likely to be at greater risk of developing depression than other sub-groups within the population. A large epidemiological study of depressive symptomatology in the total population carried out by Comstock and Helsing (1976) found that psychopathology was most prevalent among young single adults who were poorly paid and poorly educated, two common characteristics of adults with learning disabilities. It is difficult to provide prevalence figures for depression among people with learning disabilities as such a diversity of samples and diagnostic criteria have been used to determine rates of psychiatric disorders in this population (see Sturmey, Reed and Corbett, 1991).

Repeated experience of failure

Throughout childhood and adolescence individuals with learning disabilities will have many experiences of failure, both at home and at school. As they pass through the education system they may attend special classes, find themselves excluded from tests and examinations or they may attend a school for children with special educational needs. Other aspects of their life are likely to reinforce these school experiences. It is very probable that a young person with learning disabilities will have to cope with seeing his or her siblings being given greater responsibilities within the home, achieving success in their chosen leisure pursuits and gradually developing their own independent life away from their parents. An individual may feel that positive outcomes are unattainable or that negative outcomes are unavoidable. As this lack of success is associated with their intellectual impairment (an internal and stable attribute of their self) young people with learning disabilities are very likely to acquire feelings of helplessness. A state of 'learned helplessness' has been identified as a potential aetiological factor in depressive disorders (Abramson, Seligman and Teasdale, 1978) and there is some empirical evidence to suggest that adolescents with learning disabilities are more likely to experience it than their non-disabled peers (Reynolds and Miller, 1985).

Prejudice from the general population

People with learning disabilities are likely to experience a number of negative social attitudes, including stigmatization, infantilisation and labelling (Reiss and Benson, 1982). Having a learning disability can mean that few people show respect for your opinions and talk to you seriously about your feelings. Reiss and Benson (1982) have provided anecdotal evidence to indicate that people with mild and moderate learning disabilities are very much aware of these conditions and are able to articulate the distress that this situation can cause (see also Jahoda, Markova and Cattermole, 1988). Mental health professionals need to consider how to provide clients with opportunities to talk about these issues. It could be argued that healthcare professionals who work with this client group have prioritised the promotion of independent living skills and the treatment of challenging behaviour at the expense of their clients' emotional well-being. It may be necessary to increase the awareness and understanding of emotional disturbance in this client group through staff training and case discussions. Individual programme planning, and the more recently developed shared action planning (Brechin and Swain, 1987), have been very effective vehicles for bringing about change in people's lives. But the goals set by these systems of care and support tend to focus on practical, concrete problems and often ignore emotional needs.

People with learning disabilities need to have sufficient self-esteem and a positive self-concept in order to protect themselves from the negative feedback they receive from the non-disabled population. They also need to have the necessary social interactional skills to deal with critical verbal comments from the rest of the population. Clearly, there is considerable scope here for programmes of counselling, social skills training and group therapy. It is interesting to note that programmes of social skills training have seldom included assertion skills and emotional awareness. In addition, their orientation tends to be towards a behavioural model rather than a cognitive-behavioural model. In a review of studies which describe programmes of social skills training for people with a learning disability, Davies and Rogers (1985) reported that only four out of thirty-two studies had attended to the development of assertion skills. It could be argued that the ability to assert oneself and to express anger and sadness in a socially acceptable and age-appropriate way is more important to the day-to-day emotional well-being of people with learning disabilities than 'learning how to be polite' in a range of different social settings. Studies carried out in this area indicate that people with intellectual impairments who have poor social interactional skills are more likely to suffer with depression (Schloss, 1982), are more likely to return to live in an institution (Stacey, Doleys and Malcolm, 1979) and are more likely to have difficulties in adjusting to work (Greenspan and Schoultz, 1981). Perhaps the needs of the non-disabled population and mental health professionals' concerns about the social acceptability of people with learning disabilities are too much to the fore when social skills training programmes are designed.

The following case vignette reports on a therapeutic intervention with Alice, a woman with Down's Syndrome, whose appearance led members of the general public to make gross underestimations of her considerable skills and abilities. One aspect of our work with Alice was to help her to find ways of coping with difficult social situations. While we are continuing to make important advances in changing the general population's attitudes to people with learning impairments, we still need to consider how to equip our clients with the necessary skills to cope with prejudice and stigmatisation from others.

At the time of referral, Alice was a 40-year-old woman with Down's Syndrome and a measured IQ of 65 who lived with her elderly mother. She was very obese and suffered with complete alopecia. Alice was referred to a mental health service as there had been a recent change in her behaviour. She had become reluctant to leave the house by herself, had bouts of sadness and crying and had gained a significant amount of weight. At assessment interview it was clear that Alice was worried about the future death of her mother and what would happen to her after this event. We were also concerned that she might be showing signs of age-related cognitive changes of an Alzheimer type. However, it was also apparent that Alice had a long-standing difficulty in coping with the attitudes and behaviour of others in her community. She was able to talk about how her 'learning disabled appearance' led others to make assumptions that she was severely intellectually impaired. She reported that people would avoid interacting with her in preference to talking to her mother.

Alice was a sociable, outgoing woman and these negative experiences were a great sadness to her. Through a programme of social skills training involving role-play we enabled Alice to deal with the behaviour of others in an assertive way. The role-play involved acknowledging her disabled appearance to others and then politely informing them of some of her skills and accomplishments. Drawing on Alice's strong religious faith, we also helped her to imagine God's protective love enveloping her like some kind of 'force field' every time she left home. This therapeutic work, along with some family intervention, brought about significant changes to Alice's mood. This increased her motivation and her ability to leave the house for solo shopping trips and other outings.

This way of coping with her disability was appropriate for Alice, but like any other intervention, this kind of approach should be tailored to the needs and wishes of the client. It seems that there is considerable potential for developing these and other similar therapeutic techniques for clients who experience negative feedback from others and may be at risk of developing emotional difficulties as a result.

Lack of social support

Reiss and Benson (1985) found that depression was associated with low levels of social support for people with mild learning disabilities. They hypothesised that the lack of a close friend or partner who could help with day-to-day problems and provide an objective perspective would be a persistent stressor for adults with mild learning disabilities. Of course, a further associated consequence of the lack of a confidant is the absence of an ongoing, loving and sexual relationship. We have limited and only anecdotal information on client views regarding how the lack of a loving and sexual relationship affects the quality of life for people with learning disabilities. However, we can hypothesise that for many individuals this is likely to have a negative effect on both self-image and self-esteem and for some individuals may act as a contributing factor in the onset and maintenance of inappropriate sexual behaviour.

The move from institution to community-based living may also have an impact on the prevalence of depression. Many clients will suffer from 'transition shock' (Coffman and Harris, 1980) when their lifestyle undergoes this major change and important personal relationships are disrupted. As a result of this, a proportion of individuals are likely to develop a depressive disorder. There is a significant lack of research data to guide professionals who are concerned about how the mental health of their clients might be adversely affected by a lifestyle change. There is also little empirical work on how to help clients to achieve optimal psychological health and well-being after such a change. This is a particular challenge for staff who work with individuals with severe and profound intellectual impairments.

Possible biological predisposition

Finally, there is a high incidence of central nervous system impairment among individuals with learning disabilities, and it has been found that they have an increased vulnerability to the development of a range of psychiatric disturbances (e.g. Lund, 1985). Through laboratory-based research and clinical trials, our understanding of the biochemical basis of mental disorders is becoming more sophisticated. It is important to ensure that people with learning disabilities are involved in future research carried out in this area.

CONCEPTUAL FRAMEWORKS FOR UNDERSTANDING THE EXPRESSION OF DEPRESSION IN PEOPLE WITH LEARNING DISABILITIES

It is only in the past decade that there has been a general acceptance among mental health professionals that people with learning disabilities can experience a psychiatric or psychological disorder and thus may carry a 'dual diagnosis'. In earlier versions of classification systems 'mental retardation' and psychiatric illness were considered to be mutually exclusive. The titles of articles from the 1980s, such as 'Do the mentally retarded suffer from affective illness?' (Sovner and Hurley, 1983), attest to past debates on this issue. Some researchers and practitioners have argued that many individuals with learning disabilities do not have the intellectual capacity to experience depression. Clinicians with a psychodynamic orientation may argue that clients with learning disabilities do not experience depression due to their limited psychodynamic development, the maturation of which is seen as a prerequisite for the occurrence of affective illness (Reid, 1982, but see also Sinason, 1992). Clinicians who use a cognitive-theoretical framework to guide their thinking and understanding about depression might also question whether people with learning disabilities can suffer from depression. For example, according to Beck (1976), depression occurs as a result of an individual holding a set of negative beliefs about self, life events and expectations for the future. Some would say that as we cannot demonstrate that people with more significant intellectual impairments are able to conceptualise their lives in this way, they therefore cannot be said to suffer from depression. In support of this view, some investigators have found that the distribution of psychiatric diagnoses among people with learning disabilities shows a different pattern from that of the rest of the population, with schizophrenia occurring more frequently than depression or anxiety (Reiss, 1982).

At present we have limited knowledge about how depression is manifested by people with learning disabilities and few studies have looked at how behaviours and symptomatology may vary across levels of intellectual impairment (Matson, 1983). For individuals without learning disabilities a diagnosis of depressive disorder is made using a standardised diagnostic classification system. It is based on a person's self-report coupled with the clinician's observations of behaviour during an assessment interview. Standardised classification systems, such as DSM-III-R (American Psychiatric Association, 1987), have been designed to diagnose psychiatric disorders in people whose intelligence and psychosocial functioning are within the normal range. A person with learning disabilities who is suffering with depression is only likely to come into contact with a mental health clinician if a third party (e.g. parent, carer) is concerned about a recent change in his or her emotional well-being or behaviour. Thus, low self-referral rates may partly account for the relatively low prevalence of depression found in mental health services for people with learning disabilities.

In the absence of a standard classification system for the diagnosis of mental illness in this population, the formulation of an individual's presenting difficulties will depend on the conceptual framework of the assessing clinician. In arriving at an understanding of the client's presenting difficulties, a clinician may collect wide-ranging information. This is likely to include self-report data from the identified client, together with information about a person's intellectual abilities, daily living skills, physical health, recent changes in emotional expression and behaviour from a parent or carer. They may also collate details of the person's current life situation, family history and own life history in order to aid the diagnostic process.

It is not clear whether depression in people with learning disabilities involves the same set of behaviours and symptoms as the intellectually unimpaired population. Some suggest that depression is not expressed directly and must be inferred from behaviours and symptoms which are 'masking' the underlying emotional disturbance (Carlson and Cantwell, 1980). In particular, physical aggression and property damage are considered as behaviours which may characterise depression in this population. It has, however, been suggested that the manifestation of depression among people with mild and moderate learning disabilities is similar to the expression of this disorder in the non-disabled population. There is some evidence to support this dichotomous view. In a study of affective illness, Sovner and Hurley (1983) found that standard diagnostic criteria were only useful for assessing the presence of affective disorder in people with mild and moderate learning disabilities. For individuals with severe and profound learning disabilities, the clinician needed to base his or her diagnosis on changes in biological functioning and behaviour, together with details of any family history of affective illness. However, the service philosophy of social role valorisation (Wolfensberger, 1983) may prompt us not to neglect the emotional lives of clients with more significant learning disabilities as this may lead to clinicians and researchers ignoring the important challenge of developing techniques for accessing internal emotional states of this sub-group, and thus devaluing these clients. Of course, it may also lead to the over-diagnosis of depression among people with severe and profound learning disabilities and the possible neglect of alternative explanations for emotional and behavioural change. There is clearly the potential for 'masked depression' to be used as a last resort diagnosis when no other formulation is forthcoming.

Glick and Zigler (1995) have proposed a theoretical explanation for the differences in the phenomenology of emotional disturbance in people with milder and more severe degrees of mental impairment. They suggest that there is a developmental progression in the expression of emotional disturbance. They argue that behaviour in the early stages of development is marked by immediate, direct and unmodulated responses to external stimuli and higher functioning is characterised by indirect, ideational and verbal or symbolic patterns. Thus, individuals with more significant mental impairment will show their emotional disturbance through their actions rather than through their cognitions and are more likely to show symptoms of turning against others rather than turning against themselves. They compared the symptomatology of psychiatric in-patients with mild learning disabilities with a matched sample of psychiatric in-patients without learning impairments. It was found that the group with mild intellectual impairments showed more symptoms indicative of turning against others (e.g. temper outbursts, physical assaults) and fewer symptoms indicative of turning against self (e.g. somatic complaints, lack of appetite) coupled with more symptoms involving expression in direct action rather than in thought. Thus they suggest that 'developmentally younger' individuals are more likely to externalise their distress, while 'developmentally older' individuals are more likely to internalise their emotional problems. This is an interesting theory which appears to have some potential for understanding how the expression of emotional disorders might vary across levels of learning disability. However, there are some difficulties with it. For example, one would imagine that self-injurious behaviours may be classified as 'self-directed', and yet these behaviours are known to be more prevalent among people with more severe and profound learning disabilities (Oliver, Murphy and Corbett, 1987).

The following case study illustrates some of the difficulties which might arise when trying to identify and make sense of a client's emotional disturbance. In addition, our work with Karen acts as a reminder of the importance of seeking information about an individual's behaviour across different settings.

Case study

At the time of referral, Karen was a 23-year-old woman with a measured IQ of 45 who attended a day centre for adults with learning disabilities and lived with her parents. Karen does not have a medical diagnosis to explain her intellectual impairment. On meeting her for the first time many people overestimated her intellectual ability as she had acquired a number of socially appropriate greetings, had an attractive appearance and was always smiling. When Karen's mother died after a lengthy illness, staff were pleased to observe that when Karen returned to the day centre she was her usual sociable and smiling self. They decided that Karen had been well-prepared for her mother's death and was receiving emotional support from her relatives. Several weeks later they were surprised to hear from Karen's father that at home she was refusing her food, not sleeping and showing stereotypic rocking behaviour. As a consequence, Karen was referred to a mental health service.

One part of the assessment was aimed at attempting to access Karen's emotional awareness. Karen could reliably identify happy, sad and angry facial expressions, but we were unable to demonstrate that she had an understanding of their meanings. We also undertook an assessment of Karen's social interactional skills and found that she had great difficulty in expressing negative emotions. These results were supported by staff reports of Karen's behaviour. In our efforts to understand Karen's behaviour, we hypothesised that for a number of years Karen had received a good deal of positive reinforcement from others, both at home and at the day centre, contingent on her 'looking happy' and being polite. As a consequence of this, assertion skills and the ability to express negative emotions did not appear to be in her repertoire of behaviours. Indeed, those closest to her reported that Karen never seemed angry or miserable. Our intervention was focused both on sharing these ideas with Karen's father and staff at the day centre and individual therapy for Karen. The initial work carried out with Karen's carers focused on enabling them to provide opportunities for Karen to express her grief over her mother's death. Some weeks later, we discussed how a programme of social skills training might help Karen to acquire a greater emotional awareness and facilitate her ability to talk about feelings.

Karen was clearly distressed by her mother's death, but did not express her sadness in a way which was readily identified by those people who were closest to her. One could argue that her sadness was 'masked' and that

Karen's inability to express her sadness in a recognisable way was a contributing factor in the subsequent onset of her emotional disturbance. We have discussed elsewhere (Clark, Reed and Sturmey, 1991) how carers and professionals may not pay sufficient attention to the emotional needs of people with learning disabilities. It may be that we do not have the skills to help clients with these difficulties or perhaps we choose to ignore the emotional disturbances of this group.

There have been several case studies reported in the literature where cognitive techniques have been used to treat depression in people with learning disabilities. Lindsay, Howells and Pitcaithly (1993) reported improvements in depressive symptomatology using a standardised questionnaire and daily monitoring by the individual. They used Beck's (1976) model of cognitive therapy and described how all the elements of this intervention approach were simplified and then used with two clients with mild intellectual impairments. Clearly, the next challenge is for researchers to investigate the efficacy of cognitive techniques in controlled clinical trials.

OBTAINING SELF-REPORTS OF PRIMARY SYMPTOMS

A logical first step towards a greater understanding of how depression can be identified is to investigate how self-reported primary symptoms might relate to other behaviours and symptoms. Dysphoria is probably regarded as the most salient symptom of depressive illness. But before an individual can accurately report on his or her emotional state, he or she must be able both to recognise different emotions and to understand what it means to be happy, sad, angry or frightened. In this discussion the term 'emotional awareness' will be used to describe the recognition and comprehension of different emotional states.

From the child development literature there are indications that some recognition of different emotions is present at a very early age. Emotion recognition begins with the child being able to discriminate between happy and unhappy emotional states. A more sophisticated classification system which enables differentiation between happiness, sadness, anger, fear, etc. occurs at a rather later stage. For example, Walker (1982) used two films of a young woman portraying different facial expressions together with a soundtrack appropriate to one of the emotions to show that 7-month-old infants will look more at the facial expression which matches the emotional quality of a voice. By 3 years the majority of children are able to identify a range of emotions and show an understanding of happiness and unhappiness by accurately assigning these facial expressions to stories with happy and unhappy endings (Borke, 1973). Thus, as a child's cognitive abilities develop, his or her emotional awareness also shows maturation.

Reed and Clements (1989) developed an emotional-awareness assessment measure which investigates the ability of adolescents and young adults with learning disabilities to recognise happy and sad facial expressions and to understand the meanings of these two emotional states as displayed by pictorial story sequences which had a happy or an unhappy ending. The assessment measure was used to discriminate between individuals who showed a specific level of emotional awareness and those who did not. The measure was created in such a way that verbal responses were not required for its completion in order to make it accessible to as many people as possible. This measure was administered alongside a test of language comprehension. The results indicated that while emotional awareness shows an association with greater intellectual ability, people with learning disabilities may have specific emotional awareness deficits which are not in line with their cognitive development. The results of other investigations with more rigorous experimental designs concur with these findings. Rojahn, Rabold and Schneider (1995) found that adults with learning disabilities were less accurate on a task that assessed emotion recognition ability in comparison to two groups of age-matched and mental age-matched participants. However, their performance on a task where individuals were asked to judge the age of a series of portrait photographs was similar to that of the mental age-matched participants. This finding supports the proposal that people with learning disabilities have a specific emotional awareness deficit which is over and above their intellectual impairment. From this, it can be recommended that clinicians will find it helpful to assess the emotional awareness of their client in order to guide their decision-making about whether or not to use self-report measures. It also adds weight to the call for further research into the efficacy of social skills training programmes that address the development of these skills.

DEVELOPING ASSESSMENT MEASURES

Another area of research is the development of valid and reliable assessment tools. The purpose of such measures is twofold: some are designed to differentiate the signs and symptoms of depression from other unusual or challenging behaviours shown by a client with learning disabilities; others are created in order to assess change in emotional disturbance over time and thus prove useful in measuring therapeutic change.

One approach has been the development of brief questionnaires specifically for this client group which can be administered to the client or to a third party or to both in order to assess or facilitate assessment of emotional disorders. An instrument of this type is the Psychopathology Instrument for Mentally Retarded Adults (PIMRA) created by Senatore, Matson and Kazdin (1985) to identify symptoms of specific and general psychopathology. This instrument is one of several assessment measures but is mentioned here as it has received a good deal of attention and psychometric investigation from other researchers. It consists of fifty-six items, based on DSM-III diagnostic criteria, which are organised into seven sub-scales. While this measure has many positive features (e.g. self-report and informant versions), it can be criticised for focusing on diagnostic criteria developed from our knowledge of the general population and failing to address the possibility of 'masked' depression. It is suggested here that questionnaires should include items which relate to diagnostic symptomatology described by DSM-III-R as well as questions enquiring about behaviours which may be 'masking' depressive disorders. Furthermore, it is recommended that researchers seek to develop paired questionnaires for administration both to the client and to a third party in order to explore the extent to which self-reports correlate with carer reports.

An examination of recent research indicates that this is an area of investigation which has been fraught with psychometric and methodological difficulties (Sturmey, Reed and Corbett, 1991). First, some studies have simplified the language of questionnaires and checklists which have been standardised on a general population without further investigation of the instrument's psychometric properties. It is very important that there is validation of revised versions of well-recognised questionnaires and checklists in order to ensure that the language-modified example is indeed a parallel form of the original measure. Second, some studies have taken questionnaires which are used with the general population to assess severity of depression and employed them as a diagnostic tool in the learning disabled population. Third, there have been no studies which have reported the relationship between checklist scores and psychiatric diagnoses. This is a surprising and significant omission as psychiatric diagnosis may both act as a validation criterion for psychometric measures and can be used to assess a measurement tool's specificity and sensitivity. Fourth, self-report measures have been drawn up and administered to people with learning disabilities without adequate assessment of the client's ability to comprehend and respond to the language of the measure. One way of overcoming this problem is to develop a pre-assessment screening procedure which can accompany the questionnaire and determine each client's ability to cope with the items on the self-report measure. Finally, some self-report measures have been created with insufficient attention to the literature on response sets which people with learning disabilities may show in their completion of questionnaires and checklists. Acquiescence, that is, the tendency to answer in the affirmative regardless of question content, is a well-documented feature of self-reporting among people with learning disabilities. Sigelman *et al.* (1981) found that acquiescence was less likely to occur when questions were immediate and concrete and more likely to happen when a question was not understood or when a correct answer was inaccessible. Thus, a self-report measure should draw on individuals' present or immediate past experiences using short, simple questions which require easily performed responses. In order to minimise the possible effects of acquiescence, questions can be balanced for positive and negative responding and items which have definite right and wrong answers can be included as further checks of comprehension. Alternatively, the problem of acquiescence could be addressed through the pre-assessment screening procedure.

A complementary line of enquiry is the development of biological markers of emotional disorders. Pirodsky *et al.* (1985) explored the use of the Dexamethasone Suppression Test (DST) as a biological marker of depression in adults with learning disabilities. If proved to be valid and reliable, this assessment method would be particularly useful when investigating the possibility that for individuals with learning disabilities depression may be 'masked' by other symptomatology. Pirodsky *et al.* (1985) found a significant relationship between the presence of two of three primary behaviours (defined by them as self-injury, physical aggression and social withdrawal) and a positive DST result. From these findings they concluded that people with learning disabilities may express depression through atypical patterns of behaviour disturbance. However, they noted a number of potential limitations to the use of the DST with this client group. First, other forms of psychiatric illness can give a positive DST result thus limiting this instrument's potential as a diagnostic device. Second, if an individual is on regular anti-convulsant medication then this can give rise to a false positive DST result. This is a significant limitation as Aman (1982) has reported that 12 to 36% of people with learning disabilities suffer from epilepsy and take anti-convulsant drugs on a regular basis. Moreover, epilepsy is associated with greater intellectual impairment and so this percentage will be higher in the sub-group of people with severe and profound learning disabilities, which is the group for whom this test might have particular applicability.

CONCLUSIONS AND EMERGING ISSUES

1 There is a need to encourage more mental health researchers and practitioners to take an interest in the emotional disorders of people with learning disabilities. The assertion that people with learning disabilities do not have the intellectual capacity to experience depression must be challenged.

2 There is a need to provide training and consultation on emotional disorders to front-line workers who care for and support people with learning disabilities in order to increase their awareness and understanding. Furthermore, we need to explain and emphasise the importance of mental health promotion for people with learning disabilities to service planners and commissioners.

3 Further work is required to advance our understanding of the development of emotional awareness in this client group and techniques for promoting the necessary skills and abilities. We need to draw on the developmental psychology literature to inform this research and carry out more controlled evaluations of social skills training programmes.

4 Through the refinement of current measurement tools, further research needs to examine the validity of our current conceptual frameworks for

depression. We need to determine how the expression of depression varies across different levels of intellectual impairment.

5 Finally, the development of effective psychological interventions for the treatment of depression in this client group is vital. We need to explore how cognitive-behavioural techniques can be used with individuals who have severe learning disabilities.

REFERENCES

Abramson, L.Y., Seligman, M.E.P. and Teasdale, J.D. (1978) Learned helplessness in humans: critique and reformulation. *Journal of Abnormal Psychology*, **87**, 49–74.

Aman, M. (1982) Psychoactive drugs in mental retardation. In J.L. Matson and F. Andrasik (eds), *Treatment Issues in Mental Retardation*. New York: Plenum Press.

American Psychiatric Association (1987) *Diagnostic and Statistical Manual of Mental Disorders*, 3rd edn, revised. Washington, DC: American Psychiatric Association.

Beck, A.T. (1976) *Cognitive Therapy and the Emotional Disorders*. New York: International Universities Press.

Borke, H. (1973) The development of empathy in Chinese and American children between 3 and 6 years of age: a cross cultural study. *Developmental Psychology*, **9**, 102–8.

Brechin, A. and Swain, J. (1987) *Changing Relationships: Shared Action Planning with People with a Mental Handicap*. London: Harper & Row.

Carlson, G.A. and Cantwell, D.P. (1980) Unmasking masked depression. *American Journal of Psychiatry*, **137**, 445–9.

Clark, A.K., Reed, J. and Sturmey, P. (1991) Staff perceptions of sadness among people with mental handicaps. *Journal of Mental Deficiency Research*, **35**, 147–53.

Coffman, T.L. and Harris, M.C. (1980) Transition shock and adjustment of mentally retarded people. *Mental Retardation*, **18**, 3–70.

Comstock, G.W. and Helsing, K.J. (1976) Symptoms of depression in two communities. *Psychological Medicine*, **6**, 551–63.

Davies, R.R. and Rogers, E.S. (1985) Social skills training with persons who are mentally retarded, *Mental Retardation*, **23**, 186–96.

Glick, M. and Zigler, E. (1995) Developmental differences in the symptomatology of psychiatric inpatients with and without mild mental retardation. *American Journal of Mental Retardation*, **99**, 407–17.

Greenspan, S. and Schoultz, B. (1981) Why mentally retarded people lose their jobs: social competence as a factor in work adjustment. *Applied Research in Mental Retardation*, **2**, 23–38.

Jahoda, A., Markova, I and Cattermole, M. (1988) Stigma and the self-concept of people with mild mental handicap. *Journal of Mental Deficiency Research*, **32**, 103–15.

Lindsay, W.R., Howells, L. and Pitcaithly, D. (1993) Cognitive therapy for depression with individuals with intellectual disabilities. *British Journal of Medical Psychology*, **66**, 135–41.

Lund, J. (1985) The prevalence of psychiatric morbidity in mentally retarded adults. *Acta Psychiatrica Scandinavica*, **72**, 563–70.

Matson, J. (1983) Depression in the mentally retarded: toward a conceptual analysis of diagnosis. In M. Hersen, R. Eisler and P.M. Miller (eds), *Progress in Behavior Modification*, Vol. 14. New York: Academic Press.

Oliver, C., Murphy, G.H. and Corbett, J.A. (1987) Self-injurious behaviour in people with mental handicap: a total population study. *Journal of Mental Deficiency Research*, **31**, 147–62.

Pirodsky, D.M., Gibbs, J.W., Hesse, R.A., Hsieh, M.C., Krause, R.C. and Rodriguez, W.H. (1985) Use of the dexamethasone suppression test to detect depressive disorders of mentally retarded individuals. *American Journal of Mental Deficiency*, **90**, 245–52.

Reed, J. and Clements, J. (1989) Assessing the understanding of emotional states in a population of adolescents and young adults with mental handicaps. *Journal of Mental Deficiency Research*, **33**, 229–33.

Reid, A. (1982) *The Psychiatry of Mental Handicap*. Oxford: Basil Blackwell.

Reiss, S. (1982) Psychopathology and mental retardation: survey of a developmental disabilities mental health program. *Mental Retardation*, **20**, 128–32.

Reiss, S. and Benson, B.A. (1982) Awareness of negative social conditions among mentally retarded, emotionally disturbed outpatients. *American Journal of Psychiatry*, **141**, 88–90.

Reiss, S. and Benson, B.A. (1985) Psychosocial correlates of depression in mentally retarded adults: I. Minimal social support and stigmatization. *American Journal of Mental Deficiency*, **89**, 331–7.

Reiss, S., Levitan, G.W. and Szyzako, J. (1982) Emotional disturbance and mental retardation: diagnostic overshadowing. *American Journal of Mental Deficiency*, **86**, 567–74.

Reynolds, W.M. and Miller, K.L. (1985) Depression and learned helplessness in mentally retarded and non-mentally retarded adolescents: an initial investigation. *Applied Research in Mental Retardation*, **6**, 295–306.

Rojahn, J., Rabold, D.E. and Schneider, F. (1995) Emotion specificity in mental retardation. *American Journal of Mental Retardation*, **99**, 477–86.

Schloss, P.J. (1982) Verbal interaction patterns in depressed and non-depressed institutionalised mentally retarded adults. *Applied Research in Mental Retardation*, **3**, 1–12.

Seligman, M.E.P. (1975) *Helplessness – On Depression, Development and Death*. San Francisco: Freeman.

Senatore, V., Matson, J.L. and Kazdin, A.E. (1985) An inventory to assess psychopathology in the mentally retarded. *American Journal of Mental Retardation*, **89**, 459–66.

Sigelman, C.K., Budd, E.C., Spanhel, C.L. and Schoenrock, C.J. (1981) Asking questions of retarded persons: a comparison of yes-no and either-or formats. *Applied Research in Mental Retardation*, **2**, 347–57.

Sinason, V. (1992) *Mental Handicap and the Human Condition*. London: Free Association Books.

Sovner, R. and Hurley, A. (1983) Do the mentally retarded suffer from affective illness? *Archives of General Psychiatry*, **40**, 61–7.

Stacey, D., Doleys, D.M. and Malcolm, R. (1979) Effects of social skills training in a community-based program. *American Journal of Mental Deficiency*, **84**, 152–8.

Sturmey, P., Reed, J. and Corbett, J. (1991) Psychometric assessment of psychiatric disorders in people with learning difficulties (mental handicap): a review of available measures. *Psychological Medicine*, **21**, 143–55.

Walker, A.S. (1982) Intermodal perception of expressive behaviours by human infants. *Journal of Experimental Child Psychology*, **33**, 514–35.

Wolfensberger, W. (1983) Social role valorisation: a proposed new term for the principle of normalisation. *Mental Retardation*, **21**, 234–9.

5 Teaching cognitive self-regulation of independence and emotion control skills

Huw Williams and Robert S.P. Jones

INTRODUCTION

People receiving cognitive-behaviour therapy (CBT) are encouraged to gain an understanding of their mood and to learn skills for coping with the causes and symptoms of their mood. Increasingly, people with learning disabilities are living in environments in which they encounter a host of stressors to do with work, finance and interpersonal relations, and as they tend to lack inter-personal and other independence skills they may be more vulnerable to these stressors and thus to low mood (Nezu and Nezu, 1994). Indeed, therapists are increasingly being asked to provide interventions for people who are 'dually diagnosed'. Fortunately, as discussed in this volume, there is a growing inter-est in, and some innovative work on, the use of CBT for this population. That the cognitive-behavioural approach is increasingly advocated for people with learning disabilities may be for two reasons. First, CBT has been shown to be a reliable and testable means of bringing about change in non-disabled people's moods and behaviours (see Hawton *et al.*, 1989). Second, given that this client population includes those who are in particular need of encouragement to learn and deploy skills for effecting change in their own lives, CBT provides the technology for effective learning of skills to occur. Unfortunately, however, as we have argued in Chapter 2, there is, as yet, too little data to suggest for whom such techniques may work best and under what circumstances.

We will explore here techniques developed for teaching skills for daily liv-ing and emotion control with the aim of assisting clinicians in designing programmes for boosting people's independence skills. The main focus of this chapter will be on the critical problem of transfer. That is, no matter what kinds of skills are taught persons with learning disabilities tend not to use those skills later without being reminded to do so, a problem which affects the teacher and clinician.

Impetus for a change in how teaching programmes are constructed has not only arisen from frustration at the lack of transfer from training. There has been growing resistance in the field of learning disability to viewing an indi-vidual as a passive recipient of environmental controls typical of traditional behavioural approaches (e.g. Carr, 1991). Dignity, status, self-determination and choice of persons with disability have become core issues for practitioners and for advocates. There is increasing awareness of the need to re-analyse technologies for teaching skills so as to enable the recipients of teaching to become more active in programmes and to learn ways of determining their own futures.

We will argue that approaches from a Vygotskian perspective within which behavioural and cognitive approaches can be readily combined, and within which there is an emphasis on the role of language for self-regulation and effectance motivation (believing that what one does actually influences what happens, see Haywood, 1986) present a timely heuristic for designing interventions that will provide transfer.

SELF-REGULATION AND THE TRANSFER PROBLEM

When a mechanic, under the hood of a car, wants someone to pass him or her one of three wrenches from a workbench, he or she could say, 'Pass me the big wrench'. The other person noticing a small wrench and two large wrenches, might ask 'Which large one? The rusty one or the new, shiny one?'. People with learning disability do not tend to know that to communicate is to check with another what they meant to say, and then to repair breakdown by, for example, asking for these kinds of selective comparisons (Abbeduto *et al.*, 1991). A lack of skills, particularly communicative skills, is highlighted as a major obstacle to the independence of people with learning disabilities and is often the main reason why learning disabled people lose jobs, and why many non-disabled are seemingly challenged in their befriending (see Lignugaris-Kraft *et al.*, 1988).

Often people are taught skills such as these by a combination of didactic instruction and behavioural modelling. However, once trained in skills in one situation, they fail to use the skills in other similar situations later. As Frazer (1992, p. 55) points out:

> The problems of transfer and maintenance have dogged skills training . . . someone taught to interact in one setting may not use these skills in another area of life. Also, once the training programme stops there is a tendency for the newly learnt skills to fall into disuse . . . the issues have been well documented but the problem remains with us.

People with a learning disability who are taught to communicate by traditional methods do not seemingly benefit from training and remain fundamentally socially disengaged without the 'skill' to use their new skills, for keeping jobs or making friendships. Recently it has been argued that this transfer difficulty reflects a more fundamental difficulty for persons with a learning disability: *That they may not see themselves as (and therefore make themselves) agents of their own behaviour* (see Jones, Williams and Lowe, 1993). This view has been drawn from Vygotsky's writings (see

Vygotsky, 1987). He was one of the first theorists to recognise how social isolation plays a role in the handicapping of disabled persons. Societies tend to respond to disabled people by displacing them from mainstream environments so they also deprive them of the social experiences they need for social and cognitive development, delaying their development still further. Moreover, such displacement has an emotional and demotivating impact.

Vygotsky's theories foreshadowed current conceptualisations of learning disability as a condition by which people (1) become overly reliant on clues from the external environment to help them guide behaviour (Haywood, 1986), (2) remain dependent and acquire an external locus of control (Beveridge and Conti-Ramsden, 1987; Zigler and Balla, 1982) and (3) have difficulty in self-regulation (Whitman, 1990).

In the main, then, it appears that the transfer problem stems from the dependent roles that persons with learning disabilities have found themselves in. They learn to rely on others to prompt or regulate their behaviour. Consequently they have great difficulty in spontaneously using their acquired skills independently.

COGNITIVE-BEHAVIOURAL APPROACHES FOR DEVELOPING SELF-REGULATION

We will attempt to represent behavioural and cognitive approaches within a Vygotskian framework. Such an integration provides a range of options for teaching skills to people with learning disabilities, from contingency management to metacognitive instruction. This range enables us to respond appropriately to the needs of this heterogeneous population and thus provides a variety of ways for people to become more expert in controlling their own behaviour.

We will first review developments in applied behavioural analysis (ABA). We will show that traditional behavioural programmes largely neglected self-motivation and self-control as agents for training for transfer. We will then show how recent advances in ABA offer the theoretical basis for 'going cognitive' by providing an understanding of the effects of language on behaviour – even for people with minimal language skills – and how language skills can be utilised in teaching self-regulation and self-motivation and, hence, be used to teach for transfer. We will then discuss the more recent cognitively based approaches which provide specific methods for training skills in combination with self-regulatory skills through the structured use of language. Unfortunately, we will then show how such approaches have not provided consistent transfer. We will then reappraise such approaches in the context of recent developments in cognitive theory regarding transfer, which, we will argue, provide new foundations for developing programmes.

APPLIED BEHAVIOURAL ANALYSIS AND SELF-CONTROL: THE IMPORTANCE OF LANGUAGE

It is generally acknowledged that ABA revolutionised the care and treatment of people with learning disabilities (see Remington, 1991 for a review). Behaviour was shown to be controllable by specific contingencies and this provided powerful means for controlling behaviour in clinical and educational settings. A number of reviews exist which summarise how behavioural techniques have been used for teaching self-help skills, social skills, leisure skills and work skills (e.g. Martin and Pear, 1992).

Self-control within an ABA perspective is understood as the giving of reinforcers to oneself and presupposes that the individual has in her or his power the ability to 'obtain reinforcement but does not do so until a particular response has been emitted' (Skinner, 1953, pp. 237–8). It involves components such as self-monitoring (recording one's behaviour), self-evaluation (rating one's behaviour against a criterion) and self-reinforcement. ABA techniques for teaching skills and self-control represent an attempt to involve the participant as an agent of control over her or his own behaviour. As will become clear, however, the focus within ABA remained with the environment; people were assisted in arranging their external world so that they gained reinforcement. There was no specific attempt to foster or provide participants with cognitive skills for self-determination, but the findings did provide valuable evidence for the need to explore cognitive variables. These self-control studies involved skills teaching and the self-management of challenging behaviour. A selection of studies is presented below to exemplify each of the three components of self-control: self-monitoring, self-evaluation and self-reinforcement.

Self-monitoring

Reese, Sherman and Sheldon (1984) asked a 22-year-old aggressive woman (with moderate learning disability) to record, by ticking on a sheet, whether she had 'handled' or 'lost' her temper. Although she hardly ever recorded her inappropriate behaviour accurately, there was a significant reduction in her aggressive behaviour. Indeed, several studies have found a low correlation between the accuracy of self-monitoring and its effectiveness in changing the behaviour that is being recorded (e.g. Kneedler and Hallahan, 1981; Shapiro, 1986; Reese, Sherman and Sheldon, 1984).

Self-evaluation

Bryon (1988) described four participants with mild learning disabilities whose behaviours included shouting and disruptive interruptions. All four showed some reductions in these behaviours when taught to self-monitor, but these decreases were greatly enhanced when they were taught to evaluate their behaviour as being either 'good' or 'bad'. No external consequences were provided for evaluation.

Self-reinforcement

Litrownik, Freitas and Franzini (1978) taught children with moderate learning disabilities to indicate that they had finished a task by placing a picture of a happy face in front of them. These children showed improved performance on the task compared to a control group. Gardner and Cole (1989) described an attempt to train adults with learning disabilities to adopt work skills in a workshop setting. They were instructed that 'whenever you decide to be a good adult worker . . . you'll earn a coin'. When an appropriate behaviour was engaged in for a designated period, the participant was prompted to self-reinforce by taking a coin.

CRITICISMS OF ABA APPROACHES TO SELF-CONTROL AND TEACHING SKILLS

On reviewing these studies the first conclusion one arrives at is that there are in fact no examples of individuals with learning disabilities using self-reinforcement to modify their own behaviour (see Jones, Williams and Lowe (1993) for a full discussion of self-control and self-reinforcement). Performance standards were set by external agents and individuals did not have free access to reinforcers. In many cases what is termed 'self-control' means, in practice, that individuals were trained to cue external agents (experimenters, teachers, etc.) to deliver stimuli labelled 'reinforcers' for certain prescribed behaviours. However, there were reductions in inappropriate behaviour and increases in on-task behaviour. When changes in behaviour emerged, they did not seem to be tied directly to particular elements of the training regime designed. More precisely, contingencies did not appear influential in effecting behavioural change.

We believe that the processes that were primarily influential for the emergence of self-control in the studies mentioned above were not those directly designed to operate within the studies (such as contingencies for ticking boxes for appropriate behaviour and so on) but rather were non-programmed factors. We would suggest that the principal non-programmed factor was the encouragement of participants' engagement in verbal behaviour to describe their behaviour for themselves (e.g. 'I handled my temper'). That is, the participants were learning verbal rules for their behaviour (Jones, Williams and Lowe, 1993). This is indicated by the finding that the accuracy of a person's self-monitoring was less crucial to a positive outcome than their engagement in the process; also that self-monitoring did not necessarily need the support of external reinforcers for there to be reductions in inappropriate behaviour. *Facilitating participants' engagement in the process of developing verbal rules therefore had a reinforcement potency in itself. Moreover, the reinforcement potency of developing verbal rules may be greater than external consequences 'programmed' in as contingent reinforcers. That is, intrinsic reinforcement, integral to motivation and self-esteem, can be targeted by attending to verbal rule formation.* It appears that it was the extent to which training methods provided a context for participants to develop verbal rules for organising and controlling their behaviour for themselves that promoted behavioural change.

However, before concluding our review of ABA, it should be stressed that the ABA studies illustrate how contingency management can be used to help participants to develop verbal control over non-verbal behaviour. Although reinforcement approaches are mostly external, they can provide some of the tools for freeing people from their environmental restraints. Indeed, it may be that although a person may learn a skill by external management, she or he may come to be able to execute such skills independent of another change agent.

COGNITIVE-BEHAVIOURAL APPROACHES TO SELF-CONTROL: MAKING AND USING INNER SPEECH

Cognitive theorists have criticised applied behavioural approaches for neglecting the individual as the desirable and, indeed, necessary agent of her or his own behavioural control (Bandura, 1976). The overall goal of integrating behavioural and cognitive approaches was to make individuals the principal agents of their own behavioural change. As Meichenbaum and Asarnow (1979, p. 11) explain: 'Whereas the operant approach focuses attention on the rearrangement of the external environment to help establish self-control, the more cognitive conceptualisation of self-control supplements the operant approach by helping individuals to alter their internal environments.' As we saw in the review of ABA and self-control, the ability of an individual to use language to describe and control his or her own behaviour represents one of the most important of all skills.

Programmes have more recently been developed which attempt to account more fully for the use of rule-governance through self-regulatory speech (e.g. Hayes, 1989). These approaches go beyond enabling participants' comprehension of contingencies to their planning of future action. Whereas the emphasis in behavioural self-control is on controlling contingencies, the emphasis in cognitive self-control (more accurately self-regulation) is on manipulating one's own cognitive processing. The most prominent example is self-instructional training developed by Meichenbaum and Goodman (1971). The programme was based on the Vygotsky/Luria socio-developmental theory of how children develop control over their behaviour by internalising the speech that others use to control them. Although the approach had been used with non-disabled children (e.g. for inhibiting hyperactive behaviour), and for non-disabled adults (e.g. for coping with anxiety by using positive coping self statements) there was some controversy regarding whether people with learning disabilities could make use of the approach (see Whitman, 1990;

Meichenbaum, 1990). Ironically, such verbally mediated approaches were seen as fundamentally inappropriate for those with a learning disability while no technology existed that could provide consistent self-regulation (see Whitman, 1990). It is often the case in learning disability research that there is a need to emphasise the heterogeneity of this population and the consequent need to identify what works for whom and why.

Vygotsky (1962) and Luria (1961) provided an understanding of the process by which language comes to function as a means by which people can regulate their own behaviour. They showed how children can be instructed by others and learn to instruct themselves to respond in certain ways and that this method of self-control becomes increasingly reliable as development proceeds. Initially, children are unable to use speech to direct their own behaviour but speech has a general 'impellant' or initiating function. As children get older they use language to develop more complex control over their behaviour (i.e. they do what they say they will do) and gradually speech becomes covert and internalised and a shift occurs in the locus of control over a child's behaviour from caregiver to the child. Luria (1959, p. 349) noted that:

> As L.S.Vygotsky has already shown, the function which at first is distributed between two people [such as an adult directing a child's behaviour] can easily turn into an internal psychological system, and what the child does today with help, he will tomorrow be able to do on his own.

SELF-INSTRUCTIONAL TRAINING (SIT)

Self-instruction provided a method by which salient aspects of interpersonal speech could be assembled in the form of a package for assisting people in developing inner speech to control their own behaviour. The transfer benefits of the approach were stated simply by Hughes and Agran (1993, p. 262).

> Because most people can learn to use their verbal behaviour to guide their own performance even though no one else is around, self-instruction seems to be an appropriate strategy to teach people to use when they are on their own, outside of an instructional setting. Because one's verbal behaviour is always available to him or herself, self-instruction may allow people with severe disabilities to live more normalized lives in settings where instructional support typically is unavailable such as on the bus, shopping at the grocery store, or a video arcade.

The SIT literature in learning disability, even now, is rather small. Hughes and Agran (1993) suggest that investigators are still reluctant to advocate the use of language-based approaches for those with limited verbal skills. However, the literature does provide striking evidence that verbally oriented approaches can help people with learning disabilities, even with apparently minimal verbal skills, to direct their own behaviour. We shall describe examples of such approaches and concentrate on transfer as an outcome, and whether predictions can be made for whom it works. We will then examine the behavioural and cognitive components of SIT to explore limitations to the approach and further directions, signposted by new developments in cognitive theory of transfer, which training in self-regulation may take.

In SIT participants are taught, by instructor modelling and feedback, verbally to rehearse instructions to set a goal, take action to fulfil that goal and to attend to whether that goal is met, and then to reward oneself for meeting the goal. Stages of training were based on Vygotsky (1962) and Luria's (1961) model as follows: an instructor performs a task, instructing aloud, while the participant observes; the participant then performs the task while being instructed; the participant performs a task while self-instructing, at first overtly, then covertly (see Hughes and Agran, 1993).

Self-instruction: examples

Agran, Fodor-Davis and Moore (1986) used SIT to teach four adults with mild learning disabilities to learn simple housekeeping skills. The participants were taught to use self-instructions, such as 'I've just brought the vacuum into the room' by modelling and verbal rehearsal, for what they had just finished doing, what they needed to do next, and what they were going to do. Following training all participants increased their percentage of job-sequencing. They also maintained the use of their skills up to three months after training. However, transfer to other tasks was inconsistent.

Agran, Salzberg and Stowitstchek (1987) used similar techniques with individuals with moderate and severe learning disabilities in the training of social interaction skills. They were taught skills for seeking assistance when they ran out of task materials. Those with moderate disabilities were able to learn the skills, and maintained skill use. However, they did not transfer the skills for initiating contact with others from 'running out of materials' to initiating contact for completing work tasks. Also, unfortunately participants with severe disabilities failed to learn the self-instructions. This suggested that participants needed to have a high degree of language skill before being able to make use of SIT.

In contrast, Hughes and Rusch (1989) and Hughes (1992) showed that SIT could be used to teach vocational skills to individuals with severe learning disability if very simple self-instructions were used. Hughes (1992), for example, taught participants to use self-instructions for solving how to plug in lamps, such as 'light out, gotta fix it, plug in'. Participants learnt the skills and went on to use the self-instruction strategy to respond appropriately to further untrained problem situations.

Criticisms of self-instruction

Although participants of SIT programmes tend to learn and maintain skills they have not been shown consistently to generalise skills to similar tasks nor to generalise instructing themselves as a problem-solving approach (see reviews by Hughes and Agran, 1993; Meichenbaum and Asarnow, 1979; Whitman, 1987). It has been argued that the inconsistent transfer of SIT is due to the fact that those participants unable to learn and generalise by self-instruction were not being partialled out from those who can. Hitherto the numbers of participants per study, usually less than five (Hughes and Agran, 1993), mitigate against adequate analyses. Researchers in self-instruction had not therefore managed to identify the precise participant characteristics which would predict the success of a self-regulation programme prior to its implementation. There have been a number of calls for analyses of the inter-action between individual differences in cognitive and linguistic skills and training effects so that predictions can be made regarding for whom self-instruction is a useful intervention (Meichenbaum, 1990; Whitman, 1987). A study by the first author who attempted to evaluate how individual differences in language and cognitive skills predict intervention success will be discussed later.

Further criticisms can be made of the approach in terms of what are supposed to be the active ingredients that are meant to deliver transfer, and whether, in fact, they should. There are operant and cognitive components within SIT for promoting transfer. Participants may generalise self-instruction for a class of tasks as a conditioned response operation (Rusch, Schutz and Heal, 1983). Hughes (1992), for example, largely attributed her participants' transfer of skills to their exposure to 'sufficient' multiple exemplars of training tasks that, she suggests, served to form self-instructing as a response class. People therefore would have a response 'trained up' to a number of situations which serve as a discriminative stimulus for that response. The wider the range of situations, the greater the number of salient characteristics of the environment that would come to serve as such stimuli. This behavioural component may be a necessary factor for promoting transfer, but it retains problematic characteristics as described above in our discussion of ABA and transfer. That is, relentless responding to the surface features of environments may lead to a 'gluing' to surface features and to negative transfer (responding with particular skills in inappropriate situations). These issues will be examined in more detail below.

Self-instruction is also supposed to contain cognitive elements for effecting transfer. Verbal rehearsal has been argued to set up retentional processes for processing information in between memory stores such that learners remember the strategy (Meichenbaum and Asarnow, 1979; and see Hale and Borkowski, 1992). Indeed rehearsal is argued to be a particularly useful strategy for people with learning disabilities as they to tend not to use such memorial strategies (Hale and Borkowski, 1992). In addition, as SIT requires learners actively to rehearse instructions, it forces their engagement, facilitating attention and concentration for a task (Meichenbaum and Asarnow, 1979). Over the past fifteen years a number of reviewers have argued that the cognitive component of SIT, faded verbal rehearsal, might be an inefficient cognitive strategy for encouraging transfer (e.g. Schleser *et al.*, 1984). It has been argued that although SIT engages learners' memory processes for reproducing self-instructional statements, it does not require the learner to integrate self-instruction as a problem-solving approach with their existing strategic knowledge and executive decision-making skills (Schleser *et al.*, 1984). Such criticisms reflect the claim that people with learning disabilities do not lack specific strategic processing, such as rehearsal, but have difficulty in spontaneous access and co-ordination of such processes, that is in metacognitive processing (Borkowski and Turner, 1988; Hale and Borkowski, 1992). This criticism is particularly relevant when considering the cognitive determinants of transfer. It is with the cognitive determinants of transfer, and how to help people develop metacognitive awareness for making use of old information in new environments, that the remainder of this chapter will be largely concerned.

METACOGNITION AND TRANSFER OF SKILLS

Gick and Holyoak (1987) argued that transfer depends heavily on participants' perception of similarity between training and transfer tasks. Perceived similarity may lie in the tasks' surface features, that is they may be topographically related. For example, the first task of discovering the causes of failure in electrical appliances, such as radios and televisions, are the same: first check the power source. Similarity may also lie deeper within task structures – they may be functionally related, in terms of similar goals and processing. For example, to check failure in a gasoline lawnmower, first, as with radios and televisions, check the power source. Topographically different tasks that may occur in different settings (e.g. in a house or in a garden) may then share structural similarities which need to be discovered by an active problem-solver for her or him to deploy previously learnt skills. Consequently learning to transfer skills by first attending to surface features of tasks for discriminative stimuli and, second, by verbal rehearsal, to give oneself a list of things to do as a response to such topographically similar tasks, may leave those people 'glued' to surface features. Such learners would remain unable to learn to explore further topographically different tasks, to discover how self-directed talk might help as a problem-solving device to be called on and, by which, to apply skills learnt previously on tasks that are topographically different. That is, they might not learn the metacognitive processing necessary for implementing 'known strategies' during new tasks (Hale and Borkowski, 1992).

Ironically, therefore, by relying on the behavioural component for transfer, SIT narrows the band of transfer that is allowed as it actively 'glues' people to the surface features of tasks. Thus people need to be taught actively to scan and adapt their strategic repertoires to meet the demands of tasks (that is, to be metacognitive) so that they may discover structural commonalties between tasks in order to transfer skills. It is this form of cognition that appears the most salient to target in training for transfer. It is actual training in cognitive self-regulation. Controversy as to the ability of people with learning disability to profit from approaches with such apparently sophisticated content is similar to the discussion over the general use of verbal mediation with this population.

The rationale for teaching metacognitive strategies to people with learning disabilities versus teaching by modelling procedures was simply stated by Vygotsky (1978). He wrote that it was understandable that educationalists concentrated on concrete thinking (or look-and-do) problems for children with learning disabilities given their difficulties with abstract awareness. However, in doing so, teachers failed to assist their learners to overcome their handicaps and, moreover, reinforced their handicaps by accustoming them exclusively to concrete thinking which, Vygotsky (1978, p. 89) argued,

> suppress the rudiments of . . . abstract thought that such children still have. . . . [Therefore, he continued] the school should make every effort to push them in that direction [towards abstract awareness] and to develop in them what is intrinsically lacking in their own development.

An anchor definition of metacognition is provided by Wellman (1983, p. 33): 'it is the difference between engaging in some form of cognition versus knowledge of that cognition itself . . . it is no different from any other knowledge one possesses'.

It is what we believe to be what Vygotsky called 'reflective awareness and deliberate (cognitive) control' (Vygotsky, 1962).

Campione, Brown and Ferrara (1982, p. 434) describe the metacognitive nature of active problem-solving as:

> *Self-regulatory mechanisms* used by an active learner during an ongoing attempt to solve problems. These indexes of metacognition include checking the outcome . . . planning one's next move, monitoring effectiveness of any attempted action, and testing and revising and evaluating one's strategies for learning (our italics).

Ironically, the traditional SIT approach – with participants observing a model, rehearsing instructions in a monologue (a list, or menu of instruction) – remains overly 'look and do as I do!' and not 'How would you do?' which might encourage such metacognitive development.

Metacognition and self-instruction

It therefore seems that if to self-instruct is to control one's own behaviour by talking to oneself, then to be metacognitive would be to know that by talking to oneself one is controlling one's own behaviour. SIT relied on learners to learn instructions that controlled them, whereas to be trained in metacognition would involve a person becoming more active in generating such self-regulatory speech.

Campione, Brown and Ferrara (1982), in common with those developing self-instructional programmes, looked to Vygotsky's theory for a method for teaching metacognitive skills to non-disabled children. The result was reciprocal teaching, a form of Socratic dialogue, which, although a systematised form of social interaction, emphasised the role of children's discovery of solutions for themselves to problems, and being supported in doing so with graded hints (e.g. Campione and Brown, 1987). Reeve and Brown (1985, p. 347) argued that, consistent with the views of Luria and Vygotsky,

> awareness of self-regulatory activity has its roots in social interactions with others. Others, in the developing child's world, initially take responsibility for articulating metacognitive processes. With time, this responsibility is ceded to the child, who is required to take charge of her or his own thinking behaviors.

Williams, Ellis and Jones (1996) investigated the effects of teaching skills to adults with learning disabilities by a traditional SIT programme and by a metacognitively enhanced programme. As would seem evident from the discussion so far, the main issue in the area of using self-regulatory programmes with people with learning disabilities was that, although there was increasing theoretical impetus for using such approaches, there was little clear evidence of whether such approaches were of use, and, if so, for whom, particularly as regards transfer. The study was therefore designed with two main aims: (1) to compare the effects of teaching self-instruction explicitly by verbal rehearsal against encouraging participants to discover solutions via a problem-solving approach which encouraged metacognitive processing; and (2) to explore whether individual differences in terms of linguistic and cognitive processing might predict training outcome.

The participants in the study were forty-five people with learning disabilities aged between 21 and 60 years. They spoke in at least two-word sentences and had no major sensory disability. Participants had expressive and receptive language skills comparable to the developmental age equivalent range of 3 years, 8 months to 5 years, 6 months and abstract reasoning skills comparable, on average, to below the non-disabled developmental equivalent age of 5 years, 5 months.

Participants were taught communication skills using maps. They were taught skills for being effective speakers, for being able to tell a listener how to find a series of target referents by making selective comparisons ('from the house, to the tree, *the evergreen not the apple tree*'). After being trained with maps as speakers they were tested for learning and transfer with a series of tasks, including being speakers with maps with novel icons (supermarket layout); being speakers on a task involving giving directions to assemble a three-dimensional object (a block model bridge which had blocks of various sizes and colours); and being listeners with maps (principally recognising that if they were given an ambiguous message ('the tree' when there are two) they could be active and ask for selective comparisons).

The participants were assigned to one of three groups – verbal self-instruction, metacognitive training or practice (didactic) – and trained as speakers with a series of nine maps over three 45-minute sessions. The verbal rehearsal self-instructions condition included modelling of task behaviour, verbal rehearsal of self-instructions (with prompting and fading) and self-reinforcement. Self-instructional statements were designed, for example, to implement 'trace and name' for map reading ('Line goes from the house to the tree'), to evaluate progress ('I'm to ask if you got there. Did you get there?') and implement a strategy for recognising situations when the listener could not select a target referent and requires a selective comparison ('No? You didn't get there. But if there's two trees, which one? The evergreen tree'), and self-reinforcing statements ('We're doing OK'). At the end of each trial the dyad's maps were compared and the participant was given an evaluation of performance: ('We didn't do too good', 'We did well', 'We did real well'). To foster transfer the participants were told, at the end of sessions, to use the instructions they had learnt that day ('When we do this again tomorrow').

In the metacognitive condition participants were engaged in a dialogue with an instructor by questions that provided a model of executive decision-making skills for tasks. Participants were not told to rehearse instructions but to ask questions of themselves. A hierarchy of questions and statements was used to guide participants to discover task demands and appropriate strategic intent and then to implement strategies and monitor performance. Questions were designed to engage participants in joint problem-solving, and provided statements to clarify and summarise task-appropriate behaviour. Questions were set to prompt participants to make predictions about the effect of strategic actions. If the participant did not provide an answer to a question, the instructor provided assistance. The instructor asked questions and made summaries in the following stages.

1 Questions for joint task analysis: 'What is this? A map – mine's got things joined up, has yours? No.' The instructor then made a statement to clarify the task characteristics: 'I've a map with a road, your map hasn't got a road.'

2 The instructor then asked a question to prompt the 'trace and name' strategy and to make predictions about sharing knowledge: 'What if I told you how my road/line goes? You could fill your map in', 'OK, the road goes from the house to the tree'.

3 After naming a referent the instructor asked the participant a question to focus on the need for perspective monitoring: 'How do I find out if you are doing OK – that you made a line from the house to the tree?'

4 The instructor then asked the participants questions for modelling the selection of a strategy for monitoring the participants' perspective as a listener and for predicting the outcome of doing so: 'What if I asked if you got there? I'd know. So, did you get there?' If the participant, confronted with two nominally similar referents, could not target a referent by name only (and either said 'No, I didn't get there' or had inappropriately selected a referent, answering 'Yes, got it') the instructor asked questions to foster the participants' 'discovery' of the need for selective comparisons: 'But, if there's two trees, how do I make sure you get the right one? What if I told you how the one you want is different to the other? You should choose the evergreen/tall one.'

5 At the end of each trial the participant was asked to monitor the dyad's performance and predict the usefulness of using such communicative strategies in future: 'Do you think we did well? What if we had the same kind of work to do again?'

The study produced results that showed quite clearly how differential transfer effects can be produced by adopting verbal rehearsal or metacognitive (Socratic) self-regulatory approaches.

• *Learning.* Participants in both self-regulatory groups learnt to make selective comparisons for a listener when using maps, such as 'Go to the larger house'.

• *Near transfer.* Participants in both self-regulatory groups used the same skills on a different kind of map with supermarket symbols, such as 'Go from the red bottle bin to the bigger checkout'.

• *Far transfer 1.* Participants in the metacognitive group used their selective comparison skills when they were asked to tell another how to assemble a three-dimensional object, such as 'Place the large yellow brick on the long red brick'

• *Far transfer 2.* Participants in the metacognitive group – when asked to be listeners – were able to ask for selective comparisons from a speaker who had given her or him ambiguous messages for finding referents on maps, such as, to the direction of 'Go to the tree', they tended to respond with requests for clarification with 'Which one? There's two trees'.

Participants who received self-instructional training to clarify ambiguous messages using verbal rehearsal had therefore learnt a routine for performing well on the training tasks but did not appear to have gained knowledge of self-instruction (or engaging their inner speech) as a problem-solving strategy for further, topographically different, tasks. In contrast, recipients of meta-cognitive instruction seemed aware of the benefits of interrogating their own strategic knowledge base and exploring whether skills learnt were applicable to tasks that were topographically different but structurally similar to the training tasks.

The study was also designed to examine how participants' individual skills, in cognitive and linguistic domains, might predict success of training. In the self-instructional condition those who had highest performance scores for language comprehension and short-term memory measures appeared most able to acquire and transfer skills, albeit near transfer. Near and far transfer effects in the metacognitive group were related to performance on measures of abstract reasoning and short-term memory, while maintenance was related to performance on language comprehension measures. Metacognitive instruction may have had an impact on participants' capacity to represent and manipulate information in an abstract fashion, while self-instruction may have had an impact on participants' potential for sheer repetition.

Interpreting these individual difference effects suggests two main implications. First, persons who readily demonstrate abstract reasoning skills may make appreciable gains from a metacognitively enriched self-instructional programme, even as brief an intervention as reported here. Second, instructional gains could be enhanced, especially for those with advanced language comprehension skills, with active verbal rehearsal.

Our data on individual differences should not serve to guide the development of exclusion criteria, to deny persons training in cognitive self-regulation, because of scores on various cognitive measures, but should serve to suggest ways of including persons as efficiently and effectively as possible in training programmes. As Jones (1991, p. 61) emphasised, 'any large group of people will include individuals who have differing verbal abilities. It is likely, therefore, that the responses of these individuals to particular interventions will differ on the basis of their ability to formulate and use verbal rules describing schedule contingencies.'

This point is crucial considering how cognitive programmes could be made useful for persons who, for example, are without readily demonstrable abstract reasoning skills. Indeed, our data suggest for whom such modifications in training programmes need to be made. Some people with moderate, and possibly severe, learning disabilities may need shorter but more numerous training sessions. They may also benefit from changes in instructional content such as shorter self-instructions and fewer questions (Hughes, 1992). Moreover, continued training over multiple exemplars would increase the likelihood of transfer (Hughes, 1992) and may foster metacognitive awareness.

In general, the findings suggest that, for teaching and clinical purposes, targeting training on metacognitive activity is fundamentally important for encouraging transfer of learning, while engaging participants in active verbal rehearsal may well consolidate learning.

People with a learning disability can therefore use metacognitive strategies for engaging and developing their inner speech for learning and transferring skills for particular tasks. Thus they can be released from a dependence on topographical similarity between tasks for transfer of skills. The inclusion of metacognitive strategies in training reduces the need to hope for generalisation to occur as either a conditioned response to a certain set of stimuli, or for a learner spontaneously to attempt to deploy self-instruction as a problem- solving stratagem. Indeed, the findings exemplify what Borkowski, Carr and Pressley (1987, p. 62–3) argued to be crucial to consider in teaching skills: 'Strategy use is never spontaneous . . . [it] is the result of a complex interaction involving . . . knowledge of strategies, knowledge about higher level co-ordinating strategies, and motivational beliefs.'

It is in training in such metacognitive strategies, which makes the process of generating and applying self-commands explicit for a learner, that 'spontaneity' is promoted. If, then, to self-instruct is to control one's behaviour by talking to oneself, to be metacognitive is to know that by talking to oneself one is controlling one's behaviour. Training in such cognitive self-regulatory skills is possible and can promote intrinsic control over behaviour.

CONCLUSIONS

Promoting intrinsic control over behaviour has emerged as the principal goal of approaches to skills teaching in learning disabilities. We have shown how the transfer problem itself reflects a more fundamental difficulty for people with learning disabilities; that they may not see themselves as, nor make themselves, agents for their own behaviour. In effecting intrinsic control over behaviour they may develop greater self-efficacy and independence.

In this chapter we have outlined a range of cognitive-behavioural approaches that may be used to enable people with learning disability to develop self-regulatory skills. We have argued that interventions, be they for skills teaching or for bringing about direct therapeutic emotional change, should be designed to account for both the cognitive and emotional determinants of apparent learning disability.

Clinicians wishing to enable people to develop specific skills for independence (e.g. social skills, employment skills), or for coping with emotional difficulties (e.g. controlling anger, developing relaxation techniques for social anxiety must, of course, tailor programmes to the strengths of each individual, be it for comprehending and setting of contingencies for oneself by verbal rule formation or for strategic problem-solving by metacognitive instruction. Programmes discussed may provide persons with learning disability with the foundation skills for managing their own behaviour, encouraging adaptivity and autonomy. However, we emphasise that the development of self-regulation, although it can be boosted by such short-term programmes, is a long-term goal.

People with learning disabilities are more likely to have experienced skills performed for them by others than to have had self-regulatory skills gradually shaped with the expectation of success. Indeed, persons with learning disabilities tend to have higher expectations of failure than non-disabled persons, and it is hypothesised that they are more likely to attribute failure to lack of ability than to controllable factors such as effort (Hale and

Borkowski, 1992). The importance of a global view of self-regulation was outlined by Whitman (1990, p. 359) who stated that:

From a developmental perspective attributional beliefs not only develop as a result of life experiences but also can be directly shaped by teaching individuals with retardation that success is a consequence of effort and proper strategy usage on their part and conversely that failure occurs through lack of effort and strategic inactivity.

True self-regulation means that an individual has both control and choice over significant aspects of her or his own life. The technology does exist for improving the skills of people with learning disabilities to take greater control over aspects of their lives, and in doing so gain the rewards inherent in being in control.

REFERENCES

Abbeduto, L., Davies, B., Solesby, S. and Furan, L. (1991) Identifying the referents of spoken messages: use of context and clarification requests by children with and without mental retardation. *American Journal of Mental Retardation*, **95**, 5, 551–62.

Agran, M., Fodor-Davis, J. and Moore, S. (1986) The effects of self-instructional training on job-task sequencing: suggesting a problem solving strategy. *Education and Training of the Mentally Retarded*, December, 273–81.

Agran, M., Salzberg, C.L. and Stowitstchek, J.J. (1987) An analysis of the effects of social skills program using self-instructions on the acquisition and generalization of two social behaviors in a work setting. *Journal of the Association for Persons with Severe Handicaps*, **12**, 131–9.

Bandura, A. (1976) Self reinforcement: theoretical and methodological considerations. *Behaviorism*, **4**, 135–55.

Beveridge, M. and Conti-Ramsden, G. (1987) Social cognition and problem solving in persons with mental retardation. *Australia and New Zealand Journal of Developmental Disabilities*, **13**, 99–106.

Borkowski, J.G. and Turner, L. (1988) Cognitive development. In J. Kavanaugh, *Understanding Mental Retardation: Research Accomplishments and New Frontiers*. Baltimore: Paul H. Brooks.

Borkowski, J.K., Carr, M. and Pressley, M. (1987) 'Spontaneous' strategy use: perspectives from metacognitive theory. *Intelligence*, **11**, 61–75.

Bryon, M. (1988) The reduction of disruptive behaviour using self-management: a component analysis. Unpublished research dissertation. Leicester: The British Psychological Society.

Campione, J.C. and Brown, A.L. (1987) Linking dynamic assessment with school achievement. In C. Schneider (ed.), *Dynamic Assessment*. New York: Guilford Publications.

Campione, J.C., Brown, A.L. and Ferrara, R.A. (1982) Mental retardation and intelligence. In R.J. Sternberg (ed.), *Handbook of Human Intelligence*. Cambridge: Cambridge University Press.

Carr, J. (1991) Recent advances in working with people with learning difficulties. *Behavioural Psychotherapy*, **19**, 109–20.

Frazer, W.I. (1992) Teaching skills. In W.I. Frazer, R.C. MacGillivray and A.M. Green (eds), *Hallas' Caring for People with Mental Handicaps*. Oxford: Butterworth Heinemann.

Gardner, W.I. and Cole, C.L. (1989) Self-management approaches. In E. Cipani (ed.), *The Treatment of Severe Behavior Disorders: Behavior Analysis Approaches*. Washington, DC: American Association on Mental Retardation.

Gick, M.L. and Holyoak, K.J. (1987) Analogical problem solving. In A. Aitkinhead and M. Slack (eds), *Issues in Cognitive Modelling*. Hillsdale, NJ: Laurence Erlbaum.

Hale, C.A. and Borkowski, J.G. (1992) Attention, memory and cognition. In J.L. Matson and J.A. Mulick (eds), *Handbook of Mental Retardation* (2nd edn). New York: Pergamon.

Hawton, K., Salkovskis, P.M., Kirk, J., and Clark, D.M. (1989) *Cognitive Behaviour Therapy for Psychiatric Problems: A Practical Guide*. Oxford: Oxford University Press.

Hayes, S.C. (1989) *Rule Goverened Behavior: Cognition, Contingencies and Instructional Control*. New York: Plenum Press.

Haywood, H.C. (1986) Intrinsic motivation and behavior effectiveness in retarded persons. *International Review of Research in Mental Retardation*, **14**, 1–46.

Hughes, C. (1992) Teaching self-instruction utilizing multiple exemplars to produce generalized problem solving among individuals with severe mental retardation. *American Journal on Mental Retardation*, **97**, 302–14.

Hughes, C. and Agran, M. (1993) Teaching persons with severe disabilities to use self-instruction in community settings: an analysis of applications. *Journal of the Association of Persons with Severe Handicaps*, **18**, 261–74.

Hughes, C. and Rusch, F.R. (1989) Teaching supported employees with severe mental retardation to solve problems. *Journal of Applied Behavior Analysis*, **22**, 365–72.

Jones, R.S.P. (1991) Reducing inappropriate behaviour using non-aversive procedures: evaluating differential reinforcement schedules. In B. Remington (ed.), *The Challenge of Severe Mental Handicap: A Behaviour Analytic Approach*. Chichester: John Wiley.

Jones, R.S., Williams, W.H. and Lowe, C.F. (1993) Verbal self-regulation. In Ian Fleming and Biza Stenfert Kroese (eds), *People with Learning Disability and Severe Challenging Behaviour: New Developments in Services and Therapy*. Manchester: Manchester University Press.

Kneedler, R.D. and Hallahan, D.P. (1981) Self-monitoring of on-task behavior with learning disabled children: current studies and directions. *Exceptional Education Quarterly*, **2**, 73–82.

Lignugaris-Kraft, B., Salzberg, C.L., Rule, S. and Stowitschek, J.J. (1988) Social-vocational skills of workers with and without retardation in two community employment sites. *Mental Retardation*, **26**, (5), 295–305.

Litrownik, A.J., Freitas, J.L., and Franzini, L.R. (1978) Self-regulation in mentally retarded children: assessment and training of self-monitoring skills. *American Journal of Mental Deficiency*, **82**, 499–506.

Luria, A.R. (1959) The directive function of speech in development and dissolution: Part I. Development of the directive function of speech in early childhood. *Word*, **15**, 341–53.

Luria, A.R. (1961) *The Role of Speech in the Regulation of Normal and Abnormal Behaviour*, ed. J. Tizard. London: Pergamon.

Martin, G. and Pear, J. (1992) *Behavior Modification: What It Is and How To Do It* (4th edn). Englewood Cliffs, NJ: Prentice-Hall International.

McConaughy, E.K, Stowitstchek, J.J., Salzberg, C.L. and Peatross, D.K. (1989) Work supervisors' ratings of social behaviors related to employment success. *Rehabilitation Psychology*, **34**, 3–15.

Meichenbaum, D. (1990) Cognitive perspective on teaching self-regulation. *American Journal of Mental Retardation*, **94**, 367–9.

Meichenbaum, D. and Asarnow, J. (1979) Cognitive-behavioral modification and metacognitive development: implications for the classroom. In P.C. Kendall and

S.D. Hollon (eds), *Cognitive-Behavioral Interventions: Theory Research and Practice*. New York: Academic Press.

Meichenbaum, D. and Goodman, J. (1971) Training impulsive children to talk to themselves: a means of developing self-control. *Journal of Abnormal Psychology*, **77**, 115–26.

Nezu, C.M. and Nezu, A.M (1994) Outpatient psychotherapy for adults with mental retardation and concomitant psychopathology: research and clinical imperatives. *Journal of Consulting and Clinical Psychology*, **62**, 1, 34–42.

Reese, R.M. Sherman, J.A. and Sheldon, J. (1984) Reducing agitated-disruptive behavior of mentally retarded residents of community group homes: the role of self-recording and peer prompted self-recording. *Analysis and Intervention in Development Disabilities*, **4**, 91–107.

Reeve, R.A. and Brown, A.L. (1985) Metacognition reconsidered: implications for intervention research. *Journal of Abnormal Child Psychology*, **13**, 343–56.

Remington, B. (1991) Behaviour analysis and severe mental handicap: the dialogue between research and application. In B. Remington (ed.), *The Challenge of Severe Mental Handicap: A Behaviour Analytic Approach*. Chichester: John Wiley.

Rusch, F.R., Schutz, R.P. and Heal, L.W. (1983) Vocational training and placement. In J.L. Matson and J.A. Mulick (eds), *Handbook of Mental Retardation*. New York: Pergamon.

Schleser, R., Cohen, R., Meyers, A.W. and Rodick J.D. (1984) The effects of cognitive level and training procedures on the transfer of self-instructions. *Cognitive Therapy and Research*, **8**, 187–200.

Shapiro, E.S. (1986) Behavior modification: self-control and cognitive procedures. In R.P. Barrett (ed.), *Severe Behavior Disorders in the Mentally Retarded*. New York: Plenum Press.

Skinner, B.F. (1953) *Science and Human Behavior*. New York: Macmillan.

Vygotsky, L.S. (1962) *Thought and Language*, ed. A. Kozulin. Cambridge, MA: MIT Press.

Vygotsky, L.S. (1978) *Mind in Society: The Development of Higher Psychological Processes*. Cambridge, MA: Harvard University Press.

Vygotsky, L.S. (1987) The problem of mental retardation (a tentative working hypothesis). *Soviet Psychology*, **26**, 78–85.

Wellman, H. (1983) Metamemory revisited. In M.T. Chi (ed.), *Trends in Memory Development*, Vol. 2. Basel: Karger.

Whitman, T.L. (1987) Self-instruction, individual differences, and mental retardation. *American Journal of Mental Deficiency*, **92**, 213–23.

Whitman, T.L. (1990) Self-regulation and mental retardation, *American Journal of Mental Retardation*, **94**, 347–62.

Williams, W.H., Ellis, N.C. and Jones, R.S.P. (in preparation) Teaching communication skills to persons with developmental disabilities: effects of teaching by self-instructive and metacognitive approaches and of individual differences on generalization of skills.

Zigler, E. and Balla, D. (1982) The developmental approach to mental retardation. In E. Zigler and D. Balla (eds), *Mental Retardation: The Developmental-Difference Controversy*, Hillsdale, NJ: Laurence Erlbaum.

6 Social problem-solving groups for adults with learning disabilities

Konstantinos Loumidis and Andrew Hill

INTRODUCTION

Social problem-solving is a cognitive-affective-behavioural process by which people attempt to identify, discover or invent ways of dealing with everyday problems (D'Zurilla and Goldfried, 1971). It is at the same time a social learning process, a self-management technique and a general coping strategy, applicable to a wide range of problems (D'Zurilla, 1988). Other terms have also been used to refer to essentially the same process, for example, inter-personal problem-solving (Shure, and Spivack, 1978) interpersonal cognitive problem-solving (Spivack, Platt and Shure, 1976) and personal problem-solving (Heppner and Petersen, 1982).

The link between social problem-solving skills and social and psychological adjustment has been supported by evidence from a variety of sources (see D'Zurilla, 1988; Marx, 1988). For example, poor social problem-solving skills are reported among a wide range of clinical populations (e.g. maladjusted adolescents, adult psychiatric patients, drug and alcohol abusers, depressed students, suicidal patients). In addition, compared to effective problem-solvers, ineffective problem-solvers report a greater number of life problems, more anxiety, more depression, more irrational beliefs and more dysfunctional thoughts. In clinical practice, social problem-solving therapy aims at: (a) equipping people with problem-solving skills to solve current life problems if problem resolution is possible; (b) helping people to change their way of thinking about the problem if problem resolution is not possible; and (c) equipping them with generalisable skills to deal with future problems more effectively and independently.

Problem-solving therapy has been successfully applied as a major therapeutic intervention (e.g. depression, stress, anxiety, agoraphobia), as a treatment maintenance strategy (smoking reduction, alcohol, expressed emotion in schizophrenia), as a competence training approach with non-clinical populations (e.g. academic achievement) and has been recommended for individuals prior to drastic environmental, social and personal changes (see Marx, 1988). In that way social problem-solving differs from other forms of general problem-solving such as the intellectually abstract process of dealing with puzzles, anagrams and arithmetic tasks that rely on different types of reasoning.

However, training in social problem-solving skills should not be confused with social skills training. According to McFall (1982) social skills training helps clients to acquire *responses* which, when displayed during interpersonal interactions, are deemed appropriate for the situation (Marchetti and Campbell, 1990). Acquired social skill responses could be non-verbal motoric behaviour, verbal behaviour, affective behaviour and social cognitive skills (Trower, Bryant and Argyle, 1978), although the inclusion of cognitive skills as a part of the social skills definition still remains controversial (see Marchetti and Campbell, 1990). In contrast, social problem-solving refers to the *process* of discovering an effective course of action, which following training could be applied in a wide range of situations and generalise to future problems.

People with learning disabilities have particular difficulties in dealing with social and interpersonal problems (Ashman and Conway, 1989; Bouffard, 1990). Maladaptive social behaviour is often a major obstacle to integration in the community (Schalock, Harper and Genung, 1981) and to a large extent such behaviour may result from a lack of ability to solve personal and social problems.

As a result individual or group training programmes have been developed with apparent success. A recent review highlighted the clinical importance of this approach with children as well as adults with mild or moderate learning disabilities (Loumidis, 1992). One of the strengths of this approach is that training can be combined with other treatments (e.g. anger management, assertiveness training) to improve general problem-solving skills or meet specific needs of people in community, residential or employment settings. Social problem-solving could then be perceived as a 'positive programming' approach (La Vigna and Donnellan, 1986) empowering people with 'functionally equivalent' responses based on problem-solving skills to enhance their quality of life in community settings.

Critical issues in the application of social problem-solving skills training to people with learning disabilities

Literature relevant to the training of social problem-solving skills in individuals with learning disabilities has been reviewed and critically evaluated elsewhere (Loumidis, 1992, 1993). On the basis of the critique, a five-stage view of the problem-solving process was then offered as a means for planning and evaluating social problem-solving training programmes, and detailed outcome criteria were proposed for assessing the effectiveness of training (Loumidis and Hill, in press). The five stages are:

1 problem recognition and definition;
2 ends-directed thinking;

3 instrumental or means–end thinking;
4 evaluative checking and decision-making;
5 solution implementation.

In the next section the literature related to the clinical application of social problem-solving skills training is reviewed.

A REVIEW OF THE LITERATURE: CLINICAL ISSUES

Number of sessions

The duration of training in social problem-solving for people with learning disabilities has often been short. For example, Bramston and Spence (1984) used four weeks of training, Ross and Ross (1973) six weeks, Vaughn, Ridley and Cox (1983) eight weeks, Foss, Auty and Irvin (1989) six weeks. Some authors have suggested that weak and transient effects of social problem-solving skills training may have been due to too short a training period (Bramston and Spence, 1984). Most studies recommend an increase in the amount of training sessions with the potential use of booster sessions to attain the maximum effect. Meta-analytic evidence from a review of fifty social problem-solving studies with children reported that interventions lasting for forty or more 1-hour sessions lead to better acquired skills (Denham and Almeida, 1987). Since training is likely eventually to build people's confidence and raise their expectations in dealing with everyday problems, extra sessions may be necessary during the practice of the acquired skills emphasising components of training that evaluate the degree of realism of problem-solving. In addition, booster sessions may be required for encouragement, support and corrective feedback to promote maintenance and generalisation.

Comprehension

According to Ashman and Conway (1989) any intervention should take into consideration the cognitive strengths and weaknesses of the client. Because the medium of training is principally verbal, it is essential to ensure that the participants in social problem-solving interventions have a sufficient level of language comprehension to benefit from training. In a review of assessment instruments for people with learning disabilities, Matson and Frame (1986) proposed ways of improving comprehension, such as using short questions, or rewording them occasionally, requiring both yes and no responses since in many cases people with learning disabilities may be influenced by a bias towards answers in the affirmative (Sigelman *et al.*, 1981). An index of ability to comprehend different levels of language can also be obtained from some of the items of the Adaptive Behaviour Scale (Nihira *et al.*,1974), although formal measures of verbal abilities should be preferred. Manuals and assessment materials should at best be formally examined by a speech therapist, or at least contain open-ended questions to indicate that the concepts are understood. Subsequently, the language and concepts used at any stage of assessment and training should be adjusted to the level and needs of the participants.

Therapeutic effects

To establish the therapeutic effects on general mental health or social adjustment solely on the basis of improvements in measures of social problem-solving skill is insufficient. Yet, in many studies, improvements in social adjustment were claimed on the basis that post-training measures of problem-solving skills (e.g. number of alternative solutions generated for hypothetical problems of questionable relevance to the life of trainees) showed statistically significant increases over pre-training measures. Such an assertion was justified on the basis of the 'quantity breeds quality' principle of social problem-solving theory. This principle was supported by a positive correlation between quantity and quality of solutions (D'Zurilla and Nezu, 1980; Spivack, Platt and Shure, 1976). However, an increase in the number of alternative solutions does not necessarily indicate an improvement in a person's ability to evaluate the alternative solutions, decide which is the best and finally implement and verify it. Thus, measuring the outcome of training in terms of the number of alternative solutions does not necessarily reflect accurately the extent to which training may have improved the ability to solve real-life problems effectively. An emphasis on qualitative aspects of solutions to problems (such as effectiveness and social acceptability) both for assessment and training purposes is likely to be much more meaningful and valid as a component of an evaluation and seems more likely to be related to psychological adjustment.

In addition, to ensure that social problem-solving training is not a simple cognitive exercise, but a powerful technique for clinical change, it is essential to evaluate the effects of training using measures of adaptive behaviour or psychological distress and not simply measures of social problem-solving skill. However, selecting measures of psychological distress that are sensitive enough to detect changes in moods or behaviour for people with learning disabilities can be a difficult task. This is due to the fact that in learning disabilities research, most measures of behavioural adjustment or psychopathology are staff report measures designed for the quite severely disabled group. Such measures tend to assess severe forms of psychiatric psychopathology such as hallucinations (Clinical Interview Schedule: Goldberg *et al.*, 1970), schizoid withdrawal (Devereux Adolescent Behaviour Rating Scale: Spivack, Haimes and Spotts, 1967), or schizophrenia (Diagnostic Assessment for the Severely Handicapped Scale: Matson *et al.*, 1990). However, some of the well-established measures of adaptive and maladaptive behaviour (e.g. Adaptive Behaviour Scale: Nihira *et al.*, 1974), have some items tapping psychological distress (e.g. poor reaction to frustration) completed by independent raters. The ABS-R therefore appears to be a potentially useful measure of adjustment but has been under-used in social problem-solving skill training for people with learning disabilities. Furthermore, there has been an increasing body of applied research in learning disabilities using self-report measures developed for people without learning disabilities (see Chapters 1, 7 and 8), although in institutional settings an attempt to apply a modified version of the General Health Questionnaire (GHQ-28: Goldberg, 1978) was shown to be problematic (see Loumidis, 1990).

Finally, it is important to obtain some feedback from the clients themselves on the process and outcome of training. Despite the inevitable risk of obtaining results contaminated by demand characteristics, any negative feedback could be used constructively to improve process variables that may be perceived as being obstacles to therapeutic success.

Generalisation

If training is to be considered therapeutically useful for people with learning disabilities, it is important to determine whether the skills are maintained and will generalise. Some previous studies failed to report any generalisation of social problem-solving skills (Castles and Glass, 1986; Ross and Ross, 1973, 1978), or have reported poor generalisation over time (Bramston and Spence, 1984; Mueser et al., 1987). The exact way in which previous researchers attempted to promote generalisation is often not mentioned (e.g. Mueser, Valenti-Hein and Yarnold, 1987; Vaughn et al., 1983), or is assumed to take place automatically. Generalisation may benefit from some of the methods proposed by Ashman and Conway (1989), namely: (a) cueing or sensitising the learner to the importance of the strategy; (b) emphasising the systematic step-by-step nature of problem-solving; (c) training the identification of the relevant attributes of a problem category (e.g. problems involving authority, peers, conflict, advocacy); and (d) using tasks that satisfy the conditions of two or more categories (e.g. conflict problems with authority figures). By emphasising the similarities and differences among and between conceptual categories, generalisation is more explicitly addressed. This application of the acquired skills to various contexts, tasks and situations has been referred to as 'subsequent generalisation' (see Ellis, Lenz and Sabornie, 1987). Finally, one could encourage the application of the trained problem-solving strategies to relatively familiar or personal problems by gradually increasing the conceptual distance between the training task and the tasks of everyday life. This seems to be an appropriate strategy, as Hammre-Nietupski et al. (1982) argued that practice with familiar stimuli can promote generalisation and transfer in other problem-solving tasks.

IMPROVING THE PROCESS OF TRAINING

In addition to the improvements needed for the above clinical purposes, there is also a need to improve the nature and content of training in several ways. These are outlined in the following section.

Comprehensive programme

Some of the studies on training people with learning difficulties in social problem-solving have focused on a small number of components of social problem-solving skill (e.g. Castles and Glass, 1986: four; Healey, 1977: five; Ross and Ross, 1978: one). However, one study with children used as many as eight components (Vaughn, Ridley and Cox, 1983) but evaluated the effects of all components using a crude global measure of the number and kind of generated solutions. Since successful problem-solving is a (comparatively) systematic procedure that involves the examination of all information and methods available (Ashman and Conway, 1989), one should attempt to apply and evaluate a comprehensive problem-solving programme equipping people with all the skills necessary for successful problem-solving in real life.

Motivational components

Zigler and Burack (1989) argued that prior to any intervention a motivational boost is required to overcome low self-efficacy and low expectancy of success which is often characteristic of people with learning disabilities. Whitman (1990) also emphasised the need to overcome motivational deficits and to correct negative attributional beliefs of people with learning disabilities by providing opportunities to self-regulate and shape self-regulatory skills in such a way that a history of success is developed. It is necessary to find ways of raising trainees' belief in their control over their lives. This stage has been referred to by Ellis, Lenz and Sabornie (1987) as 'antecedent generalisation', engaging the learner in activities which aim at increasing motivation and interest while changing negative attitudes that may affect the transfer of learning.

Therapeutic components

People with learning disabilities often exhibit challenging behaviour as a means of coping with frustration, anxiety and stress (Menolascino, 1977; Reiss and Benson, 1984). In addition, many people with learning disabilities have problems with self-control which affect their interpersonal functioning. However, training in anger management using self-control procedures has produced positive results (Benson, 1986; Chapter 3 in this volume). Furthermore, the success of cognitive interventions managing negative cognitions with this population (see Chapter 8) demonstrates the utility of similar emotion-focused interventions. For these reasons, it seems to be important to address the therapeutic nature of training more explicitly, first by including components focusing on the role and control of emotions in problem-solving, second by encouraging the expression and management of individual problems both during training and in real life, and finally by promoting generalisation and transfer to future personal and interpersonal problems.

Solutions or statements

There is evidence to suggest that children with learning disabilities (mean IQ = 59) generate significantly fewer solutions to hypothetical problems and more irrelevant responses as compared to children without learning disabilities (Herman and Shantz, 1983). As a result, the process of training people with learning disabilities should include specific components differentiating between statements (which include irrelevant responses) and solutions. Such a distinction has not always been evident in published research on the effectiveness of training.

Autonomy components

According to Williams and Schoultz (1981) there are plenty of self-advocacy groups training people to take control over their lives. However, in the absence of effective problem-solving skills, frustration and distress may arise if raised expectations are not met. A component of self-advocacy has a valuable place in the problem-solving process, provided that this is based on realism and not ideologically driven optimism. Social problem-solving – although cognitively mediated – by definition takes place in interpersonal and social systems with a wide range of ideologies and fully independent problem-solving may not always be possible (for a conceptual critique of the ideological premises of cognitive therapies see Chapter 10).

Decision-making components

During the decision-making stage of training, the criteria used to evaluate decisions should include something more than simply the consequences (Mueser *et al.*,1987; Tymchuk, Andron and Rahbar, 1988) or the probability of success in solving the problem (Bramston and Spence, 1984). A set of meaningful criteria to evaluate decisions generated in training could be the probable degree of social acceptability of the solution, the potential degree of effectiveness of the solution and finally the impact on other people's thoughts and feelings. An 'effective' solution is only effective if it is socially acceptable and does not have an adverse impact on other people.

Comparative components

One component of training notably missing from the literature is training people to select an alternative on the basis of its 'relative effectiveness' in comparison to the effectiveness of other possible solutions generated. There is evidence to suggest that people with learning disabilities often fail to evaluate the progress towards a goal (Campione, 1987) and deal with problems in a random, trial-and-error manner (Ashman and Conway, 1989). Emphasis should be placed on encouraging people to consider the whole range of alternatives and 'question' or 'justify' their own choices, rather than choosing arbitrarily what seems to be the best alternative at that instance.

Justification components

Compared to social skills training which involves the training of specific responses to specific problems (such as eye-gaze in dating-behaviour, intonation of voice, etc.), social problem-solving training encourages people to generate, evaluate and implement their own choices of behaviour. However, it is surely important to ensure that people are able to justify their own choice by encouraging them to offer explanations or justifications for the probable efficacy of their selected response. With reference to self-regulation, Kanfer and Hagerman (1981) emphasised that individuals must understand the importance of a particular activity in order to be sufficiently motivated to self-regulate.

Pre-action thinking components

In addition to a wider range of decision-making criteria, it seems desirable to encourage trainees to generate as many thoughts as possible prior to action (i.e. obstacles, intermediate goals, social and interpersonal reactions, evaluative criteria, etc.). Such a training component would aim to reduce impulsive attempts to attain a goal, while utilising or incorporating previously taught components.

Realistic means–ends components

Although generating a large number of 'means to ends' increases the possibility of selecting an appropriate one, training people with learning disabilities to consider the realism of these means is a neglected component of social problem-solving skills. It is important to consider realism as a useful component of training, complementing the existing literature. If 'means to ends' are unrealistic, the effectiveness of problem-solving will almost certainly be lessened which in turn is likely to decrease people's motivation and self-confidence.

Verification component

This component of training aims at integrating all the acquired skills, executing the behavioural component of the problem-solving process and evaluating the outcome of the problem-solving process. Again, the outcome could be evaluated in terms of the degree of social acceptability of the solution, the degree of effectiveness of the solution, the impact on other people's thoughts and feelings, the long- and short-term effects. This is the last stage of the problem-solving process which could restart the problem-solving process once again, if the outcome proves to be unsatisfactory. It is surprising how some studies have neglected this valuable component (Vaughn, Ridley and Cox, 1983; Castles and Glass, 1986), in the absence of which problem-solving is incomplete.

A NEW PROGRAMME OF SOCIAL PROBLEM-SOLVING SKILLS TRAINING FOR PEOPLE WITH LEARNING DISABILITIES

On the basis of the extensive theoretical and empirical evidence on the use of problem-solving training with various populations (D'Zurilla, 1988), and the changing philosophy towards social role valorisation (Wolfensberger, 1972) and community care for people with learning disabilities (Department of Health and Social Security, 1989) a new training programme was compiled.

Training methods

Open conversation, counselling

This was in some cases necessary especially when current problems emerged that required immediate attention. Failure to attend to these highly emotionally disturbing situations could result in some people being distracted from the process of training.

Reviewing previous session

Each session started with a review of the previous session to: (a) recall vital components which could have been forgotten; (b) ensure that the occasionally absent members of the group would be aware of the content of sessions; (c) review and give feedback on the homework exercises which were not always completed; and (d) set the previous session in context with the present one, to reinforce a sense of continuity.

Teaching the new component

Once the component was explained each individual was encouraged to reword, repeat or give examples of the application of each component. Role-play, modelling and a lot of praise were necessary at this stage. In addition, the participants were encouraged to relate the newly acquired component to previous sessions and place it in the context of a whole problem-solving process.

Exercise on problem vignettes

During each session, individual vignettes were presented ranging in difficulty from impersonal practical problems to interpersonal problems with different roles (authority, peers, strangers). Again, praise and reinforcement were offered for people's attempts.

Individual practice on own problems

In addition to the exercise on the problem vignettes presented, individual problems were also addressed, usually in the initial 'counselling' stage of the session. This was considered to be a useful contribution for the following reasons: (a) the transfer of learning from hypothetical problems to real-life personal problems might be enhanced and (b) the link between training in cognitive social problem-solving skills and the therapeutic application of such skills in people's everyday life was emphasised, making the nature of training more interesting and more personally relevant.

Occasional homework assignments

Occasionally, homework exercises were assigned, where the participants were asked to apply the acquired problem-solving skills in real life. However, in most cases these assignments were successfully completed by a small number of participants and in most cases by the very able ones only.

Review of session and relaxation

The final stage of all sessions was to review the session and set any homework assignments. This was followed by a few minutes of relaxation with some visualisation tasks whenever the session was too intense or the participants seemed unusually excited.

Materials used

The materials used included self-generated and predefined problem vignettes, audiovisual aids (e.g. cards with the components of training, tape recordings), homework exercises and diaries.

For the purposes of training a set of thirty-two vignettes presenting problems was selected. Problems were classified in two dimensions: (a) *source of problem* involving impersonal practical problems, problems relating to personal needs and desires, and problems relating to interpersonal conflict; and (b) *social contact* including problems regarding peer issues, problems involving authority and problems involving strangers. The problems for which vignettes were written were as follows:

1 impersonal practical problems with no social contact (e.g. getting help in case of an emergency or an injury, losing money or other objects);
2 impersonal practical problems with no social contact (e.g. missing the bus, being lost in a new place);
3 problems satisfying needs/wants in relation to authority (e.g. expressing negative feelings towards people in authority, advocating wishes, asking people to keep their promise if broken);
4 problems satisfying needs/wants in relation to peers (e.g. borrowing money off a peer, getting help at work);
5 problems satisfying needs/wants in relation to strangers (e.g. asking strangers for some help, preparing for an interview);
6 problems in conflict resolution with authority figures (e.g. dealing with unpleasant sarcastic comments from staff, staff rationing your cigarettes);
7 problems in conflict resolution with peers (e.g. peer bosses you around, non-constructive criticism from peers);
8 problems in conflict resolution with strangers (e.g. being called names in the community, controlling anger when provoked, neighbours blame you for things you haven't done).

In addition to working on these vignettes, participants were encouraged to consider and manage problems as they arose in the groups, or in their everyday life.

Components of training

In the following section the aims, content and theoretical basis of each component of training is described. The number of sessions required for each component was different for the community (one session per component) and the hospital groups (one-and-a-half sessions per component).

Component 1: introducing the aims, rules, process and rationale

The introductory component aimed at introducing the members of the group to each other, familiarising the participants with the group activities, clarifying the short-term and long-term aims of training and drafting a set of working group rules (Camp and Bash, 1981; McClue *et al.*, 1978; Gesten, 1982; Hawton *et al.*, 1989; Platt, Prout and Metzger, 1987; D'Zurilla, 1986; Kanfer and Busenmeyer, 1982; Weissberg *et al.*, 1979; Larcen, 1980). In this component of training, the terms 'problem' and 'solution' were clarified by the trainer. Following this, each person was asked to provide an example from their own personal and interpersonal environment. It is important to notice that some people needed extra encouragement and praise to talk for the first time in a group setting, while others preferred to talk about 'other people's problems' rather than their own. Exercise on hypothetical problems was offered to enhance generalisation and transfer.

Component 2: impulse control and motivational boost

The aim of this component was to highlight the importance of impulse control (Kanfer and Busenmeyer, 1982) and increase people's motivation and beliefs in self-efficacy (D'Zurilla, 1986). In this component, the following topics were examined and discussed: (a) problems, frustration and aggressive outbursts are related; (b) importance of impulse control ('stop and think'); (c) examples of positive effects of impulse control; and (d) examples of adverse effects of lack of control. As part of the motivational boost (for the least motivated clients), self-motivating statements were repeated ('I can problem-solve'). In addition, each participant was invited to provide an example of successfully having done something about a problem. Exercise on hypothetical problems was encouraged to enhance generalisation and transfer.

Component 3: use of feelings as cues to problem-solving

The aim of this session was to examine the facilitatory role of emotions in the problem-solving process (D'Zurilla, 1986) by highlighting an existing problem which may not necessarily be evident (Gesten, 1982; Hawton *et al.*, 1989; Platt, Prout and Metzger 1987; D'Zurilla, 1986). In this component, the following topics were examined and discussed: (a) negative feelings are reactions to a stressful, upsetting or threatening life situation requiring a coping or a problem-solving response; (b) negative feelings signify the presence of a problem; and (c) emotional problems are associated with maladaptive ways of thinking. Subsequently, examples of life situations (both positive and negative) were offered and each participant was invited to offer their emotional reaction to that event, followed by practice on hypothetical problems to promote generalisation and transfer across domains.

Component 4: problem identification

This component aimed at facilitating people's ability to identify the existence of a problem by examining the characteristics of problems, while addressing some of the consequences of problems (Camp and Bash, 1981; McClue *et al.* 1978; Gesten, 1982; Hawton *et al.* 1989; Platt, Prout and Metzger, 1987; D'Zurilla, 1986; Kanfer and Busenmeyer, 1982; Weissberg *et al.*; 1979; Larcen, 1980). This component assists individuals in identifying their problems 'by themselves', without relying on external sources of help or advice which could be misinterpreted as being critical or dogmatic. In this session participants were helped to identify problems by the use of the following cues: (a) negative feelings; (b) inefficient behaviour; and (c) social feedback. Each participant was then requested to provide an example of a problem where: (a) the participant identified a problem by using a personal feeling as a cue; (b) the participant identified a problem by identifying an inefficient behaviour; and (c) the participant identified a problem because other people were not happy. This component was backed up by exercises on hypothetical problems followed by some real problems to enhance generalisation and transfer.

Component 5: emotional ABC: antecedents and consequences

This component addressed the relationship between antecedents and consequences of negative emotions, by encouraging people to identify the triggers of maladaptive responses (D'Zurilla, 1986; Dryden and Ellis, 1987). The following issues were addressed: (a) negative feelings are related to problems while positive feelings are associated with mastery over one's environment; (b) impulse control helps us to prevent negative consequences; (c) consideration of one's own feelings and thoughts can aid problem identification; and (d) negative emotional feedback from other people can aid problem-solving. Participants were encouraged to attempt to discover the antecedents of negative emotions ('What made me sad?' 'What was I thinking before?'). Further exercise on hypothetical problems was provided to enhance generalisation and transfer.

Component 6: problem definition

The aim of this component was to train people in defining a problem as clearly as possible and to appreciate that a problem may consist of two or more interrelated problems (Platt, Prout and Metzger, 1987; D'Zurilla, 1986; Kanfer and Busenmeyer, 1982). In this session, participants were encouraged to define a problem, aided by the following questions: who, what, where, when and why (e.g. Why is your peer abusing you?). Exercises on hypothetical problems were offered and participants were given corrective feedback and praise while defining a problem. This component of training utilised components addressed in previous sessions.

Component 7: realistic self-advocacy

The aim of this component was to enhance the participants' assertiveness and motivation to self-advocate, provided that change is realistically possible (Loumidis, 1993). In this component a distinction was made between problems that realistically did or did not require external assistance. In a simplified language, the distinction between autonomous, semi-independent and independent problem-solving was addressed. This component included elements from the previous motivational components. In addition, participants were encouraged to make an appraisal of the realistic possibility of change and autonomous management of a problem. Examples of hypothetical problems were used to exercise the acquired skill and particular emphasis was placed on problems involving 'conflict with authority figures'.

Component 8: definition of needs/goals

The aim of this component was to establish and operationalise the short- and long-term goals of problem-solving. Specifying goals and breaking down complex problems into simpler subgoals is a major component in many problem-solving approaches (Kanfer and Busenmeyer, 1982; McClue *et al.*, 1978; Gesten, 1982; Hawton *et al.*, 1989). In this component, goals were explicitly defined and appraised, breaking complex problems into simpler subgoals. Participants were encouraged to define the goal ('What is it that I want') when presented with a hypothetical but personally relevant problem.

Component 9: generation of alternative solutions

The aim of this component was to equip people with the fundamental problem-solving skill of 'generating alternative solutions' which is included in social problem-solving programmes for people with learning disabilities (Castles and Glass, 1986; Ross and Ross, 1973) and without learning disabilities (Camp and Bash, 1981; McClue *et al.*, 1978; Gesten, 1982; Hawton *et al.*, 1989; Platt, Prout and Metzger, 1987; D'Zurilla, 1986; Kanfer and Busenmeyer, 1982; Weissberg *et al.*, 1979; Larcen, 1980). For this component the quantity principle was employed ('Think of as many things/solutions to do about it'). Each participant was encouraged to generate at least three alternative solutions to hypothetical problems, linking them to personal, real problems to enhance generalisation and transfer.

Component 10: introduction to decision-making

Here, participants were encouraged to select one of the previously generated alternative solutions (i.e. choose the best). Components of previous sessions highlighting the importance of impulse control and the use of emotions in aiding problem-solving were addressed and rehearsed. Subsequently hypothetical problems were presented with a wide range of alternative solutions and each individual was encouraged to select the one most likely to solve the problem. At this point the participants generated a number of different criteria upon which solutions could be evaluated. The criteria employed to evaluate solutions included safety (Camp and Bash, 1981), fairness (Camp and Bash, 1981), feelings (Camp and Bash, 1981), emotional well-being (D'Zurilla, 1986), time and effort (D'Zurilla, 1986), effectiveness (D'Zurilla, 1986; Camp and Bash, 1981), and consequences (Gesten, 1982; Platt, Prout and Metzger, 1987).

Component 11: decision-making criteria: I: Effectiveness

The aim of this component was to examine effectiveness as a criterion of decision-making (Camp and Bash, 1981; D'Zurilla, 1986). During this session participants were presented with a hypothetical problem, were required to generate a number of alternative solutions and were encouraged to evaluate each of the solutions using the criterion of effectiveness. Self-addressed questions included: 'What will happen if I choose this one?', 'Which one is the best?' The use of role-play was a powerful method to illustrate and examine each alternative.

Component 12: decision-making criteria: II: Social acceptability

Although 'social acceptability' *per se* has not been considered as an evaluative criterion during the decision-making process of social problem-solving training, some programmes consider 'the facts from an other person's viewpoint' (Platt, Prout and Metzger, 1987). In the present study, using social acceptability as a criterion of decision-making was based on the realisation that some of the participants scored highly on measures of social adaptation. During this session participants were presented with a hypothetical problem, were required to generate a number of alternative solutions and were encouraged to evaluate each of the solutions using the criterion of effectiveness as well as social acceptability. Examples of ineffective but socially acceptable, effective but not socially acceptable and both effective and socially acceptable responses were addressed. Components of previous sessions examining self-advocacy and feelings as a cue to problem-solving were also included. Self-addressed questions included: 'What will other people think?' and 'How will other people feel?'

Component 13: decision-making criteria: III: Consequences

Consequential thinking is a major skill and training component of social problem-solving (Camp and Bash, 1981; McClue *et al.*, 1978; Platt, Prout and Metzger, 1987; Weissberg *et al.*,1979; Larcen, 1980; Gesten, 1982; D'Zurilla, 1986). In session, participants were presented with a hypothetical problem, were required to generate a number of alternative solutions and were encouraged to evaluate each of the solutions using the criterion from previous sessions. Furthermore role-play was employed as a method to test each of the alternatives in terms of the likely consequences. Participants were encouraged to consider as many consequences as possible, by using the 'generation of alternative solutions skill' that was addressed in previous sessions. Self-addressed questions included: 'What things can happen if I choose this one?' The criteria used for hypothetical problems were related to personal real problems to enhance generalisation and transfer.

Component 14: consideration of means to ends and obstacles

'Means–ends planning', being one of the fundamental social problem-solving skills, has been a component of training (sometimes called 'elaboration' (McClue *et al.*, 1978; Larcen, 1980)) based on the relationship between the number of relevant means and positive mental health (see D'Zurilla 1988 for a review). During this session, the following issues were explored: (a) what is a means?; (b) what is an obstacle?; (c) what can we do to get what we want? Vignettes depicting hypothetical problems were offered for exercise providing the beginning and the end of a problematic situation. Participants were encouraged to provide as many means (or steps) as they could to achieve the desired end. Components from previous sessions were also included, especially the criteria to evaluate the effectiveness, social acceptability and consequences of a response.

Component 15: solution implementation and verification

This component of 'solution implementation and verification' is included in all problem-solving approaches (Camp and Bash, 1981; McClue *et al.*, 1978; Gesten, 1982; Hawton et al., 1989; Platt, Prout and Metzger, 1987; D'Zurilla, 1986; Kanfer and Busenmeyer, 1982; Weissberg *et al.*, 1979; Larcen, 1980), emphasising the importance of feedback that could initiate the problem-solving process all over again. During this component, the following issues were discussed: (a) does the social problem-solving process end with the behavioural implementation of the selected action?; (b) should emphasis be placed on the feedback received on the implemented action?; (c) if a solution does not prove to satisfy the desired goal, can the process of problem-solving start again?; (d) challenging self-defeating statements in case the desired goal is not achieved; and (e) the importance of behavioural overt social skills. Examples of hypothetical problems were offered and behavioural plans to execute the decision were tested. Once again, role-play was a powerful method to test this component. Self-addressed statements included: 'Did it work?', 'Did I get what I wanted?', 'Was I a good problem-solver?' However, D'Zurilla and Nezu (1982) warn about the negative consequences of unrealistic, perfectionistic and overly strict performance standards.

EVALUATING THE NEW PROGRAMME

The programme was evaluated on a sample of people with learning disabilities (n = 46) with a wide range of age (21–81 years, mean age = 40 years), intellectual ability (Silverstein, 1982: 4SF-WAIS IQ = 40–77, mean IQ = 57), adaptive behaviour (Nihira *et al.*, 1975: ABS-I = 165–282, mean ABS-I = 252) and maladaptive behaviour functioning (Nihira *et al.*, 1975: ABS II = 0–148, mean ABS-II = 18.5) from both residential and community settings.

In the first part of the study, twenty-two people with learning disabilities living in hospital and twenty-four people who lived in the community and attended one or another of two day centres were assessed to establish baseline measures of intellectual functioning (WAIS-4SF: Silverstein, 1982) and adaptive and maladaptive functioning (ABS: Nihira *et al.*,1975). A structured individual interview was used to assess the ability to solve hypothetical social and interpersonal problems relevant to such individuals.

In order to overcome the limitations of traditional problem-solving measures, the following scoring criteria were developed and scored by two raters:

Criterion 1 Nature of problem definition (implicit, explicit, absent);
Criterion 2 Problem-solving style (autonomous, dependent, semi-independent);
Criterion 3 Number of independent solutions generated;
Criterion 4 Number of alternative statements generated (solutions and irrelevant responses);
Criterion 5 Number of irrelevant responses generated;
Criterion 6 Degree of comparative reasoning;
Criterion 7 Ability to justify the selected solution;
Criterion 8 Degree of social acceptability of solution;
Criterion 9 Degree of effectiveness of solution;
Criterion 10 Number or relevant pre-action thoughts;
Criterion 11 Number of means to achieve the ends;
Criterion 12 Degree of realism of the means employed;

During the training part of the study twenty-nine of the forty-six participants were selected to satisfy the following criteria for inclusion:

1 satisfied the AAMR criteria for 'mental retardation' (Grossman, 1983);
2 were able to use and understand sentences and complex instructions (ABS-I sub-scales);
3 were able and willing to interact in group settings;
4 were either considered for resettlement into the community or exhibited challenging behaviour.

The twenty-nine people selected for training were assigned to two hospital groups (n = 6 and 7) and two community groups (n = 8 and 8), each receiving a total of 15 hours of group training on a weekly basis. Training was delivered by the first author. Due to client characteristics, the duration of each session was different for the community group which received fifteen 1-hour sessions and the residential group which received twenty-three sessions lasting 40 minutes. The remaining seventeen people formed two control groups that did not receive training in social problem-solving skill.

In the third part of this study, the effects of training were assessed by comparing performance on the measures of problem-solving and adaptive behaviour. Comparisons were made between trained and untrained groups both before and after training. In addition, changes occurring over the period of training within trained and untrained groups were assessed. An additional structured interview was delivered by an independent interviewer to examine the clients' views about the group.

RESULTS

Following training, statistically significant improvements were found in the trained group, but not in the control group, on the degree of maladaptive behaviour as rated by independent judges (members of staff that were not informed about who was in the treatment group) and some components of social problem-solving skill.

A brief summary in Table 6.1 illustrates the post-training gains on the measures employed, highlighting the implications for further clinical work. In the degree of maladaptive behaviour, although the interaction Group × Time was not significant at the conventional 5% level of significance, a Tukey test indicated that only the trained group showed a significant change ($p < 0.001$) over time (46.8%). The trained group (but not the untrained) also showed significant improvement in some components of social problem-solving skill, namely 'solution effectiveness' (12.4%), 'number of relevant means to ends' (123%), and 'mean number of relevant pre-action thoughts' (41.7%). However, no other components of social problem-solving skill showed significant differential changes over time between the trained and untrained groups in which the trained group improved.

OBSTACLES AND DIFFICULTIES IN IMPLEMENTING THE PROGRAMME

Various difficulties were encountered while implementing the programme, which are not atypical in group therapy.

1 *Adapting the original programme.*
  The process and style of training had to be constantly modified including concrete examples, visual aids, self-instructions and plenty of humour. Some components of the original protocol were not easily comprehended and as a consequence were excluded. It is important to ensure that in clinical practice the individual characteristics of the client are taken into account in a collaborative manner.

2 *Maintaining interest.*
  Some members lost interest and perceived the group as not addressing their own needs. Apparently, the transfer of training to everyday problems should be more explicitly addressed with an emphasis to individual 'problem vignettes'. In this way, motivation can be enhanced and generalisation of training can become more probable.

3 *Attending to emotional needs.*
  Occasionally, the group had to attend to the needs of some emotionally distressed people and consequently the scheduled agenda had to be slightly

Table 6.1 Possible range of scores for each component of social problem-solving skill, with mean performance before and after training for the untrained and the trained group on the five components of social problem-solving skill and the ABS-II (Maladaptive Behaviour)

Skill component	Score	Untrained		Trained		2-WAY ANOVA (sig.p)		
		Pre	Post	Pre	Post	Group	Time	G×T
1 Problem definition								
1 Problem definition	(0–2)	1.14	1.04	1.14	1.17	NS	NS	NS
2 Ends-directed thinking								
2(a) No. of statements made	(1 =)	3.21	2.16	3.51	2.84	$p < 0.01$	$p < 0.0001$	NS
2(b) No. of solutions given	(1 =)	1.92	1.49	2.14	1.97	$p < 0.03$	$p < 0.002$	NS
3 Means–ends thinking								
3(a) No. of relevant means	(1 =)	0.23	0.46	0.39	0.87	NS	$p < 0.0001$	NS
3(b) Degree of realism of means	(1–5)	0.97	1.62	1.52	2.28	$p < 0.08$	$p < 0.0001$	NS
3(c) No. of pre-action thoughts	(1 =)	0.46	0.52	0.96	1.36	$p < 0.003$	$p < 0.009$	$p < 0.05$
4 Evaluative checking and decision making								
4(a) Ability to justify solution	(0–5)	2.04	1.97	2.36	2.83	NS	NS	$p < 0.05$
4(b) Degree of comparative reasoning	(0–5)	0.39	0.54	0.52	0.94	NS	$p < 0.03$	NS
5 Overall effectiveness of solution								
5(a) Degree of effectiveness of solution	(0–5)	2.90	2.80	3.31	3.72	$p < 0.02$	NS	$p < 0.04$
5(b) Degree of autonomy in solution	(0–3)	2.47	1.99	2.34	2.43	NS	$p < 0.02$	$p < 0.0001$
5(c) Social acceptability of solution	(0–5)	4.87	4.18	4.86	4.59	NS	$p < 0.0001$	$p < 0.056$
Maladaptive behaviour	(ABS)	24.94	20.76	26.51	14.1	NS	$p < 0.003$	NS

modified. Complicated bereavement, disclosure of abuse, relationship breakdowns and unmet expectations may require immediate crisis interventions while abiding to a social problem-solving model.

4 *Modifying clients' expectations.*
In some cases, people's expectations of the group were inaccurate as a result of previous groupwork that aimed at totally different goals (i.e. non-directive groupwork, specific work-related skill acquisition). Clarifying the aims and goals of this group was difficult and time-consuming, but is essential to ensure that clients share the same expectations about the group.

5 *Allowing for restricted experiences.*
Some of the older people in the hospital group had limited experiences of community life. Tailoring the content of training to accommodate such diverse experiences is essential.

6 *Facing low motivation.*
Some people did not perceive anything as being a problem. As a consequence, their motivation and group participation were limited. To overcome this, the authors would recommend a thorough pre-treatment screening procedure to allow more time on the 'problem definition' component of training.

7 *Confronting the status quo*
Some people tried to exercise their problem-solving skills only to find that the existing systems (family, institutions, society) were too rigid to allow self-advocacy or change. Indeed, some types of problems may be enmeshed in dysfunctional interrelating systems (family, services, professionals) and totally independent problem resolution may not be possible.

CONCLUSIONS

Despite the obstacles and difficulties mentioned above evidence emerged to support the view that individuals with learning disabilities can benefit in some respects from training in social problem-solving skill. More specifically, the effectiveness of problem solutions and some aspects of cognitive functioning associated with the production of effective solutions, in particular instrumental (means–ends) thinking and pre-action thought, improved with training. Very importantly, training was also associated with a decline in maladaptive behaviour. In many ways this last finding was the most important as a major rationale for offering training is that it may improve social adjustment and reduce problem behaviours which impair capacity to live independently in the community. In the sense that the present research provides some positive findings on this point, it presents hope for the future. Despite the difficulties encountered at a clinical level, it is essential to continue working towards a better understanding and service delivery for this underserved population.

REFERENCES

American Association on Mental Retardation (1993) *Mental Retardation: Definition, Classification and Systems of Support* (9th edn). Washington, DC: American Association on Mental Retardation.

Ashman, A.F. and Conway, N.F. (1989) *Cognitive Strategies for Special Education: Process Based Instruction.* London: Routledge.

Benson, B.A. (1986) Anger management training. *Psychiatric Aspects of Mental Retardation Reviews*, **5**, 51–5.

Bouffard, M. (1990) Movement problem solutions for educable mentally handicapped individuals. *Adapted Physical Activity Quarterly*, **7**, 183–97.

Bramston, P. and Spence, S.H. (1984) Behavioral versus cognitive social-skills training with intellectually handicapped adults. *Behavior Research and Therapy*, **23**, 239–46.

Camp, B.W. and Bash, N.A. (1981) *Think Aloud: Increasing Social Cognitive Skills. A Problem Solving Programme for Children.* Campaign, IL: Research Press.

Campione, J.C. (1987) Metacognitive components of instructional research with problem learners. In F.E. Weinert and R. Kluwe (eds), *Metacognition, Motivation and Understanding.* Hillsdale, NJ: Laurence Erlbaum, pp. 117–40.

Castles, E.E. and Glass, C.R. (1986) Training in social and interpersonal problem solving skills for mildly and moderately mentally retarded adults. *American Journal of Mental Retardation*, **91**, 35–42.

D'Zurilla, T.J. (1986) *A Social Competence Approach to Clinical Intervention.* New York: Springer-Verlag.

D'Zurilla, T.J. (1988) Problem solving therapies. In K.S. Dobson (ed.), *Handbook of Cognitive Behavioural Therapies.* Guilford: New York, pp. 85–135.

D'Zurilla, T.J. and Goldfried, M.R. (1971) Problem solving and behaviour modification. *Journal of Abnormal Psychology*, **78**, 107–26.

D'Zurilla, T.J. and Nezu, A.M. (1982). A study of the generation of alternative solutions process in social problem solving. *Cognitive Therapy and Research*, **4**, 67–72.

Denham, S.A. and Almeida, M.C. (1987) Children's social problem solving skills, behavioral adjustment and interventions: a meta-analysis evaluating theory and practice. *Journal of Applied Developmental Psychology*, **8**, 391–409.

Department of Health and Social Security (1989) *Caring for People.* London: HMSO.

Dryden, W. and Ellis, A. (1987) Rational emotive therapy (RET). In W. Dryden and W.L. Golden (eds), *Cognitive Behavioural Approaches to Psychotherapy.* Cambridge: Hemisphere Press.

Ellis, E.S., Lenz, B.K. and Sabornie, E.J. (1987) Generalisation and adaptation of learning strategies to natural environments, Part 1: Critical agents. *Remedial and Special Education*, **8**, 6–20.

Foss, G., Auty, W.P. and Irvin, L.K. (1989) A comparative evaluation of modeling, problem-solving, and behavior rehearsal for teaching employment-related interpersonal skills to secondary students with mental retardation. *Education and Training in Mental Retardation*, **24**, 17–27.

Gesten, E.L. (1982) The Rochester social problem solving training programme. *Special Services in Schools*, **2**, 19–39.

Goldberg, D.P. (1978) *The Manual of the General Health Questionnaire.* Institute of Psychiatry, London: NFER-Nelson.

Goldberg, D.P., Cooper, B., Eastwood, M.R. and Kedward, H.B. (1970) A standardised psychiatric interview for use in community surveys. *British Journal of Social and Preventive Medicine*, **24**, 18–23.

Grossman, H.J. (1983) *Classification in Mental Retardation.* Washington, DC: American Association on Mental Deficiency.

Hawton, K., Salkovskis, P.M., Kirk, J. and Clark, D.M. (1989) *Cognitive-behaviour Therapy for Psychiatric Problems: A Practical Guide.* Oxford: Oxford Medical Publications.

Hammre-Nietupski, S., Nietupski, J., Vincent, L. and Wambold, C. (1982) Effects of strategy training on the free recall performance of mildly and moderately retarded adolescents. *American Journal on Mental Retardation,* **86,** 421–64.

Healey, K. (1977) An investigation of the relationship between certain social cognitive abilities and social behavior and the efficacy of training in social cognitive skills for elementary retarded-educable children. Unpublished doctoral dissertation. Bryn Mawr, PA: Bryn Mawr College.

Heppner, P.P. and Petersen, C.H. (1982) The development and implication of a personal problem solving inventory. *Journal of Counselling Psychology,* **29,** 66–75.

Herman, M.S. and Shantz, C.U. (1983) Social problem solving and mother child interactions of educable mentally retarded children. *Journal of Applied Developmental Psychology,* **4,** 217–26.

Kanfer, F.H. and Busenmeyer, J. (1982) The use of problem solving and decision making in behavior therapy. *Clinical Psychology Review,* **2,** 239–66.

Kanfer, F.H. and Hagerman, S. (1981) The role of self regulation. In L.P. Rehm (ed.), *Behaviour Therapy for Depression: Present Status and Future Directions.* New York: Academic Press.

Larcen, S.W. (1980) Enhancement of social problem solving skills through teacher and parent collaboration. Unpublished PhD thesis. University of Connecticut.

La Vigna, G.W. and Donnellan, A.M. (1986) *Alternatives to Punishment: Solving Behavior Problems with Non-aversive Strategies.* New York: Irvington Publishers.

Loumidis, K.S. (1990) The relationship between social problem-solving performance, intellectual performance and general psychological distress in a sample of institutionalised adults with a learning disability. Unpublished MA dissertation. Keele: Keele University.

Loumidis, K.S. (1992) Can social problem solving training help people with learning difficulties? In D.R. Trent (ed.), *The Promotion of Mental Health.* Aldershot: Avebury Press, pp. 77–87.

Loumidis, K.S. (1993) Learning disability and social problem solving skill: evaluation of a therapeutic training programme. Unpublished PhD thesis. Keele: Keele University.

Loumidis, K.S. and Hill, A.B. (in press) Training social problem solving skill in learning disability groups: a controlled outcome study. Paper submitted for publication.

Marchetti, A.G. and Campbell, V.A. (1990) Social skills. In J.L. Matson (ed.), *Handbook of Behavior Modification with the Mentally Retarded* (2nd edn). New York: Plenum Press.

Marx, E. (1988) Problem solving therapy. In F.N. Watts (ed.), *New Developments in Clinical Psychology,* Vol. 2. Leicester: British Psychological Society.

Matson, J.H. and Frame, C.L. (1986) *Psychopathology among Mentally Retarded Children and Adolescents.* Beverly Hills, CA: Sage Publications.

Matson, J.H., Coe, D.A., Gardner, W.I. and Sovner, R. (1990). Diagnostic assessment of the severely handicapped (DASH) scale. Unpublished manuscript. Baton Rouge: Louisiana State University.

McClue, L.F., Chinsky, J.M. and Larcen, S.W. (1978) Enhancing social problem solving performance in an elementary school setting. *Journal of Educational Psychology,* **70,** 504–13.

McFall, R.M. (1982) A review and reformulation of the concept of social skills. *Behavioral Assessment,* **4,** 1–33.

Menolascino, F.J. (1977) *Challenges in Mental Retardation: Progressive Ideology and Services.* New York: Human Services Press.

Mueser, K.T., Valenti-Hein, D. and Yarnold, P.R. (1987) Dating skills for the developmentally disabled, social skills and problem solving versus relaxation training. *Behavior Modification*, **11**, 2, 200–28.

Nezu, C.M., Nezu, A.M. and Arean, P. (1991) Assertiveness and problem solving training for mildly retarded persons with dual diagnoses. *Research in Developmental Disabilities*, **12**, 371–86.

Nihira, K., Foster, R., Shelhaas, M. and Lelland, H. (1974) *American Association on Mental Deficiency: Adaptive Behavior Scale*. Washington, DC: American Association on Mental Retardation.

Platt, J.J., Prout, N.F. and Metzger, D.S. (1987) Interpersonal cognitive problem solving therapy (ICSP). In W. Dryden and W.L. Golden (eds), *Cognitive Behavioural Approaches to Psychotherapy*. Cambridge: Hemisphere Press.

Reiss, S. and Benson, B.A. (1984) Awareness of social conditions among mentally retarded, emotionally disturbed outpatients. *American Journal of Psychiatry*, **141**, 88–90.

Ross, D.M. and Ross, S.A. (1973) Cognitive training for the educable mentally retarded child: situational problem solving and planning. *American Journal on Mental Deficiency*, **78**, 20–6.

Ross, D.M. and Ross, S.A. (1978) Cognitive training for educable mentally retarded children: choosing the best alternative. *American Journal on Mental Deficiency*, **82**, 598–601.

Schalock, R.L., Harper, R.S. and Genung, T. (1981) Community integration of mentally retarded adults: community placement and program success. *American Journal of Mental Deficiency*, **85**, 478–88.

Shure, M.B. and Spivack, G. (1978) *Problem Solving Techniques in Childrearing*. San Francisco: Jossey-Bass.

Sigelman, C.K., Budd, E.C., Spanhel, C.L. and Schoenrock, C.L. (1981) Asking questions of retarded persons: a comparison of yes-no and either-or formats. *Applied Research in Mental Retardation*, **2**, 347–58.

Silverstein, A.B. (1982) Two- and four-subtest short forms of the WAIS-R. *Journal of Consulting and Clinical Psychology*, **50**, 3, 415–18.

Smith, D.C. (1986) Interpersonal problem solving skills of retarded and non-retarded children. *Applied Research in Mental Retardation*, **7**, 431–42.

Spivack, G., Haimes, P.E. and Spotts, J. (1967) *Deveraux Adolescent Behavior Rating Scale Manual*. Devon, PA: The Deveraux Foundation.

Spivack, G., Platt, J.J. and Shure, M.B. (1976) *The Problem-Solving Approach to Adjustment*. San Francisco: Jossey-Bass.

Trower, P., Bryant, B. and Argyle, M. (1978) *Social Skills and Mental Health*. Pittsburg, PA: University of Pittsburg Press.

Tymchuk, A.J., Andron, L. and Rahbar, B. (1988) Effective decision making problem solving with mothers who have mental retardation. *American Journal on Mental Retardation*, **92**, 510–16.

Vaughn, S.R., Ridley, C.A. and Cox, J. (1983) Evaluating the efficacy of an interpersonal skills training program with children who are mentally retarded. *Education and Training in Mental Retardation*, **18**, 191–6.

Weissberg, R.P., Gesten, E.L., Liebenstein, N.L., Doherty-Schmid, K.D. and Hutton, H. (1979) *The Rochester Social Problem Solving Program: A Training Manual for Teachers of 2nd–4th grade children*. Rochester, NY: Centre for Community Study.

Welch, J., Nietupski, J. and Hammre-Nietupski, S. (1985) Teaching public transportation problem solving skills to young adults with moderate handicaps. *Education and Training in Mental Retardation*, **20**, 287–95.

Whitman, T.L. (1990) Self regulation and mental retardation. *American Journal on Mental Retardation*, **94**, 347–62.

Williams, P. and Schoultz, B. (1981) *We Can Speak for Ourselves*. London: Souvenir Press.

Wolfensberger, W. (1972) *Normalisation*. New York: National Institute on Mental Retardation.

Zigler, E. and Burack, J.A. (1989). Personality development and the dually diagnosed person. *Research in Developmental Disabilities*, **10**, 225–40.

7 Cognitive-behaviour therapy for people with learning disabilities

Assessment and intervention

Dave Dagnan and Paul Chadwick

INTRODUCTION

Mansdorf and Ben-David (1986) describe a bereaved parent who is depressed and receives a standard cognitive therapy. Her son, who has a learning disability and had begun to show aggressive behaviour that was hypothesised to be a sign of a bereavement-related depression, received a behavioural programme with a self-instructional component. The authors stated that the self-instructional component served to create a situation where aggressive outbursts could be reduced so that his mother could find positive behaviour to reinforce. The authors do not report having considered using a cognitive approach with the son similar to that used for his mother. There is no report of assessment or other clinical decision-making processes. In this chapter we consider how a clinician might assess the suitability of a person with learning disability for cognitive-behaviour therapy and we conclude with a case example of cognitive therapy.

WHAT DO WE MEAN BY COGNITIVE-BEHAVIOUR THERAPY

It is hard to define *the* cognitive model in clinical psychology because there is no one cognitive theory and therapy. Rather, over the last twenty or more years there has been a proliferation of theories and therapies called cognitive, some specific to one disorder and others pertaining to all human behaviour. Brewin (1988) suggests that these therapies share little other than a commitment to a cognitive mediational view of behaviour. Two distinct approaches to cognitive-behaviour therapy are particularly relevant to people with learning disability. The first is concerned with teaching skills and maintaining on-task behaviour, and is largely derived from the self-instructional or self-management literature. The self-instructional approach is based within a *deficit* model hypothesising that people with a learning disability do not effectively self-instruct (Whitman, 1990) either because they have no verbal behaviour or because their verbal behaviour is functionally inadequate. There is now quite a substantial body of published work concerning the application of this approach to cognitive-behaviour therapy for people with learning disabilities (Martin *et al.*,1988; Harchik *et al.*,1992; Chapters 2 and 5 in this volume).

The second approach to cognitive-behaviour therapy has developed from psychotherapeutic methods and is concerned with emotional and behavioural disturbance. Disturbed behaviour and emotion are thought to be products of *distorted* cognitions (images, inferences, evaluations). Cognitive-behaviour therapy of this type is represented by the approaches of Beck *et al.* (1979) and Ellis (1977). There is little work other than a small number of case studies describing the use of this approach with people with learning disabilities (e.g. Williams and Moorey, 1989; Lindsay and Kasprowicz, 1987; Lindsay *et al.*, 1993). In this chapter we shall concern ourselves with this second type of cognitive-behaviour therapy.

Trower, Casey and Dryden (1988) present a useful Antecedent-Belief-Consequence model. In this model an event happens and the client's attention is drawn to this event which is then described. This process is classified as the antecedent. The interpretation, appraisal or evaluation of this event is classed as the belief. In the cognitive model it is the belief rather than the antecedent that is most strongly related to the consequence, which may include an affect and a behavioural tendency. A distinction can be made between beliefs that are inferential and those that are evaluative (Trower, Casey and Dryden, 1988). *Evaluations* may be defined as good–bad judgments, or preferences as opposed to inferences (Zajonc, 1980): for example, 'I prefer John to David', 'John did a bad thing', etc. It is Ellis who has most clearly and consistently separated inferences and evaluations and it is one of the fundamental principles of rational emotive therapy that extreme and disabling emotion is functionally associated with different kinds of negative evaluation (Trower, Casey and Dryden, 1988). *Inferences* are situational-specific hypotheses which are true or false: for example, 'He does not like me', 'I am going to fail', 'This table was made from oak', or, 'People are spying on me'. Inferences tend to be sudden, or automatic, and they occur in abbreviated (often crude) language. Beck *et al.* (1979) have demonstrated how, in clinical problems, inferences in the form of anticipations and recollections tend to be distorted or biased because of the influence of mood. Clients are usually aware of their inferences (though not as inferences!) and some of their evaluations.

Using this ABC framework it is possible to abstract a set of three essential requirements for an intervention to be described as cognitive therapy of the type we are interested in. First, a person should correctly distinguish or identify an event (the antecedent), an associated inferential thought (the belief) and a corresponding emotional and/or behavioural consequence (the consequence). Second, the person should recognise that the consequence is most closely linked to the belief and not the antecedent. Finally, the belief should be amenable to disputation or testing. To illustrate this we can take a hypothetical scenario. *I walk down the street and see my friend. He crosses the street before he reaches me and he does not say hello.* Here, one inferential belief is,

'He is ignoring me' (preceded by an implicit, 'He saw me'). In this case the emotional consequence may be *sadness* with a possible behavioural consequence of *avoidance*. In terms of the ABC model, a person needs to be able to: (1) distinguish the antecedent events from the associated cognitions and emotions; (2) recognise that it is not the event that principally determines the emotional consequence but that the mediating cognition influences how the antecedent is responded to; and (3) be amenable to the disputation of the cognition, perhaps by exploring and testing other possible inferences such as, 'He didn't see me' or 'He was in a rush'.

These three steps are very basic and do not capture the depth and subtlety of cognitive therapy, but they are nevertheless cognitive. This type of intervention might therefore be labelled *simple* cognitive therapy, that is concerned solely with inferential cognitions. A more sophisticated understanding and use of the ABC model requires that evaluations also be considered and that these core beliefs be connected to the individual's history; such therapy might be thought of as *elegant* cognitive therapy (Ellis, 1977). Thus 'simple' cognitive therapy is primarily concerned with short-term or context-specific alleviation of mood; generalization and maintenance of change may depend on changing evaluations, a necessary ingredient of 'elegant' cognitive therapy (Williams and Moorey, 1989; Safran *et al.*,1986).

The work described in this chapter is an attempt to devise assessments of those cognitive processes involved in simple cognitive therapy. Our commitment is to provide education for those clients who lack specific skills, but we recognise that some people with learning disabilities will be unable to use even simple cognitive therapy. We describe an approach to assessment that shows an individual's strengths and needs in relation to these cognitive and emotional aptitudes – for example, being able to identify and label an emotion. We describe a study of the ability of people with learning disabilities to use these skills and clinical experience of using assessment based upon these procedures. We then present a brief case study where cognitive therapy was successfully used that illustrates some issues for further development in this area.

ASSESSMENT

Several therapeutic approaches employ pre-therapy assessments of component activities required within that therapy. For example, Davanloo (1980) offered trial interpretations during a pre-therapy interview prior to short-term psychotherapy. Safran *et al.* (1993) identify a number of specific cognitive tasks as part of a comprehensive assessment before cognitive therapy with an interpersonal focus. The cognitive elements of this assessment include:

1 *Accessibility of automatic thoughts.* This assesses the client's ability to access 'negative, self-critical thinking' concerning the presenting problem.

This is the person's ability to identify cognitions associated with their emotions and behaviour.

2 *Awareness and differentiation of emotions.* This assesses the client's ability to identify emotions and to experience them in the therapeutic session. The ability to generate emotions within the session has been described as an important element in the process of gaining access to automatic thoughts (e.g. Muran, 1991). Several therapists have recognised the need to use active methods such as role-play, or *in vitro* assessment within therapy to access associated emotions (e.g. Muran, 1991).

3 *Compatibility with the cognitive rationale.* This assesses the person's ability to work with the tasks and goals of cognitive therapy. This includes elements such as understanding the relationship between cognitions and affect and establishing short-term goals for therapy.

Safran *et al.* (1993) further identify six factors for assessment that are less specific to cognitive therapy. They include acceptance of personal responsibility for change, ability to form relationships, chronicity of problems, the presence of defensive information processing strategies and the client's ability to focus on the problem. They describe a study where this assessment battery was administered to forty-two clients of a clinic for people with anxiety and depressive disorders prior to beginning therapy. The assessment was then related to success in therapy defined by change on a number of specific and general measures of psychological distress. The study found that all indicators could be reliably rated and were significantly associated with positive outcomes. A similar approach may be adopted for working with people with learning disabilities. A cognitive-emotional assessment based upon the three core activities for simple cognitive therapy are described below.

Identify the antecedents, beliefs and consequences

We interviewed twenty-nine people being seen by members of a local Community Team for People with Learning Disabilities. Participants were chosen who were considered by the team members to have a level of verbal ability sufficient to give some responses to the type of questions that would be asked. The group consisted of fifteen men and fourteen women and had a mean age of 39 years (SD = 14). Twenty-seven were willing to be tested using the British Picture Vocabulary Scale (BPVS: Dunn *et al.*, 1982). This is a test of receptive vocabulary and requires the participant to indicate which of four pictures best illustrates a particular word. The group had a mean BPVS raw score of 73 (SD = 26), indicating that the group is made up of people with mild to moderate learning disabilities.

Wessler and Wessler (1980) suggest that cognitions may be best elicited by focusing on a specific event where the person felt distressed. They recommend clarifying first the emotional consequence (C), then the antecedent (A) and finally exploring the beliefs (Bs) and their link with the consequence. This study followed the same structure. Each participant was presented with a sad face and an angry face, which they were asked to label. They were then asked to state two recent things that had made them sad and two that had made them angry. Finally, they were asked what they were thinking at the time. Responses were categorised according to how well they were judged to mediate the event and emotion. Beliefs were judged inappropriate if they were: a further elaboration of the antecedent (Category 1), an account of the behavioural consequence (Category 2) or emotional consequence (Category 3), an inappropriate response (Category 4), or no response (Category 5). Table 7.1 shows that over 20% of respondents gave an appropriate mediating belief for both scenarios involving sadness and anger. Although only one person gave a belief that could be clearly interpreted as evaluative, a number of people could immediately supply suitable inferences.

Table 7.1 Cognitions offered by participants in initial study

	Sad				Angry			
	Presentation 1		*Presentation 2*		*Presentation 1*		*Presentation 2*	
	n	*%*	*n*	*%*	*n*	*%*	*n*	*%*
Evaluative cognition	1	4						
Inferential cognition	5	19	7	26	8	30	8	30
Restates antecedent	4	15	4	15	7	26	2	7
Elaborates emotional consequence	4	15	4	15	5	19	1	4
Elaborates behaviour consequence	6	22	4	15	2	7	6	22
Unclear	3	11	1	4	1	4	1	4
No response	4	15	7	26	4	15	9	33

Linking belief and consequence

Having established that some people with learning disabilities are able to carry out the basic task of discriminating between events, beliefs and emotions, the second requirement is then to recognise the B–C link. This part of the assessment combines original techniques and established measures, and is as follows.

1 An initial assessment of general language and intellectual ability. This is either an assessment of receptive vocabulary using the British Picture Vocabulary Test (Dunn *et al.*, 1982) or the Revised Weschler Adult Intelligence Scale (Weschler, 1981).

2 A simple assessment of ability to recognise emotions using line drawings of happy and sad faces.

3 A more demanding assessment of the ability to recognise emotions using the Test of Perception of Emotion from Facial Expression from the social skills package of Spence (1988). This presents ten small photographs of male and female faces and people are asked to indicate which face is showing each of ten emotions. For some people we have also completed a parallel test of the recognition of emotion from body posture.

4 An assessment of the person's ability to recognise a simple event–emotion (A–C) link using the screening test developed by Reed and Clements (1989). This assessment offers six scenarios and for each the person is asked to identify whether they would feel happy or sad in that situation (see also Chapter 4).

5 An assessment of the person's ability to understand how thoughts and beliefs mediate emotional responses to events. In this assessment we supply a simple scenario and a facial expression of an emotion and ask the person what they consider the person may be thinking. The six scenarios in this assessment are:

- 'You are in bed one night and hear a loud noise downstairs';
- 'You walk into a room where there are a group of your friends. As you walk in they start to laugh';
- 'You want to go on a special trip, but there is only one place and your friend is chosen to go instead';
- 'You see a group of your friends but they do not say hello';
- 'You have been asked to go and see the day centre manager';
- 'It's your first day at a new job that you have not done before'.

We have applied this package in full to a number of people in clinical settings. Data for six people for whom the full assessment battery has been completed are presented in Table 7.2. It can be seen from this table that all

Table 7.2 Performance of six participants on the various components of the cognitive-emotional assessment

Participants	WAIS	Spence (1988)		Happy/sad	Reed and Clements (1989)	Dagnan and Chadwick
	(Verbal, performance, total)	Face	Body			
Person 1	56, 57, 42	0	1	Y	Y	1
Person 2	62, 67, 62	4	7	Y	Y	3
Person 3	71, 65, 66	3		Y	Y	6
Person 4	69, 68, 68	6	6	Y	Y	4
Person 5	77, 78, 77	7	6	Y	Y	3
Person 6	74, 60, 66	5	5	Y	Y	5

people completed the Reed and Clements (1989) task, and recognised line drawings of happy and sad faces. Most were able to identify a number of photographic representations of emotion. All were able to provide at least one appropriate mediating cognition although some people found the task quite difficult. All those who scored three or less provide an appropriate mediating link only for scenarios where the event could be processed by using an 'intuitive' or rule-governed approach (e.g. Chaiken and Stangor, 1987). For example, scenario four may be processed using the heuristic, 'Being ignored is bad'. So when the scenario is matched with a negative emotion then a response derived from this will be judged an appropriate link to the emotion. In these cases it is not possible to tell whether the response is based on a simple heuristic applied to the antecedent or based on an appropriate effort to give a belief that will produce the emotion in the context of the event. In considering this it is useful to illustrate some actual responses obtained with this assessment. Examples of three people's responses are presented. Person three consistently gave inferences that linked the scenario and the emotion presented. For example, when presented with scenario one and a happy face she responded, 'There are people downstairs enjoying the music'. When presented with scenario three and a happy face she responded, 'Oh well, next time, I'm pleased my friend gets to go', when presented with scenario four and a happy face she responded, 'Oh well, they never saw me'. It should be noted that in some cases the scenario and emotion might be thought counter-intuitive, or heuristically incongruent. When people gave beliefs judged inappropriate the commonest mistake was to link the belief to the antecedent but not to the emotion (an example of heuristic responding). For example, person five responded to scenario three and a happy face with, 'I wish I could go with them', person one responded to scenario one and a happy face with, 'Don't bang, it's getting on my nerves'. The other form of error was to give a response that was not a cognition but a statement or elaboration about the antecedent or the emotion. For example, when person one was presented with scenario four and a happy face he responded, 'I'm happy, smiling at last'. This suggests that the best evidence for understanding the cognitive model will be obtained when people are able to link appropriately an antecedent and a heuristically incongruent emotion.

Engaging in collaborative empiricism

The third feature of simple cognitive therapy is to engage in some disputing and testing of a belief, the process Beck *et al.* (1979) call collaborative empiricism. The following extract is from a taped interview with person five. This interaction was recorded during an initial assessment; the young man had not been presented with the cognitive model previously. This extract illustrates that some people with learning disabilities are well able to work with cognitive material.

DD   You are walking down the road and you see a group of your friends. You walk past them but they don't say hello. You feel like that (sad face).

AA   Feel cross.

DD   Why would you feel like that?

AA   Because they're being really horrible to me.

DD   What would you be thinking to yourself?

AA   They're a bunch of horrible people, shouldn't speak to them, like that.

DD   What would you think?

AA   Treating me like dirt, they shouldn't treat me like that.

DD   Is there anything you could think that would make you feel like this (shows happy face)?

AA   Let's wait a bit, wait 'til they've talked to me a bit.

DD   Wait for a bit . . . So you might be thinking, they've walked past and they haven't said hello, what might you be thinking?

AA   Thinking? . . . Thinking that they've forgotten to say hello, at first.

DD   Good. So you'd be thinking, oh they've forgotten to say hello and you'd wait for them to say hello. Then you'd feel quite happy.

AA   Yes.

DD   But if you'd thought, 'Oh they're rotten to me, they haven't talked to me', you'd feel?

AA   Unhappy.

DD   So you'd be feeling unhappy . . . so what have you done? You've got the same thing happening to you, you're walking down the road and your friends have not said hello. If you're thinking one thing you'll be unhappy . . .

AA   You could think another.

DD   And you'd feel differently, is that right?

AA   Yes.

Measurement of change

One of the many stimulating challenges in using cognitive therapy for this client group is that of measuring change in intensity of beliefs and emotions. Such measurement is usually an important part of initial and outcome assessment. The first author has addressed this issue in two recent studies that show how people with learning disabilities are able to express beliefs in ways that may be quantified and used to detect change (Dagnan *et al.*, 1994; Dagnan and Ruddick, 1995). These studies show that people with learning disabilities are able to use sophisticated self-report measures of belief strength. Even when this is not possible, more imaginative approaches often succeed. A clinical illustration of one such measure follows.

Andrew (person five in Table 7.2) experienced strong anger that was concerning to staff. In the standard ABC fashion, a particular scenario was isolated. The hostel where he lived had a rule that the television could not be watched on Saturday mornings. In particular there was a music programme that he always wished to watch. Despite the questionable appropriateness of this rule, this was a good example of a situation where he tended to think that not getting something that he wanted was awful, the worst thing he could possibly imagine, and he felt angry to a degree that prevented his achieving a satisfactory outcome. As a concrete analogue measure Andrew would hold his hands apart to illustrate how terrible this was! Initially this was as wide apart as he could get his hands. We returned to this scenario and began to challenge his sense that this was the worst possible thing that could happen. This was done in an initially light-hearted way working through other possible awful scenarios. We considered how bad it would be if he were not able to watch any of the music programmes he liked. Compared to this possibility the current situation was slightly reduced in terribleness. We considered how bad it would it be if the hostel did not have a television, and this again produced a big reduction in how bad the current situation was perceived to be. We then looked for possible solutions to the problem, such as asking his family to video the programme, asking the hostel to video the programme or advocating that the rule be changed. These were carried out and the programme was regularly videoed. Again the terribleness of the situation was reduced. A key part of the cognitive intervention is to introduce an understanding of the processes involved. In this case Andrew was able to see that as we thought about different alternatives we were able to change how bad the situation seemed. The use of quantifiable and specific measures of change in cognition as a result of specific cognitive interventions will clearly demonstrate the potential effectiveness and integrity of cognitive therapeutic approaches.

Conclusion

The assessment process described here indicates that some people with learning disabilities can easily understand and work with a simple cognitive intervention. At present we are exploring further developments. First, for those people unable to complete one or more of the three requirements, how best might the skills be learned? Second, how are the subtler features of elegant cognitive therapy to be reduced to conceptual tasks? Our hope is that the assessment approach may come to be a useful aid when deciding the viability of cognitive therapy for this client group, and thereby increase its occurrence.

COGNITIVE THERAPY

We have shown that certain people with learning disabilities can carry out tasks considered to be components of cognitive therapy. Case examples citing change in beliefs and emotional and behavioural consequences have been described by Williams and Moorey (1989), Lindsay *et al.* (1993) and Lindsay, Neilson and Lawrenson (Chapter 8, this volume). At this point we also present a case to illustrate some key assessment issues that will need to be developed in future work.

Jane

Jane is 58 and single. She has a WAIS (Weschler, 1981) full-scale IQ of 65 and lives in a social services hostel with eighteen other people. She was referred to the first author by the local psychiatrist because of a long history of major depression that presented as extreme fatigue and listlessness, tearfulness and sleep disturbance. She was seen in her home twice weekly for twenty-three sessions, seven for psychological assessment (including our procedure) and sixteen for intervention. Jane was able to achieve all three requirements for simple cognitive therapy. She recognised emotions in others and in herself, spontaneously made inferential and evaluative self-statements, and could connect the two.

Jane's beliefs were accessed in the standard way: first, to get a specific A and associated Cs, and only then to probe for the beliefs (Trower *et al.*, 1988). In practice the therapist would focus on a specific self-reported incident of crying and ask Jane what she was thinking at the time. Recalling upsetting incidents usually triggered tears and this made the beliefs more accessible.

Therapy focused on beliefs and feelings that were strongly associated with two major life events; the death of her sister some seven years previously, whom she had been unable to visit when dying, and an isolated unwanted sexual experience in her early twenties. The associated feelings were guilt and sadness. Her beliefs about these events, which were disputed and tested, were demanding thinking such as 'I should have done things right', 'I should have done things differently', 'this shouldn't have happened' and a core self-evaluative belief, 'I'm a bad person'. The global and stable features of the self-evaluation were evidenced by comments like 'I've done things wrong, I'm a bad person, I'll never be any good'. All target beliefs, and the associated sadness and guilt, were triggered by day-to-day events like not having done the washing up.

Intervention focused on beliefs about guilt (e.g. that she was fully to blame for the unwanted sexual experience) and sadness (e.g. challenging the issue of guilt). For example, in relation to the unwanted sexual experience, she came to acknowledge that the other person involved in this incident shared a responsibility with her. The core self-evaluation was challenged by means such as disputing the idea that a few isolated incidents of bad behaviour make a person totally bad. Jane was able to recognise that she evaluated herself according to different rules from those she used to judge others.

Outcome

In cognitive therapy the desired goal is for the person to be less distressed and disturbed, and this is pursued by challenging associated beliefs. Before and during therapy care staff kept a record of behavioural and emotional signs of depression. Records were completed for three periods during the day: morning, afternoon and evening. Emotion was measured in terms of the number of periods in a week during which episodes of crying were observed. Behaviour was measured by the number of periods in a week during which Jane did not show any specific behavioural signs of depression. These measures are plotted in Figure 7.1. In Jane's case no measurement of belief strength was used. The records kept by staff indicate an improvement in mood and support the argument for more extensive use of cognitive therapy in people with learning disabilities.

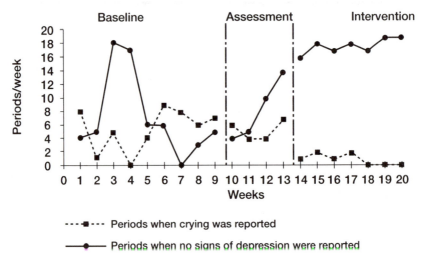

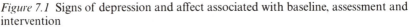

Figure 7.1 Signs of depression and affect associated with baseline, assessment and intervention

GENERAL CONCLUSIONS

This chapter has described an approach to using cognitive therapy for people with learning disabilities. First, we described a basic assessment battery, derived from the ABC framework, which seeks to establish people's ability to carry out the minimal tasks of a simple cognitive therapy. Second, we described a single case of cognitive therapy which appeared to be of benefit to the woman concerned. We believe this approach to be consistent with the constructional approach adopted in many other areas of work with people with learning disabilities (Goldiamond, 1974). For example, in teaching independent living skills to people with learning disabilities an assessment of the person's abilities, reinforcement preferences and environmental opportunities can be carried out and skill teaching planned that builds on the person's existing level of functioning (e.g. Yule and Carr, 1980). Whilst teaching programmes are in operation assessment will show whether explicit criteria are being reached within each stage of the programme. It can usually be shown that any changes in behaviour are directly related to the intervention (e.g. Barlow *et al.*, 1984). Such approaches have not been replicated in cognitive therapies for people with learning disabilities. However, the approach described here would allow basic cognitive-emotional skills to be assessed and developed.

It is particularly surprising that cognitive therapy for people with learning disabilities and emotional problems has not received greater attention. It is well documented that the cognitive and behavioural problems to which these approaches are commonly applied in populations without learning disabilities are more prevalent in people with learning disabilities (e.g. Prout and Schaefer, 1985; Eaton and Menolascino, 1982; Borthwick-Duffy and Eyman, 1990; Ineichen, 1984; Szivos-Bach, 1993; Szivos and Griffiths, 1990; Gibbons, 1985). It has not yet been clearly shown for people with learning disabilities that specific cognitive interventions are associated with specific and predicted cognitive changes and that these changes are linked to predicted changes in behaviour. Indeed, it may well be that a perceived difficulty in accessing self-report data has contributed to the predominance of behavioural work. However, methods for measuring strength of belief in people with learning disabilities are emerging (Dagnan *et al.*,1994; Dagnan and Ruddick, 1995; Lindsay *et al.*, 1993) and show that people with mild and moderate learning disabilities are reliable in their use of sophisticated measures of belief intensity.

A further issue that requires discussion is whether cognitive therapy can be possible for people with learning disability who have little or no language. We would suggest that it is not. It may be that an assessment procedure like ours could help clinicians to separate those who are able to use cognitive therapy, perhaps with some preparatory training, and those who are not. We are optimistic that this will greatly increase the use of cognitive therapy for people with learning disabilities.

REFERENCES

Barlow, D.H., Hayes, S.C. and Nelson, R.O. (1984) *The Scientist Practitioner: Research and Accountability in Clinical and Educational Setting.* New York: Pergamon.

Beck, A.T., Rush, A.J. Shaw, B.F. and Emery, G. (1979) *Cognitive Therapy of Depression.* New York: The Guilford Press.

Borthwick-Duffy, S.A. and Eyman, R.K. (1990) Who are the dually diagnosed? *American Journal of Mental Deficiency*, **94**, 586–95.

Brewin, C.R. (1988) *Cognitive Foundations of Clinical Psychology.* Hove/London: Lawrence Erlbaum.

Chaiken, S. and Stangor, C. (1987) Attitudes and attitude change. In M.R. Rosenweig and L.W. Porter (eds)., *Annual Review of Psychology*, **38**, 575–630.

Dagnan, D., Dennis, S. and Wood, H. (1994) A pilot study of the satisfaction of people with learning disabilities with the service they receive from a Community Psychology Service. *British Journal of Developmental Disabilities*, **40**, 38–44.

Dagnan, D., and Ruddick, L. (1995) The use of analogue scales and personal questionnaires for interviewing people with learning disabilities. *Clinical Psychology Forum*, **79**, 21–4.

Davanloo, H. (1980) A method of short-term dynamic psychotherapy. In H. Davanloo (ed.), *Short-term Dynamic Psychotherapy*. New York: Aronson.

Dunn, L., Dunn, L., Whetton, C. and Pintillie, D. (1982) *The British Picture Vocabulary Scale*. Windsor: NFER-Nelson Publishing Co. Ltd.

Eaton, L.F. and Menolascino, F.J. (1982) Psychiatric disorders in the mentally retarded: types, problems and challenges. *American Journal of Psychiatry*, **139**, 1297–1303.

Ellis, A. (1977) The basic clinical theory of rational emotive therapy. In A. Ellis and R. Grieger (eds), *Handbook of Rational-Emotive Therapy*. New York: Springer-Verlag.

Goldiamond, I. (1974) Towards a constructional approach to social problems. Ethical and constitutional issues raised by applied behavior analysis. *Behaviorism*, **2**, 1–84.

Gibbons, F.X. (1985) Stigma perception: social comparison among mentally retarded persons. *American Journal of Mental Deficiency*, **90**, 98–106.

Harchik, A.E., Sherman, J.A. and Sheldon, J.B. (1992) The use of self-management procedures by people with developmental disabilities: a brief review. *Research in Developmental Disabilities*, **13**, 211–27.

Ineichen, B. (1984) Prevalence of mental illness among mentally handicapped people: discussion paper. *Journal of the Royal Society of Medicine*, **77**, 761–5.

Lindsay, W., Howells, L. and Pitcaithly, D. (1993) Cognitive therapy for depression with individuals with intellectual disabilities. *British Journal of Medical Psychology*, **66**, 135–41.

Lindsay, W. and Kasprowicz, M. (1987) Challenging negative cognitions. *Mental Handicap*, **15**, 159–62.

Mansdorf, I.J. and Ben-David, N. (1986) Operant and cognitive intervention to restore effective functioning following a death in a family. *Journal of Behavior Therapy and Experimental Psychiatry*, **17**, 193–6.

Martin, J.E., Burger, D.L., Elias-Burger, S. and Mithang, D.E. (1988) Applicating self-control strategies to facilitate independence in vocational and instructional settings. In N.W. Bray (ed.), *International Review of Research in Mental Retardation*, **15**, 155–94.

Muran, J.C. (1991) A reformulation of the ABC model in cognitive psychotherapies: implications for assessment and treatment. *Clinical Psychology Review*, **11**, 399–418.

Prout, H.T., and Schaefer, B.M. (1985) Self-reports of depression by community-based mildly retarded adults. *American Journal of Mental Deficiency*, **90**, 220–2.

Reed, J. and Clements, J. (1989) Assessing the understanding of emotional states in a population of adolescents and young adults with mental handicaps. *Journal of Mental Deficiency Research*, **33**, 229–33.

Safran, J.D., Segal, Z.V., Vallis, T.M., Shaw, B.F. and Samstag, L.W. (1993) Assessing patient suitability for short-term cognitive therapy with an interpersonal focus. *Cognitive Therapy and Research*, **17**, 23–38.

Safran, J.D., Vallis, T.M., Segal, Z.V. and Shaw, B.F. (1986) Assessment of core cognitive processes in cognitive therapy. *Cognitive Therapy and Research*, **10**, 509–26.

Spence, S. (1988) *Social Skills Training with Children and Adolescents*. Windsor: National Federation for Educational Research.

Szivos-Bach, S.E. (1993) Social comparisons, stigma and mainstreaming: the self-esteem of young adults with a mild mental handicap. *Mental Handicap Research*, **6**, 217–36.

Szivos, S.E. and Griffiths, E. (1990) Group processes involved in coming to terms with a mentally retarded identity. *Mental Retardation*, **28**, 333–41.

Trower, P., Casey, A. and Dryden, W. (1988) *Cognitive-Behavioural Counselling in Action*. London: Sage.

Weschler, D. (1981) *Weschler Adult Intelligence Scale – Revised*. New York: Psychological Corporation.

Wessler, R.A. and Wessler, R.L. (1980) *The Principles and Practice of Rational Emotive Therapy*. San Francisco: Josey Bass.

Whitman, T.L. (1990) Self-regulation and mental retardation. *American Journal of Mental Retardation*, **94**, 347–62.

Williams, J.M.G. and Moorey, S. (1989) The wider application of cognitive therapy: the end of the beginning. In J. Scott, J.M.G. Williams and A.T. Beck (eds), *Cognitive Therapy in Clinical Practice: An Illustrative Casebook*. London: Routledge.

Yule, W. and Carr, J. (eds) (1980) *Behaviour Modification for People with Mental Handicaps*, 2nd edn. London: Croom Helm.

Zajonc, R.B. (1980) Feeling and thinking: preferences need no inferences. *American Psychologist*, **35**, 151–75.

8 Cognitive-behaviour therapy for anxiety in people with learning disabilities

William Lindsay, Clare Neilson and Helen Lawrenson

This chapter will discuss the use of cognitively based therapy for people with learning disabilities who suffer with anxiety problems. Discussion will focus on individuals for whom anxiety symptoms predominate, that is to say they may have additional problems but these are not greater than their anxiety. Consideration will be given to anxiety symptoms in general, rather than any one form of anxiety as listed in ICD10 or DSM3.

There is an immense literature on anxiety, panic and related disorders within the general population. This literature covers a range of the therapies including relaxation treatments, anxiety management treatments and cognitive therapies. Within these therapeutic groups there is research support for various elements of the treatment and there is a range of therapeutic options within the generic terms (for example, cognitive therapy now includes treatment options such as cognitive-behavioural treatment, schema-focused cognitive therapy and cognitive-analytic therapy). Research focuses on critical variables and symptoms within the anxiety-related disorders. We are aware of the importance of several variables including fear of negative evaluation, safety signals, anxiety sensitivity, cognitive bias (Watson and Friend, 1969; Matthews and MacLeod, 1985; Taylor, 1995; Matthews *et al.*, 1995) and the relative effectiveness of various treatments with agoraphobia, panic disorder and generalised anxiety (McNally, 1990; De Ruiter *et al.*, 1989; Van den Hout *et al.*, 1994; Ost and Westling, 1995).

We mention this range of research effort to point out the contrast with our dearth of knowledge of anxiety in people with learning disabilities. Here there is hardly any research effort, even on the simple effectiveness of treatments. There is little research on anxiety and even less on cognitive therapy. There are several possible reasons for this. First, it may be that people with a learning disability are a devalued population of little interest to the clinical/research community. This would be an indictment on us as clinical research workers, and remains a possibility. Second, there may be an assumption that people with an impoverished cognitive system do not have as stable and potent cognitions as those without a learning disability. If individuals do not have stable cognitions then it is impossible to ensure that changes are a result of clinical manipulations. Likewise, if one does not have a stable cognitive system research cannot ascertain the variables that effect and impinge upon that system since changes could be for any reason, rather than the variable under investigation. Lindsay *et al.* (1994b) investigated this hypothesis by assessing the convergent validity of various assessments for anxiety and depression in people with learning disabilities. The assessments were revised so that they would be easily understood and used by the participants. A remarkably high degree of convergent validity was found in responses to the Zung Anxiety (Zung, 1971) and Zung Depression Scales (Zung, 1965), the General Health Questionnaire (Goldberg, 1978) and the Eysenck–Withers Personality Inventory Test (Eysenck and Withers, 1965). As a further indication of validity the assessments of emotion correlated significantly with the neuroticism scale on the Eysenck–Withers Inventory but not the extroversion/introversion scale. There appears to be a high degree of consistency in the responding of individuals with a learning disability, in relation to emotion. Therefore, the assumption that this is a population with a less stable cognitive system than the general population would seem to be unfounded.

A third possibility is that there is an assumption that anxiety in people with learning disabilities functions in the same way as in the general population and therefore there is no need for specifically focused research. The present authors feel that this may be unjustified. Intellectual disability itself may determine that cognitions function in a different way. This is not necessarily detrimental to the employment of cognitive techniques; it may be that cognitions have relatively greater power and thus are more important determinants of anxiety-related symptoms and behaviour. There may also be variations in the development of dysfunctional beliefs and maladaptive strategies for coping with anxiety-related critical incidents and situations. People with learning disabilities are often brought up in relatively protected environments either with their own families or in institutional settings. Thus, they will not have had the same opportunities as others in the general population to develop coping skills and cognitions in relation to anxiety-provoking situations. Indeed, independent and self-reliant beliefs may have been discouraged. This would lead to maladaptive and dysfunctional cognitions which would mitigate against adaptive coping in critical situations. However, hypotheses such as these should be tested and we remain unaware of the relationship between protected upbringing, the nature of chronic conditions and their effects on the development of anxiety-related cognitions. Therefore, an assumption that anxiety in people with learning disability functions in the same way as in other populations is unjustified.

Levine and Langness (1983) have found that people with learning disabilities show greater levels of performance-related anxiety than non-disabled individuals. In athletic competition, people with learning disabilities responded in a fundamentally different manner from non-disabled individuals, with the former showing a reduction in performance when measured against practice conditions. Levine (1985) also found consistent relationships between individuals' reported anxiety and competence in social and work situations. Stack *et al.* (1987) suggest that people with learning disabilities who experience stressful life events may present atypical symptom profiles when compared to non-disabled controls. They found a greater level of aggression towards self and others and fewer intrapsychic symptoms. Chaney *et al.* (1985), in a study of peptic ulcers in people with learning disability, found that people in protected institutional environments developed more peptic ulcers than the general population. They concluded that helplessness in responding to environmental demands produces stress sufficient to induce peptic ulcers. Individuals who developed ulcers tended to be less able and had more physical limitations. While some of these studies are inconsistent in detail, they do provide some evidence that people with a learning disability may cope with anxiety in a different way from those in the general population. In addition, anxiety may produce different effects in this population.

Having dealt with the lack of research into anxiety in people with learning disabilities and possible reasons for this state of affairs, it has to be said that such research as there is is very encouraging. Studies evaluating effectiveness of relaxation treatment (Clare *et al.*, 1992; Lindsay and Baty, 1986), anxiety management training (Turk and Francis, 1990; Williams, 1990; Lindsay *et al.*, 1989), treatment for phobia (Dixon and Gunary, 1986; Jackson and Hooper, 1981; Lindsay *et al.* 1988), biofeedback treatments for anxiety (Calamari *et al.*,1987) and cue-controlled treatment for anxiety (Wells *et al.*,1978; Lindsay *et al.*, 1994a) have been positive. Hudson and Pilek (1990) reported the successful treatment of a case of post-traumatic stress disorder in an individual with learning disabilities. Reports of the effects of cognitive therapy in people with learning disabilities have been similarly positive with Lindsay (1991), Lindsay and Kasprowicz (1987) and Lindsay *et al.* (1993) reporting good outcomes.

The present study describes the use of cognitive therapy for anxiety in people with learning disabilities. The essential components, principles and procedures of cognitive therapy have been adhered to. However, they have been considerably revised to allow for the intellectual capabilities of the client group. The method is illustrated using two cases of cognitive therapy for anxiety with clients who have mild intellectual disability.

TREATMENT PROCEDURES

For clients with a learning disability the methods of cognitive therapy have been considerably revised and simplified. However, the essential principles, components and procedures as developed by Beck *et al.*,(1979) and subsequent developments by other cognitive therapists have been maintained as far as possible. Thus, during therapy the therapist and client follow familiar procedures. They will:

1 set an agenda;
2 develop an awareness of the role of underlying beliefs in determining thought;
3 establish the relationship between thoughts, experiences of anxiety and behaviour;
4 monitor automatic thoughts;
5 determine the content of underlying beliefs through themes in automatic thought;
6 challenge maladaptive beliefs;
7 develop adaptive automatic thoughts;
8 practise these thoughts during therapy sessions, role-plays and *in vivo* sessions;
9 review evidence to contradict maladaptive beliefs and construct new underlying assumptions about the self;
10 establish homework assignments to review malaptive cognitions and test out new underlying assumptions and adaptive automatic thought.

Setting an agenda

This has now become fairly standard in our approach to cognitive therapy for people with learning disabilities. Although with the first few cases we felt it might be a difficult concept to understand, in fact the opposite was the case and having an agenda for the session allows clients to cope with conceptually difficult material in an organised and systematic way. Therefore, the agenda has become a more important and explicit aspect of a treatment session. We now frequently use a flipchart on which the agenda is written at the beginning of the session and salient points on each agenda item are emphasised. It is important to use a very few simple words to ease understanding.

Isolating negative thoughts

Lindsay and Kasprowicz (1987) and Lindsay (1991) have discussed methods of eliciting negative automatic thoughts through role-play. This can be done while re-enacting some of the difficult events which have taken place in the client's recent past. Take the case of one of the clients to be discussed (Mr P) who had a fear of being in a room with females. Such a situation was role-played after three sessions of therapy during which the client had become more comfortable and felt safer with the methods. During this role-play Mr P's anxiety was clearly evident and the therapist simply asked him what he was thinking. In this way the automatic thoughts tumbled out: 'I can't stay here', 'I've got a red face', 'They'll be laughing at me', 'This is terrible', 'I don't like girls', 'This is bad to talk to girls'. These thoughts were so powerful and so pervasive that there was no opportunity for the therapist to intrude into them and the subject actually ran out during the session. On this occasion, because the therapeutic context of the sessions had been established, it was very easy to bring him back in, whereas on previous occasions he had refused to return to the day centre.

Negative thoughts are also elicited in the normal way through therapeutic interviews. Some clients are extremely able to review their automatic negative thoughts during interviews; others find it very difficult to say what they have been thinking and in Mr P's case he would simply say 'I just don't like it'.

Another method used during treatment is to reverse roles of therapist and client. The client, as therapist, then has to ask what 'the client' is thinking. The 'therapist' may then ask very leading questions of 'the client' such as 'Do you worry in bed at night that somebody might be breaking into your house?' In this way clients reveal very clearly the nature of the thoughts that they consider to be important in their own lives. Negative thoughts may also be elicited through plotting the sequence of events leading to anxiety or panic attack. This should be done in as much detail as possible, reviewing the client's thinking at each stage of the sequence. This method is also used to develop awareness of the link between belief, thought, emotion and behaviour.

Eliciting underlying assumptions

This is generally done by identifying themes across automatic thoughts. In one of the cases to follow (Mr K) the client had the automatic thoughts, 'Someone is breaking into the house', 'Someone will attack me if I go out', 'No one will find me if I stay here'. These automatic thoughts were linked to an underlying belief that he was completely alone in the world. The thoughts and his belief of being alone increased his agitation to such a pitch that he was unable to sleep at night, felt that it was impossible to go out of the house, had panic attacks when he went out of the house and became extremely anxious and agitated when he remained in the house. This tremendous level of anxiety and agitation led to more serious thoughts and beliefs that will be discussed later (see pp. 131–4).

It may be that underlying assumptions about the self cannot be identified from the automatic thoughts. For example, in Mr P's case it was not clear if the automatic thoughts were an extension of an underlying assumption since he was quite clear that he did not dislike girls – he simply became extremely anxious when in their presence. Some of the automatic thoughts might indicate a more basic feeling towards females (e.g. 'It's bad to talk to girls'). However, during treatment this was dealt with at the level of automatic thoughts rather than underlying assumptions.

Testing the accuracy of cognitions

As with all other aspects of cognitive therapy for people with learning disabilities, simplicity and clarity are essential aspects of treatment. To test the accuracy of cognition, simple and more direct methods should be used.

When Mr P says 'It is bad to talk to girls' we would review the evidence on why it might be bad to talk to girls. This would lead to the obviously ridiculous proposal that if it is indeed bad to talk to girls then no male would ever talk to any female. Therefore, Mr P's thoughts are being undermined through logical evidence and humour. Other thoughts and beliefs have been challenged using more personal evidence. With Mr K it was possible to review the number of times his house had been broken into (none) and continue to question how sensible it was to have the thought that someone was breaking in four or five times a night when in fact no one had ever broken in.

Generating alternative cognitions

Once again the simplest cognitions suggested by the evidence were used in treatment. Where possible this is done by using the converse of the negative thought. Therefore, where Mr P has said to himself 'The girls will be laughing at me', the converse of the thought was used – 'No one's laughing at me', 'No one's bothered about me', 'They're all getting on with their own work'. Where he has thought 'It's bad to talk to girls' the converse thought, 'It's good to talk to girls', was used. In this way his thought can be enabling and reassuring in anxiety-provoking situations rather than frightening and undermining. In Mr K's case the alternative cognitions used relied on the review of evidence and he was encouraged to say to himself, 'No one has ever broken in – go back to sleep'. In this case the converse thought is inappropriate and Mr K was acutely aware, and argued, that on this occasion it might just be the time that someone was breaking in. Thus cognitions based on past evidence, his security arrangements and comparisons with others were also used. Consequently he was able to think, 'I've locked all the doors and windows and no one can get in without making a big noise', 'Why would they break into my house, I have only got things I would want'.

Monitoring thoughts and feelings

The present authors have used one particular system for monitoring thoughts and feelings over the past few years. This involves cartoon representations of the emotion and an analogue scale aided by descriptive histograms on which to record degrees of emotion. The system was developed by Helsel and Matson (1989) and has been described by Lindsay (1991) and Lindsay *et al.* (1993). The analogue scale is flexible and can be used for daily rating of emotion and thought or, in the case of Mr P to follow, hourly ratings. Colleagues have used this scale for a variety of variables such as embarrassment, depression and even attention and time spent on work throughout the day.

Figure 8.1 shows the analogue scale for anxiety which incorporates hourly ratings and descriptive histograms to assist the subject's rating. The client is taught that the low bar indicates no anxiety, intermediate histograms indicate degrees of anxiety and the largest histogram indicates a great deal of anxiety

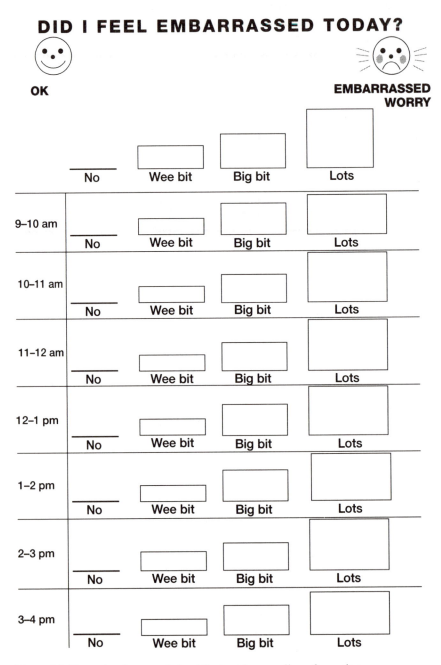

Figure 8.1 Example of a record sheet for hourly recording of emotion

during the particular period. Clients with mild intellectual disability have been able to use this scale consistently and in a way which appears to relate to others' description of their moods.

Role-play

Role-play is used to identify negative automatic thoughts. Anxiety-provoking situations are re-enacted in order to help the client to understand the relationships between their thoughts and anxiety-related feelings and behaviour. Role-play is also used frequently to help the client practise more adaptive ways of thinking in critical situations. This would be done as a precursor to homework tasks where the client could use these thoughts in the real situation. Therefore, role-play is used frequently in therapy.

Other specific tasks

Other tasks are used where appropriate. For example, in Mr P's case, a series of pictures and slides of men and women talking together was used to assess his degree of discomfort and to allow him to practise more adaptive ways of thinking about these situations. They also provide a stimulus for discussion of the realistic basis for his ways of thinking.

Homework

Setting homework tasks is extremely important both to monitor the extent of maladaptive thinking that has occurred during the week and to provide situations in which more adaptive responses can be practised. In the present examples people were encouraged to practise positive thoughts when faced with seriously anxiety-provoking situations. They were also encouraged to monitor their degree of anxiety and the extent of their maladaptive automatic thinking throughout the week or, in Mr P's case, throughout the day. All homework was reviewed carefully at the following therapeutic session.

TREATMENT PROCESS AND OUTCOME

Case 1

Mr K is a 27-year-old man with a measured IQ of 67 (WAIS-R, Wechsler, 1981). He had lived on his own in a flat. He lived a very isolated life and had become increasingly agitated over a period of months. He developed acute anxiety attacks whenever he thought about going out of his flat and became increasingly agitated when he stayed in. He was unable to sleep at night believing that someone was breaking into the flat and constantly wanted to get out when he was at home. This produced an impossible dilemma for him in that he was extremely agitated while staying at home and experienced panic attacks as soon as he went out of the house. His solution to this dilemma was to set fire to his flat. He was then taken into custody and the first author assessed him in the local police cells. It was clear that the fire-setting was the result of extreme distress and agitation. Mr K is one of the most anxious and agitated individuals with whom the service has been faced and his responses to cognitive therapy for anxiety are correspondingly interesting and illuminating.

Mr K had several automatic thoughts and these were elicited through plotting the sequence of events in his agitated and anxious episodes. He would misinterpret and misconstrue his feelings and the events that happened around him in a catastrophic manner. Automatic thoughts included those related to loneliness, such as 'I'm completely alone', 'No one wants to be with me', 'I haven't seen anyone for weeks'; thoughts which he called 'bad thoughts', such as 'I should do something about it', 'I could kill myself', 'I would be better off dead', 'I could burn the place down'; and thoughts associated with anxiety, such as 'I am uptight', 'I look odd', 'I think someone is going to harm me', 'Someone is trying to break into the flat'.

Looking across these thoughts for underlying beliefs about the client, the therapist and Mr K came to identify certain assumptions which formed the basis of Mr K's view of the world. The bad thoughts and angry thoughts seemed related to an assumption that Mr K was to blame for all his unhappiness and that he didn't like himself. Therefore, he held the dysfunctional belief that it would be appropriate for him to kill himself and that it would be appropriate for him to burn his house down and deny himself a place to live. The thoughts of loneliness and fear of being attacked at night were related to an underlying assumption that he was a solitary person who would never have any friends and never have any support. These basic dysfunctional beliefs led him to stop going out because he feared someone would attack him, which resulted in panic attacks. Moreover, he experienced extreme anxiety when he stayed in to the extent that he constantly checked his flat for intruders, injured himself and, in the end, set his flat on fire.

Treatment was conducted over one year as described above and, after reviewing Mr K's life, the skills he possessed and the relationships which he possessed, the following adaptive cognitions emerged. In relation to feeling scared and lonely Mr K reviewed all of the relationships which he had in his life. He had a number of relatives who visited him regularly and he was encouraged to think about them when he experienced thoughts related to fear of loneliness. He was also encouraged to substitute previous maladaptive thoughts with more functional thoughts such as 'I only feel scared because I'm lonely'; 'I've only been lonely today'; 'I saw my brother yesterday'; 'I will go and see my friends tomorrow'. Thus, using methods previously described, simple adaptive thoughts were substituted for thoughts that produced anxiety and agitation.

A similar procedure was used with the very frightening 'bad thoughts'. Since a degree of self-dislike was involved in these he was encouraged to review his competencies and ways in which people liked him. Therefore, he was encouraged to substitute simple positive thoughts such as 'I am a good cook'; 'I can keep my house'; 'I know lots of people and I can go to see them any time'; 'If I do something or go to see someone I will feel okay'. In relation to his fear of intruders he was encouraged to think simple practical thoughts such as 'I've locked all the doors and windows – I know I'm safe', 'No one can get in without making a big noise' rather than continually checking for strangers.

Figure 8.2 shows Mr K's scores on the Beck Anxiety Inventory and the Beck Depression Inventory from before treatment, at 4 months, at 8 months, at 12 months, at the end of treatment and at 18 months follow-up. As can be seen his anxiety fell from extremely dysfunctional levels to levels which he

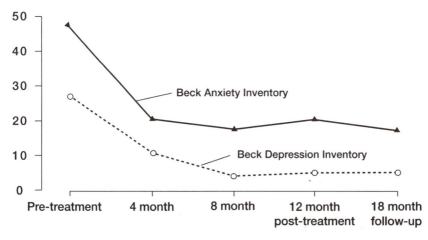

Figure 8.2 Beck Anxiety Inventory and Beck Depression Inventory scores for Mr K at baseline, 4-month, 8-month, 1-year and 18-month assessments

found much more comfortable. Mr K also showed a degree of depression at pre-treatment assessment. This depression fell to more normal levels after 4 and 8 months of treatment. These improvements maintained to follow-up.

Mr K is an excellent case illustration since he kept very good records both of his thoughts and of his behaviour each week. The content of his thoughts and behaviour have already been described and Figure 8.3 shows the total number of thoughts he recorded weekly. Both 'bad thoughts' and thoughts related to anxiety and loneliness are shown. As can be seen these thoughts reduced over the weeks of treatment from extremely high levels to relatively low levels. The 'bad thoughts' reduced from around fifty or sixty per week to under ten. The anxiety-related thoughts reduced less dramatically from around thirty or forty per week to between ten and twenty per week. However, in both cases there was a positive response to treatment.

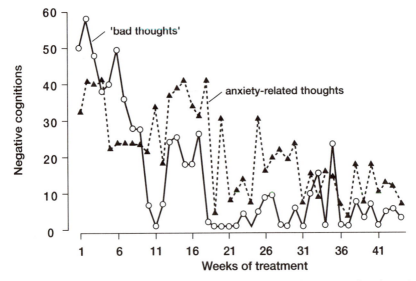

Figure 8.3 The number of anxiety-related and 'bad' thoughts reported each week by Mr K

Case 2

Mr P was a 19-year-old man with a measured IQ of 66 (WAIS-R, Wechsler, 1981). He was referred from the centre in which he worked because he was having acute panic attacks when asked to work beside women. He had run out of the centre on several occasions and refused to return after being asked to sit or work beside women. He had also become quite aggressive when somebody tried to stop him leaving. It soon became clear that Mr P's problems were acute embarrassment with women leading to panic attacks. This was a life-long problem that had been allowed to continue and had been accommodated at school and at home. It was only now that he had left school that the extent of his embarrassment became clear.

Mr P's automatic thoughts were elicited in two main ways. The therapist and Mr P went through the sequence of events leading to the anxiety attacks and Mr P mentioned a number of thoughts that he experienced when he went into a room with women, when he was asked to sit down beside women, when he was asked to work beside women or when he was asked to work with them. In addition, we looked at a few slides in which men and women were talking together and Mr P reported his thoughts. From these methods several automatic thoughts related to his embarrassment with women were isolated: 'I can't stay'; 'They will be laughing at me'; 'This is terrible'; 'I don't like girls'; 'It's bad to talk to girls'. These thoughts were challenged through examining how logical and sensible they were. For example, how could it be bad to talk to girls when millions of men do it all over the world; how can they be laughing at you when they've got their own work to get on with; if they're not looking at you and not laughing how can they be laughing at you? Other self-statements were countered by encouraging Mr P to use the opposite self-statement in situations with women, i.e. 'I can stay here for a while'; 'I'll manage to do this alright'; 'I like girls, they've never done me any harm'. These very simple self-statements would enable interaction with women rather than undermine his ability to stay in a room with women.

In addition to reviewing his thoughts, part of each session (around half an hour) was given over to practising positive cognitions when watching couples together. The slides were taken from the Life Horizons II Course (Kempton, 1988). On each occasion eight slides were presented (there were five different sets to avoid habituation). These slides increased in their anxiety-provoking nature for Mr P. The slides were pictures of a girl on her own; a couple talking; a couple talking in a café; a couple holding hands; a couple in the street with arms around each other; a couple kissing; a couple kissing and embracing; a couple in bed. These last two proved so difficult for Mr P that they were not used after baseline and the first treatment session. However, since they had been scored at baseline, for the purposes of data analysis to follow, they were given maximum scores throughout the data collection period.

Figure 8.4 shows Mr P's BAI and BDI scores before treatment, at a mid-way point in treatment, after the treatment sessions were finished and at 3 months' follow-up. It can be seen that his BDI scores were low and support the view that Mr P's problems were wholly related to anxiety and embarrassment. His BAI scores fell from very high levels before treatment to intermediate but still clinically significant levels after 8 weeks, to relatively low levels at post-treatment and follow-up.

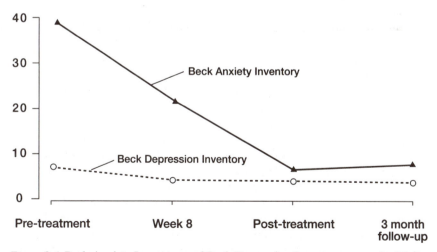

Figure 8.4 Beck Anxiety Inventory and Beck Depression Inventory scores for Mr P at baseline, 8-week, post-treatment and 3-month follow-up assessments

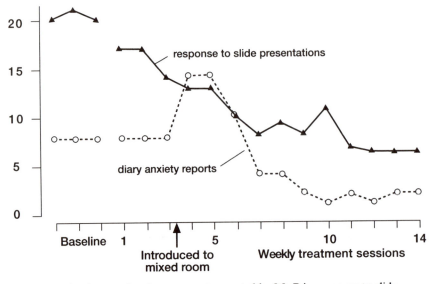

Figure 8.5 The degree of embarrassment reported by Mr P in response to slide presentations and target environments

Figure 8.5 shows the results of two assessments. The first shows Mr P's response to the slide presentations. On each of eight presentations Mr P was asked to rate his anxiety on a four-point analogue scale from 'no' anxiety, through a 'wee bit' of anxiety, a 'big bit' of anxiety to 'lots' of anxiety. These reference points were chosen as meaningful to Mr P in that they were the words he used. As has been mentioned the two most difficult slides were not used after the first treatment session because they were so anxiety-provoking. However, they continued to be scored at a maximum, i.e. six points were added to his total score. As can be seen in Figure 8.5 Mr P's baseline scores were around the maximum possible for eight presentations (scoring was 0, 1, 2, 3). He quickly began to become more comfortable with the less anxiety-provoking slides and towards the final sessions became somewhat more comfortable with the slides that provoked a greater degree of anxiety. His progress here was very smooth. The second set of scores on Figure 8.5 shows Mr P's reported anxiety on a daily diary. He found it extremely difficult to keep the diary every day and so it was decided to record his anxiety through one particular day each week in the day centre. It was possible for a member of staff to make themselves available at certain points during the day to help Mr P fill out his diary. He made a rating of embarrassment for each hour of the day (0 = no embarrassment, 3 = lots of embarrassment). Each set of ratings was recorded on a single sheet. The maximum possible score was twenty-one. As can be seen Mr P reported moderate levels of embarrassment throughout baseline and the first 3 weeks of treatment. However, the three treatment sessions were spent orientating Mr P's awareness of the relationships between belief, thought, feeling and behaviour, eliciting the automatic thoughts and looking for themes within the automatic thoughts, reinterpreting his beliefs and thoughts and questioning the evidence supporting and challenging his thoughts. These processes are described above. It was not until after the third session that he was reintroduced into a room with women. Figure 8.5 shows that his reported embarrassment increased sharply for 2 weeks after joining females in the room and this embarrassment began to reduce after a further 3 weeks of treatment. It then came down to stable, low levels for the final 6 weeks of treatment. Both Mr P and members of staff who worked with him reported that he used the alternative cognitive statements frequently throughout the day. Therefore there was a very clear perception that his enabling cognitions were promoting an ability to stay for longer periods with women. However, during the session, when looking at the slides, Mr P often said 'I still don't like this'. This was true up to and including the last session and indicates that although there was a considerable improvement in Mr P's ability to stay with women, he retained some residual anxiety.

DISCUSSION

This chapter has outlined the way in which the techniques of cognitive therapy for anxiety can be adapted and simplified for people with learning disabilities. Two case studies are presented to illustrate the methods and adaptations. Mr K was an extremely agitated and anxious man who had several deep-seated beliefs related to unworthiness, loneliness and fear of being attacked. Mr P was a man who was embarrassed in the presence of females and with little evidence of depression.

While the procedures of cognitive therapy were simplified and adapted, all of the main elements were retained. Therefore, therapist and client continued to set an agenda for the session, review homework, elicit negative automatic thoughts, challenge these negative automatic thoughts, identify themes in automatic thoughts related to dysfunctional beliefs, review the evidence for and against these dysfunctional beliefs, role-play more positive ways of thinking and encourage the client to use these more positive ways of thinking in their life. We also set homework and monitored feelings during the week. Thus the basic principles of cognitive therapy were adhered to closely and the evidence of improvement supports the use of these techniques with this client group.

Both men showed very high levels of anxiety before treatment as measured by the BAI. One showed moderately high levels of depression. In both cases the BAI scores showed significant clinical improvements as therapy progressed. By the end of treatment and at follow-up, anxiety had improved to tolerable levels for Mr K and normal levels for Mr P. In the case of Mr K his BDI scores fell to normal levels. Mr K's treatment lasted approximately a year and his anxiety levels remained low at 6 months' follow-up. Mr P's treatment lasted 14 weeks and again his anxiety levels remained low at

3 months' follow-up. For the purposes of this paper both men were followed up recently using the BDI and BAI Inventories. In both cases anxiety levels have remained stably low at 18 months' follow-up. The staff who work with both men report no significant problems in relation to anxiety. There were certainly no reports of any of the problems which led to referral.

Both men monitored their anxiety-related cognitions throughout the therapy period. In both cases there were considerable reductions in anxiety-related cognitions although both men retained low levels of residual dysfunctional thinking related to their particular problem at the end of therapy.

SUMMARY AND CONCLUSIONS

This chapter has reviewed the field of cognitive therapy for anxiety, panic and related disorders in people who have learning disabilities. It was noted that there has been very little research effort in identifying anxiety-related disorders in this population and there have been even fewer studies investigating the effectiveness of cognitive therapy in the client group.

In our introduction we have presented evidence to suggest that cognitive therapy may be an eminently suitable approach for people with learning disabilities. Subjects seem to possess a consistent reliable cognitive system which is amenable to therapeutic manipulations. We also presented some evidence suggesting that anxiety in this population may differ in its function, process and presentation, when compared to other more cognitively sophisticated populations. Therefore, we would suggest that there is a need for research on cognitive therapy for anxiety and other emotional disorders that is specifically addressed to the field of learning disabilities. This chapter, and the clinical illustrations given, would suggest that such research endeavours might prove positive.

REFERENCES

Beck, A.T., Rush, A.J., Shaw, B.F. and Emery, G. (1979) *Cognitive Therapy of Depression*. New York: John Wiley.

Calamari, J.E., Geist, G.O. and Shahbazian, M.J. (1987) Evaluation of multiple component relaxation training with developmentally disabled persons. *Research in Developmental Disabilities*, **8**, 55–70.

Chaney, R.H., Eyman, R.K., Givens, C.A. and Valdes, C.D. (1985) Inability to cope with environmental stress: peptic ulcers in mentally retarded persons. *Journal of Psychosomatic Research*, **29**, 519–24.

Clare, I.C.H., Murphy, G.H., Cox, D., Chaplin, A.H. (1992) Assessment and treatment of fire setting: a single case investigation using a cognitive behavioural model. *Criminal Behaviour and Mental Health*, **2**, 253–68.

De Ruiter, C., Rijken, H., Garssen, B. and Kraaimaat, F. (1989) Breathing retraining, exposure and a combination of both, in the treatment of panic disorder with agoraphobia. *Behavior Research and Therapy*, **27**, 647–55.

Dixon, M.S. and Gunary R.M. (1986) Fear of dogs: group treatment of people with mental handicaps. *Mental Handicap*, **14**, 6–9.

Eyesenck, H. and Withers, A. (1965) *Eyesenck–Withers Personality Inventory.* London: Hodder & Stoughton.

Goldberg, D. (1978) *The General Health Questionnaire.* Windsor: NFER–Nelson Publishing Company Ltd.

Helsel, W.J. and Matson, J.L. (1989) The relationship of depression to social skills and intellectual functioning in mentally retarded adults. *Journal of Mental Deficiency Research*, **32**, 411–18.

Hudson, C.J. and Pilek, E. (1990) PTSD in the retarded. *Hospital and Community Psychiatry*, **41**, 97.

Jackson, H.J. and Hooper, J.P. (1981) Some issues arising from the desensitisation of a dog phobia in a retarded female: or should we take the bite out of the bark? *Australian Journal of Developmental Disabilities*, **7**, 9–16.

Kempton, W. (1988) *Life Horizons 1 and 2.* Santa Monica, CA: James Stanfield & Company.

Levine, H.G. (1985) Situational anxiety and everyday life experiences of mildly mentally retarded adults. *American Journal of Mental Deficiency*, **90**, 27–33.

Levine, H.G. and Langness, L.L. (1983) Context ability and performance: comparison of competitive athletics among mildly retarded and non-retarded adults. *American Journal of Mental Deficiency*, **87**, 528–38.

Lindsay, W.R. (1991) Psychological therapies in mental handicap. In W. Fraser, R. MacGillivray and A. Green (eds), *Hallas 'Caring for People with Mental Handicaps'.* London: Butterworth.

Lindsay, W.R. and Baty, F.J. (1986) Behavioural relaxation training: explorations with adults who are mentally handicapped. *Mental Handicap*, **14**, 160–2.

Lindsay, W.R. and Kasprowicz, M. (1987) Challenging negative cognitions: developing confidence in adults by means of cognitive therapy. *Mental Handicap*, **15**, 159–62.

Lindsay, W.R., Michie, A.M., Baty, F.J. and MacKenzie, K. (1988) Dog phobia in people with mental handicaps: anxiety management training and exposure treatments. *Mental Handicap Research*, **1**, 39–48.

Lindsay, W.R., Baty, F.J., Michie, A.M. and Richardson, I. (1989) A comparison of anxiety treatments with adults who have moderate and severe mental retardation. *Research in Developmental Disabilities*, **10**, 129–40.

Lindsay, W.R., Howells, L. and Pitcaithly, P. (1993) Cognitive therapy for depression with individuals with intellectual disabilities. *British Journal of Medical Psychology*, **66**, 135–41.

Lindsay, W.R., Fee, M., Michie, A.M. and Heap, I. (1994a) The effects of cue control relaxation on adults with severe mental retardation. *Research in Developmental Disabilities*, **15**, 425–37.

Lindsay, W.R., Michie, A.M., Baty, F.J., Smith, A.H.W. and Miller, S. (1994b) The consistency of reports about feelings and emotions from people with intellectual disability. *Journal of Intellectual Disability Research*, **38**, 61–6.

Matthews, A. and Macleod, C. (1985) Selective processing of threat cues in anxiety states. *Behavior Research and Therapy*, **23**, 563–9.

Matthews, A., Mogg, K., Centish, J. and Eyesenck, M. (1995) Effect of psychological treatment on cognitive bias in generalised anxiety disorder. *Behavior Research and Therapy*, **33**, 293–303.

McNally, R.J. (1990) Psychological approach to panic disorder: a review. *Psychological Bulletin*, **18**, 403–19.

Ost, L.G. and Westling, B.E. (1995) Applied relaxation vs cognitive behaviour therapy in the treatment of panic disorder. *Behavior Research and Therapy*, **33**, 145–58.

Stack, L., Haldipur, C.V. and Thompson, M. (1987) Stressful life events and psychiatric hospitalisation of mentally retarded patients. *American Journal of Psychiatry*, **144**, 661–3.

Taylor, S. (1995) Anxiety sensitivity: theoretical perspectives and recent findings. *Behavior Research and Therapy*, **33**, 243–58.

Turk, V. and Francis, E. (1990) An anxiety management group: strengths and pitfalls. *Mental Handicap*, **18**, 78–81.

Van den Hout, M., Arntz, A. and Hoekstra, R. (1994) Exposure reduced agoraphobia but not panic, and cognitive therapy reduced panic but not agoraphobia. *Behavior Research and Therapy*, **32**, 447–51.

Watson, D. and Friend, R. (1969) Measurement of social–evaluative anxiety. *Journal of Counselling and Clinical Psychology*, **33**, 448–57.

Wechsler, D. (1981) *The Wechsler Adult Intelligence Scale – Revised*. San Antonio: The Psychological Corporation/Harcourt Brace Jovanovich.

Wells, K.C., Turner, S.M., Bellack, A.S. and Hersen, M. (1978) Effects of cue control relaxation on psychomotor seizures: an experimental analysis. *Behavior Research and Therapy*, **16**, 51–3.

Williams, J. (1990) Helping people to relax in overstimulating environments. *Mental Handicap*, **18**, 160–2.

Zung, W.K. (1965) A self rating depression scale. *Archives of General Psychiatry*, **12**, 63–70.

Zung, W.K. (1971) A rating instrument for anxiety disorders. *Psychosomatics*, **12**, 371–9.

9 Applying cognitive-behavioural approaches to the carers of people with learning disabilities who display challenging behaviour

Albert Kushlick, Peter Trower and Dave Dagnan

INTRODUCTION

In recent years a great deal of research has been developed in the area of working with people with learning disabilities who have additional challenging behaviours (e.g. Jones and Eayres, 1993; Emerson *et al.*, 1994a). Challenging behaviour has been defined as

> behaviour of such an intensity, frequency or duration that the physical safety of the person or others is likely to be placed in serious jeopardy, or behaviour which is likely to seriously limit or delay access to and use of ordinary community facilities.
>
> Emerson *et al.* 1987

Such a definition introduces the idea that one aspect of challenging behaviour is that it prevents people from participating in a high quality of life. Many services for people with learning disabilities use the concept of 'quality of life' as an outcome (Kushlick, 1975; Kushlick *et al.*, 1983; Felce and Perry, 1995; Dagnan *et al.*, 1995; Schalock *et al.*, 1989). Challenging behaviours may exist throughout life (Emerson, 1992) and we assert that, even when the challenging behaviours remain, it is still vital that the opportunities for a high quality of life with ensuing opportunities to develop functional alternative behaviours are offered despite the challenging behaviours.

We suggest that seeking a high quality life for oneself and others is a valuable and widely accepted goal. A definition of challenging behaviour as a behaviour that impedes our achievement of this allows us to understand our own behaviour and that of our clients in the same way. This chapter shows how one of the most well-accepted and ecologically valid behavioural technologies, positive programming (La Vigna and Donnellan, 1986), can be integrated with a cognitive psychotherapy approach for carers. This cognitive-behavioural method will be described in some detail in the context of a training course for carers of people with learning disabilities. The approach described assumes that the goal of working with people with learning disabilities and challenging behaviour is to enable our clients and ourselves to work creatively and effectively towards a high quality of life.

Behavioural approaches

By far the biggest contribution to understanding and intervention in challenging behaviour has come from the behavioural approach. A major advance within this has been the shift from behaviour-reducing techniques to suppress or eliminate behaviours labelled 'challenging' to using non-aversive contingencies to develop new and maintain existing positive behaviours – the constructional approach (Goldiamond, 1970).

Positive programming

One of the most widely used multi-component packages of non-aversive behavioural interventions is that assembled by La Vigna and Donnellan (1986). This approach begins to offer the techniques needed to maintain a high quality of life in 'ordinary' environments. They offer a constructional approach that celebrates, rewards and extends each person's existing current valuable repertoire. The approach has three components.

1 *Assessment.* Positive programming requires thorough assessment. This should involve assessment of the strengths of the client, their preferences and their adaptive behaviour. It will also involve assessment to identify the functions of the challenging behaviour. One of the main components of the 'non-aversive' approaches is an emphasis upon functional analysis (Bijou and Baer, 1961; Bijou et al., 1968; Carr, 1988; Horner et al.,1990). Functional analysis is the attempt to identify factors affecting a particular behaviour. These include events immediately preceding and following the behaviour and broader ecological variables. From this it has been possible to infer some possible communication functions of challenges. For example, 'I feel . . .', 'I want . . . .', or 'I don't want . . . '. Using such formulations it has been possible to teach carers to respond immediately to the challenging behaviour in the 'hot' situation as if the person had communicated more effectively and appropriately and to begin to teach the person presenting the challenges in the 'cold' situation to communicate more effectively (Carr and Durand, 1985).

2 *Positive proactive interventions* to teach more appropriate ways for the person to communicate their needs and feelings. This may include positive programming of the constructional development of general skills and skills that are functionally equivalent to the challenges presented. This may then replace the challenging behaviour provided it achieves the same function as the challenging behaviour at least as easily. Proactive interventions may also include direct behavioural treatment such as arranging differential schedules of reinforcement and stimulus control methods and ecological manipulations to change settings, styles of interaction, etc.

3 *A range of reactive strategies* to be implemented to keep clients, carers and others safe and to limit any damage caused by the challenging behaviours

until the proactive strategies have an effect. This may include active listening, stimulus change and other forms of crisis intervention.

The importance of staff behaviour

The positive programming approach requires staff and carers to implement a complex set of procedures over long periods. Increasingly there has been recognition of the cognitive, behavioural and emotional challenges presented to carers if they are to arrange high quality environments for their clients. Evidence shows that, without accessible support, care staff 'survive' by responding to challenges in the best way known to them (Hall and Oliver, 1992; Hastings and Remington, 1994a). Such reactive strategies may successfully stop the behaviour in the short term, but they may have long-term negative effects. For example, giving the client what they want, or removing what they don't want in response to challenging behaviours, may reduce escalations to more serious behaviours. However, unless also accompanied by procedures to increase frustration tolerance, and to teach appropriate alternative ways of attaining objectives, they will strengthen the earlier component of the challenging behaviour in the long term. This is so particularly if such consequences are delivered only intermittently (Ferster and Skinner, 1957).

Effective intervention packages will often be complex and must be carried out consistently over long periods of time if they are to work. There have been few attempts to study the barriers to successful implementation of such behavioural programmes. Indeed, Hastings and Remington (1994a, p. 281) point out that 'researchers and practitioners have rarely considered the motivational factors that may underlie the origins and current determinants of staff behaviour'. Hastings and Remington (1994b) recommend that, in trying to understand the determinants of staff behaviour, we should look at the relationships between a behaviour and its consequences as a two-term contingency. They suggest that components of staff behaviour may be 'under the control of contingencies relating to the aversive nature of challenging behaviour itself' (p. 282). Some care staff behaviour may arise from attempts to reduce their aversive experiences.

Cognitive-behavioural models

In this section we turn to cognitive-behavioural approaches which we believe can provide us with an understanding of staff responses to challenging behaviour. The virtue of these approaches is that they provide a framework for explaining such staff responses at the emotional and cognitive as well as the behavioural level. These approaches also enable us to specify and test the kind of cognitive-behavioural training intervention that may be effective in producing beneficial change in carer behaviour. We draw mainly on rational-emotive behaviour therapy (REBT; see Ellis, 1962).

The results of a study by Dagnan *et al.* (1996) and other studies that show a relation between staff attitudes and staff behaviour can be understood within a rational-emotive behaviour therapy (REBT; see Ellis, 1962) perspective. Ellis offers an ABC model in which A is an activating event, B is a belief about that activating event and C is the consequence in behaviour or emotion. For example, the A may be a client's challenging behaviour in a particular situation. B is a belief about that behaviour: for example, the inference that 'the behaviour is under the person's control' and that the person is 'attention seeking' and hence is 'bad' or 'worthless' and 'should be punished or avoided'. C is the emotional or behavioural consequence that may involve feeling anger and avoiding the person. The main point of the theory is that the person's feelings and behaviour can be predicted from a knowledge of their beliefs. Rational-emotive behaviour therapy is then designed to help a person identify their beliefs, feelings and behaviours. Beliefs that are found to be 'irrational' (i.e. unsupported by evidence) and that appear to be an obstacle to working towards a high quality of life may be systematically appraised. They may then be changed for beliefs that are supported by evidence and that empower the individual to work for the attainment of a high quality of life for themselves and others.

In setting the scene for describing the training workshops we make the following assumptions. Humans want to live high quality lives for themselves and, where they can see ways of doing it, to help other humans to live high quality lives also. However, challenging behaviour by definition is a barrier to high quality living. It is predictable that we all will, at times, respond unhelpfully at the behavioural level, experience anxiety or anger at the emotional level, and make negative attributions to the challenger ('blame' the client) at the cognitive level (Weiner, 1980; 1985). We may also make inappropriate positive attributions to the challenger.

Ellis and Harper (1975) have drawn attention to the tendency of most humans with sufficient expressive language to exaggerate and overgeneralise their healthy 'preferences' about themselves, others and the universe into unhealthy 'demands'. For example, a healthy preference may take the form, 'I like to perform well', and a healthy inference, 'If I want to get things the way I prefer, I had better accept my uncomfortable feelings and work creatively towards getting what I want'. Our tendency to exaggerate and overgeneralise 'demands' may take the form 'I must, ought and should always perform perfectly', and unhealthy inferences drawn from this may include, 'If I don't get what I demand of myself then I deserve condemnation and punishment as a worthless wimp, I feel totally depressed, the future is hopeless and it is awful and terrible and I can't stand it'. Because of these very widespread and fallible tendencies in most humans, we conclude that most will need special forms of support if they are to problem-solve effectively and implement detailed multi-component procedures of the constructional behavioural approach over long periods that will include both successes and severe setbacks.

OVERVIEW OF AN INTEGRATED COGNITIVE-BEHAVIOURAL TRAINING APPROACH

In describing a substantial cognitive-behaviour training approach in the space available here we inevitably have to be selective. We therefore concentrate at the level of detail on the innovative and cognitive components of the training. In order to make use of this material readers will need to have a detailed knowledge of positive programming from sources such as La Vigna and Donnellan (1986). The bulk of this chapter takes the form of a description of the framework and some of the content of a training course developed by the first author. The training takes the form of two or more workshops that are best integrated with ongoing supervision of carers and people themselves, focusing on issues of concern.

Preparation

Before the first training meeting participants are asked to collect data concerning an individual client. The data may consist of:

1 The Behavioral Assessment Guide (Willis and La Vigna, 1989). This substantial assessment provides descriptive data on the person's strengths and the daily routine they follow. It provides sufficient data on the challenging behaviour to make an informed hypothesis about its function;

2 Staff are requested to send a video of parts of the client's daily activities. People sometimes apologise that the video taken does not include illustrations of the challenging behaviours. However, examples of the client's behaviours that are not challenging provide the key information on what is already working and it is on this type of material that future interventions can be built. Staff are asked to take about 1 or 2 hours of video 'as it occurs' so that the sequence can be seen in 'real time';

3 If the client has an extensive verbal repertoire or is self-conscious about being videoed, staff are asked to do a tape recording of a conversation or a counselling session and send that;

4 Staff are asked to keep a daily diary of 'good news' and 'bad news'. If the client is able to write, the client is asked to do this with as much support as they need. Some clients do this using pictures and symbols, otherwise staff do it with them.

Who constitutes the 'service'?

Before starting the workshops we review the service in which people work. Participants are often unaware of the numbers of professionals whose participation will need to be supported and aligned if procedures are to be effectively and efficiently implemented. In particular it is useful to highlight the different amounts of time carers of different types spend with clients. This varies from clients, parents, residential and day-care staff who interact intensively with one-another over long periods of the day or night to the interactions of professionals who interact intensively, and often individually, for much shorter periods of any day, and who may only do so at long intervals (weekly, or monthly, or even annually). The failure of service managers and planners to address this challenge may result in a waste and duplication of effort that is often ineffective. It is also often perceived very negatively by clients, parents and other front-line workers.

The training

To work successfully with people with learning disabilities and challenging behaviour it is important to:

1 have a goal and know what we are trying to achieve;
2 know how to achieve this goal;
3 have a way of 'surviving' the journey; that is to be able to act constructively, calmly and lovingly to ourselves and others despite the setbacks we will experience and the accompanying emotions that will be felt during the journey.

The goal is to attain a high quality of life for the client and those working or living with them. The method of attaining this goal is the constructional, non-aversive behavioural approach (Skinner, 1953; Goldiamond, 1970, 1974; La Vigna and Donnellan, 1986). The ways of keeping calm and accepting along the way involve the use of techniques and ideas from rational-emotive behaviour therapy (Ellis and Harper, 1975) by those working or living with the client and by the client themselves if they are able to participate.

What are our goals?

We begin this section with a discussion of our goals. Through discussion these are brought together under the heading of achieving a high quality of life. We use the abbreviated form 'HQL' to make this a specific goal rather than a general concept. Table 9.1 lists some components of a 'menu' of what constitutes a high quality of life for most people. Most people seeing the menu agree that the main challenge they face is the priority given to different components of the menu. 'How much time should I spend on my house, my clothes, my finances, my relationships, my spiritual life or being creative?' Few people find a good balance for very long. We strongly emphasise that our most important relationship is with ourselves. Ellis (1962) summarises this as 'me first, others a close second'. Participants may claim that this is a selfish position, and that their most important relationship is with their partner, parent, or children. During discussion, most agree that the better I am getting on with myself, the better I am also likely to respond to the interests of others

Table 9.1 A menu for a high quality of life

Housing, shelter, clothing, food, furnishings, money, paid work
Social relationships with: ourselves, children, parents, family, friends, partners, colleagues, neighbours, town
Privacy and choice
Expression of sexuality
Security from abuse
Education, qualifications, information
Physical and emotional health
Recreation
Political decision-making, protesting, access to legal help, rights
Exploring and creating, helping self and others
Spiritual

and help them towards their own high quality life. On the other hand, if I am relating badly with myself and putting myself down, I am less likely to notice others and their needs. The commitment to work for goals relating to a high quality life constitutes what Ellis calls 'medium and long-term (as opposed to short-term) hedonism' (Ellis, 1962).

There is a qualification to a high quality life menu. This is that it is very important to be committed to work for a high quality of life despite failure. Most people have a tendency to work for their own and others' high quality life, 'as long as I don't have failures or too many of them'. We will discuss the issue of 'failure' (we offer Table 9.2 as a 'menu') and help participants to the conclusion that 'failure' is best defined as, 'not getting what I want', or, 'getting what I don't want'. The items on the failures menu are discussed in some depth later. It is noted that the items listed on Table 9.2 are either synonyms for failure, or particular forms of it (e.g. 'obstacles', 'hassles', or, in the case of 'uncertainty' or 'risk', predictions that I may not get what I want, or that I may get what I do not want).

The value to the species of the commitment to work at HQL activities despite discomfort is illustrated from the observation that very important valued activities take place despite the fact that people are experiencing extreme forms of discomfort. For example, women continue to bear children despite the fact that the confinement and birth are clearly uncomfortable and painful. Parents of very young children who do not sleep choose to practise walking and doing other parenting tasks when they are virtually asleep! Similarly, important and valuable tasks are carried out despite the fact that the people doing so feel depressed, panicky, or angry. Indeed, the evidence suggests that people 'get better' and even 'feel better' to the extent that they

Table 9.2 A menu for setbacks in working towards a high quality of life

Failure
Obstacles
Hassles
Uncertainty
Risk
Just and unjust criticism
My own and others' obnoxious behaviour
Inadequate resources
Physical impairments, mental health impairments, intellectual impairments
Feeling 'yukkie': depressed, panicky, angry, jealous, tired, nauseous, in pain, sweaty, shaky, breathless
Severe challenging behaviour

practise and learn to work for high quality lives despite their negative feelings and the discomfort of 'failing'.

Often for people working in health and social services lack of resources is a big issue and people frequently resist committing themselves to working for a high quality of life for themselves or others because their resources are inadequate. However, whenever we are working towards high quality lives we use those resources that are available to us (if our resources were not adequate to do what we are doing, we would not be doing what we are!). If we want to do new things, we had better budget for what we want to do and set about getting or rearranging our resources to do what we want.

A quick exercise we often use is to ask participants to raise their hands if on the day of the meeting they have already not got some things they wanted or got others they did not want; all do. Some add comments about what the failures have been, such as attending the workshop when they would rather be doing something else. We point out that this exercise shows that people have experience of working towards a high quality of life despite the fact that they experience failures. The commitment to work and support others to work for their high quality life, despite failing some of the time, is what is referred to by Ellis (1962) as 'high frustration tolerance'. The commitment to procrastinate or give up because it is too difficult at present and to wait until things get better before working toward high quality life is usefully categorised as 'low frustration tolerance'.

Low frustration tolerance relates directly to the issue of challenging behaviour. A challenging behaviour is one that gets in the way of us or others attaining a high quality of life. Self-harming behaviours such as smoking, overeating and procrastination (putting off completing assignments, taking up issues to improve relationships) are usually acknowledged by workshop participants as challenging behaviours that they have. Next they are asked if they believe that they will ever be able to give them up entirely. Wisely, very few think they will. Nevertheless, most can conclude that they are committed to continue working for their own and others' high quality of life despite their own continuing challenging behaviours. The same principle can be applied in working with the challenging behaviours of others.

Why are challenging behaviours so difficult to give up?

We explore with trainees the idea that challenging behaviours virtually always have a function: for example, under some conditions they get the person immediate results or relief from discomfort. This relief is often exaggerated by the person: for example smokers say they are 'dying' for a smoke and proceed to kill themselves smoking; overeaters say they are 'starving' despite being overweight and munch cheese sandwiches; procrastinators say 'I'll do it later' and leave important tasks undone. The immediate common result of each challenge is the 'relief' felt by the person expressing the challenge. In this way, challenging behaviours can be seen as having a 'communicative function' (i.e. they communicate, 'I feel . . . ', 'I want . . , ' and 'I don't want . . . '). We set trainees the task of working out what their own challenging behaviours communicate.

One of the aims of this section is to help participants to identify the power of immediate relief from discomfort as a motivator of human behaviour. We also identify the tendency of humans to use their creative verbal behaviour to derive inaccurate inferences on which they then proceed to act as if they were true or a part of their real experience. This helps to introduce them to what Ellis (1962) calls 'irrational beliefs' or 'inferences'; a point we return to later.

What tools do we have to work towards a high quality of life for our clients?

This part of the training includes a checklist of procedures drawn largely from the package developed by La Vigna and Donnellan (1986). These procedures are the tools that people will need in order to work towards and maintain a high quality life for themselves and for the people with challenging behaviour. Later in the training and in subsequent supervision meetings they will be going over and implementing these components in detail. At this stage the aim is to familiarise participants with all of the components and to highlight that many of them are similar to the 'ordinary' activities that they and others now do. Most of what we cover here can be found in other works (La Vigna and Donnellan, 1986). In this chapter we give an overview with issues highlighted where they are of particular interest.

Assessment

We continually stress that we are taking a constructional approach and that any new developments will take place 'on top' of what is already there. Therefore, we stress that we assess the challenging behaviour in great detail and also assess the strengths of the person and people working with them. We add to the non-verbal behavioural assessment an assessment of the person's verbal (cognitive) behaviour.

Direct treatment and reinforcers

At this point the value of 'catching people getting it right' rather than 'getting it wrong' is raised. If we want to teach new behaviours effectively we need to reward people more for getting things right than for getting things wrong. In doing this it is important that we find out what are the things that function as rewards for individuals, and that we do not assume that these are the same for everyone. We also highlight issues surrounding schedules of reinforcement.

Positive programming

A number of staff or carer skills are discussed here including Discrete Trial Compliance Training (Koegel *et al.*, 1977), an effective and non-aversive way of getting compliance for practising skills, and Functional Communication Training (Carr and Durand, 1985) which is an approach that teaches people an appropriate way to communicate the preference or demand expressed by the challenging behaviour.

At this stage participants are also introduced to the procedures of 'thank you for saying "no" ' and 'I'll come back soon and ask again' (Kushlick, 1988). This is very helpful in allowing staff to back off appropriately from a request to a client who says or indicates 'no'. Staff who have been told 'no!' can then get on with other tasks before going back to try another way with the client. Without such a procedure, carers tend to feel very rejected by the person's refusal. They may tell themselves catastrophic things about their having 'no power' or 'a low value', and about being 'manipulated'. They may then express these beliefs and engage in nagging, over-prompting, abuse or avoidance of the client.

Within this section participants also learn to value high frustration tolerance referred to earlier. That is, the carer will at first respond immediately to the client's want or not want only because at that stage the evidence is that the client is unable to respond appropriately to the frustration of not getting what they want immediately. However, it is the medium- and long-term aim to teach the client the skill of tolerating frustration for longer periods, without escalating. Staff and parents will therefore be supported in gradually increasing the delay in responding to the client's requests. In relation to clients with conversational skills, this aim can be agreed with them. For clients without such skills, the increases in delay are arranged subtly so that they are not noticed by the client.

If this strategy is to work, staff have to agree to comply by 'actively listening' to (e.g. Egan, 1986) and problem-solving around the clients' requests. This has to be done repeatedly and with great precision if the client is to learn that it works better than interacting in ways that do not involve active listening. The regular participation of clients in goal-setting and problem-solving relating to their high quality of life is a key ingredient for those clients with the skills to participate in this way. Staff who learn to 'actively listen' also have to learn the importance of accepting, without arguing, what clients express as their beliefs at that time, however unlikely these may be.

Ecological strategies

In the past most attention in this domain was focused on conditions like noise, crowding and temperature (e.g. Aiello and Thompson, 1980; Boe, 1977; Rago *et al.*, 1978). These conditions are still relevant, but more attention is now focused on the staff–parent interaction with the client, and the training is aimed at familiarising participants with these competencies. These may include the manner in which staff approach a client before making a request, whether the client's attention is negotiated before making requests or giving instructions, the clarity and tone of the instruction, whether the person repeats the instruction several times (nags), whether and how prompts are given, how client successes are rewarded, how clients' requests are responded to, how carers respond to the client's non-compliance.

Reactive strategies

These are procedures aimed at limiting damage to the client and others, and returning the client to agreed high quality of life activities as soon as possible. Reactive procedures are needed to keep people safe when challenges occur until the other components of the overall package begin to render challenging behaviour less relevant as a form of communication. Indeed, we believe that parental and staff credibility in the skills of an outside consultant who uses a non-aversive, constructional approach is seriously reduced if the consultant fails to address the vital issue of 'What do we do that is acceptable (and will not result in our being disciplined) to keep safe when the challenging behaviour occurs?' On the other hand, experience shows that staff and parents who have got agreed, safe and well-practised reactive procedures (preferably agreed and role-played with the client), will work creatively and lovingly, despite the persistence of challenging behaviours over long periods.

Reactive procedures are taught in the form of a hierarchy from the least intrusive to the most. The most valuable by far, particularly in relation to people who have some conversational or verbal receptive and expressive skills, is active listening (Egan, 1986). Simply listening to the person can diffuse difficult situations and allows jointly prioritising clarified issues in a way that can lead to creative problem-solving. Where this fails or is not applicable other strategies are needed. These include ignoring or diverting to high quality living activities, stimulus change and blocking to limit the impact of physical violence. Where other methods fail restraint and relocation may be needed. All of these procedures are better designed individually for (and wherever possible with) the client during emotionally 'cold' periods of calm discussion. They had better be practised, with feedback, regularly in role-plays, if they are to be used effectively when emotionally 'hot' situations arise.

Setbacks

We ensure that our trainees will also have strategies for coping with 'set-backs'. The aim in this work is not to eliminate setbacks, but to monitor them systematically, and to use the data to modify the procedures used. Indeed, the most important component of the workshop is to communicate the value of accepting the data of the situation in relation to the high quality life of staff, parents and client just as it is at any time, and working energetically and creatively at nearly all times towards high quality lives despite the severe challenging behaviours. In this context, setbacks, although always healthily uncomfortable, had better be viewed as useful data indicating that changes are needed to prevent damage, and to enable a high quality of life to be attained. Another way of putting this is that setbacks illustrate that the strategies being followed do not work. The challenge to staff is to describe what will happen in that situation if the strategy works and to set about problem-solving to find ways of making things work.

The A-B-C of emotions

The next part of the workshop addresses the ways staff, parents and some clients with sufficient verbal skills can apply rational-emotive procedures to help the task of working creatively for a high quality of life as calmly and effectively as possible. This is developed through the 'birthday exercise'. The aims of the exercise are:

1 to help participants to distinguish feelings from beliefs;
2 to identify and name negative and positive feelings;
3 to clarify that there are healthy and good negative feelings that protect us through highlighting situations in which we are not getting what we want or getting what we do not want;
4 to distinguish healthy negative feelings which help us to defend and expand our high quality of life and that of those we care about, from unhealthy negative feelings which help us to destroy and sabotage high quality life goals.

The birthday exercise

First we ask participants to rate their own feelings as they are at that point in time. They are told, 'Rate yourself zero if you are feeling such that you are considering suicide as a solution to your problems. Rate yourself 10 if you are feeling so energised that you are looking forward to making this workshop/ session the best you have ever created'. We then ask some participants to volunteer their score and the reasons for this. Their responses usually illustrate the A-C theory of emotions; that events cause the emotional consequence. For example, someone may say, 'My score is two, the baby didn't sleep last night, my partner was in a foul mood at breakfast, the car didn't start for an hour and the credit card account shows we owe £500'. We point out that if the events (the As) are the cause of the feeling (the Cs), then until the events are changed, the feeling (C) would not change. However, most people experience that their score does indeed change during the day even though the As remain the same.

Participants are then introduced to the cognitive A-B-C theory. There are still activating events and emotional consequences. However, between 'A' and 'C' we now consider our beliefs (B) or thoughts about 'A' or 'C'. At its simplest level this theory suggests that if one's beliefs about 'A' or 'C' are positive, one feels 'cheery' and does 'cheery' things; if one's beliefs about 'A' or 'C' are negative, one feels 'yukkie' and does 'yukkie' things.

We then suggest that we test this theory out. We ask for volunteers who are told that they will be given an activating event that occurs regularly in everyone's life. The volunteers will be asked to share with the group their beliefs or thoughts in relation to this 'A'. The first volunteer is asked to give us depressed thoughts in relation to the 'A'. It is explained that depressed thinking is offered to the earliest volunteer because most people are very good at it. Indeed, participants are told that they will now be given a recipe for having a 'great depression' because if they know how to create one, they will also know how to get out of it. A second volunteer is then sought for the equally easy task of offering anxious thoughts. Participants are reassured that like depressed thinking, this too is well developed among most people. Recruiting of volunteers continues until they are also available for angry, calm, and loving.

Volunteers are told that the 'A' for the experiment is, 'It's your birthday', and they have woken up with depressed thoughts. They are then asked 'What are these thoughts?' The first volunteer may start with 'I'm a year older. I haven't done the things I had wanted to do. No one has remembered my birthday. I'm a year closer to death. I have wrinkles on my face/I am getting bald or grey'. (It is useful to stop the listing at three to make the exercise manageable). It is asserted that these beliefs will not cause depression. If at one's birthday one believes that one is other than a year older, it would be a source for serious concern. The point is made that scientifically accurate thinking supported by evidence may well be accompanied by healthy feelings of sadness. This is appropriate because this may set the occasion for healthy problem-solving. However, with only healthy sadness people will not succeed in the task of creating depression. It is asserted at this stage that additional effort will be needed for this. If no one has already offered this, we then prompt participants in the core belief leading to depression (as opposed to healthy sadness), that of global negative self-rating. Thus the accurate beliefs – people have forgotten my birthday, that I have not attained my targets, that I am now nearer death – will only lead to depression if they are linked by a common cause, that I am 'a failure, a loser, a nobody, a fool'. We suggest that this is covered by the general label of 'a worthless shit'.

Most 'depressed' beliefs follow logically from the belief, 'I am a worthless shit'. In giving the recipe for depression this can be taken as the first ingredient. The second ingredient is a response to the question, 'What is the future for us worthless shits?', with the reply, 'The future is bleak, none, hopeless'. We then ask 'How should the future be?' and the third ingredient is offered, 'It should be perfect and easy like it is for everyone else and I should get the things I want, and I should not get the things I don't want'. We add 'like it is for every one else'. This leads to the fourth ingredient: 'Poor me!' The participants then complete the sentence 'I can't . . .' with 'I can't cope' or 'I can't stand it' as the fifth ingredient. We suggest that the repetition of these five beliefs many thousands of times in all the waking hours of each day will probably be accompanied by 'yukkie' feelings labelled 'depressed'. It is also suggested that this sequence occurs because it has been reinforced by expressions of sympathy, special forms of attention, and relief from unpleasant activities that attain high quality of life, 'until the person feels better again'.

We then ask the participants to address systematically the evidence supporting or challenging the five beliefs. Participants have so far enjoyed laughing at the expression of the beliefs without examining the appropriateness of their humorous rejection of the beliefs. First they are asked if they know a 'worthless shit'. We remind participants that people who, like us, behave 'shittily some of the time' do not count. We make the point that if the rating was to be used meaningfully it would have to be applied only to humans who behave worthlessly 24 hours of the day and 365 days of the year. We suggest that fallible humans like us who try hard to be committed to such 'worthless' behaviour all of the time would, occasionally, by mistake, get something 'right' and do something 'worthy'. We suggest that the only generalisation which can, therefore, be usefully made about people is that we are all 'fallible human beings' (FHBs) who sometimes get things right and sometimes get things wrong. Most people are delighted to see themselves in this way. They are advised that as FHBs, they will continue to use global ratings of themselves and others as they have been doing (like all of us) for many years. However, if they practise the new skills from the workshop, they may do so less frequently, may not take their global ratings so seriously, and they may treat them more humorously than they have done in the past. We highlight the value of giving up the habit of giving general values or ratings to themselves and other humans.

We then take the same approach to the belief that 'the future is hopeless'. Participants quickly conclude that they and others cannot predict the future because they do not have crystal balls or time machines. They note the extent to which they are in control of vital care activities like getting up, washing up, getting dressed, eating, going to work. These are activities that are more valuable if performed in difficult circumstances. They are also helped to see that the things they have gained in their own high quality lives have been attained by their own work and efforts (sometimes supported by others). Participants also note that the behaviour of fallible human beings other than themselves is very much more difficult to predict, let alone to control. They therefore note the folly of making their efforts to work for their or others' high quality of life dependent on whether other FHBs act lovingly to them. They note, often for the first time, that they are their own best and most reliable friends.

The belief that 'the future should be great, and that I should get everything I want and nothing that I don't want' is addressed by asking participants for evidence that this is so. The first author describes how he asks clients to look out of the window to check whether it is written in the sky that they should have a great life. It is pointed out how some depressed clients with a developed healthy sense of humour, say 'It was there but someone's rubbed it out'. The belief that, 'everyone else is having a better time than I am' is addressed by asking what evidence would be required to support it. It is agreed that a telephone or door-to-door survey is required but that this is not often done by people who feel depressed.

If we take the depressed thoughts and feelings that we have on our birthday seriously, how does this affect our behaviour? The first volunteer is asked: 'If you were energetically rehearsing the five beliefs that lead to depression, which room of the house would you be in?' The volunteer generally replies 'In my bedroom. I would probably be in bed looking very gloomy'. In reply to the question 'And how would the bedroom look if these thoughts have been practised for several weeks?', the person generally replies, 'The curtains would be drawn; the floor would be covered with dirty clothes, unwashed cups and plates, filled ashtrays, empty beer cans or other containers of alcohol, unopened mail and unread newspapers'. Asked what arrangements they have made about their birthday, volunteers shake their heads and say 'none'.

In this exercise we have begun to demonstrate the links between the beliefs and the emotional and behavioural consequences. We then proceed to carry out the same process for anxious, angry, calm and loving thoughts. This chapter does not allow enough space to describe these in the same detail as we have for depressive thoughts. However, we summarise some points of these discussions below.

For 'anxious' thoughts the prompt is given that anxious thinking is generally about the terrible things that will happen today in relation to my birthday. The person starts listing things like 'No one will turn up', 'I will not have enough food'. We point out that expert panickers can catastrophise in both directions. For example, 'Either no one will turn up or there will be droves of people', 'Either there will not be enough food and drink or there will be too much'. Whatever happens, other people will discover today that 'I'm a worthless shit and I will feel very yukkie'. Participants list details of their 'yukkie' symptoms associated with panic. They note two key fears: the fear of being uncomfortable and the fear of getting depressed, discovering that they are worthless and having a 'nervous breakdown'. They note that most discomforts are not damaging and can be relieved. They note that 'nervous breakdowns' do not happen and that depression only arises out of practising depressed beliefs.

For the angry volunteer the clue is to find someone who has let them down on their birthday and to think angry thoughts about them. For example, 'Joe didn't send me a birthday card or sent me the wrong present'. The volunteer is then asked 'And what are you planning to do to Joe on Joe's birthday?'. The volunteer usually responds 'I'm not going to send him a card or I'm going to send him an inappropriate present'. The workshop leader then asks the volunteer what they will be if they do not do this, but merely send Joe a card or an appropriate present. The volunteer usually replies 'I will be a fool/ idiot/doormat/worthless shit'. The leader emphasises how the main feature of angry thinking is the need to exact revenge against the person who was at fault. It is also pointed out how the revenge is believed necessary if the person perceiving themselves as victim is to avoid becoming depressed and 'worthless'. Finally, participants are helped to see that expression of anger (calling others a worthless shit) is a very inefficient anti-depressant.

The calm volunteer generally begins with 'I feel really calm because I have everything prepared for today's celebrations; the invitations, the food and the house is organised and I can now choose to go back to sleep until I need to get up to go to work'. We challenge them 'to assume that they have the radio on and hear the weather forecast. It is that it will rain for the next two days and that they have prepared to have a barbecue in the evening'. The volunteer responds 'Oh well, we will grill the food inside'. We then challenge further 'But you also note there has been no card from your partner'. The person responds 'She probably forgot', 'But why did she forget?', 'Because she was very busy arranging other things for the party, or because she is fallible'.

The loving volunteer is first told that there are two components to loving, loving of yourself and loving of others. The person is asked to start with loving thoughts about themselves, for example, to list some of their performances during the last year about which they are proud. This generally seems to take the volunteer by surprise. We ask other participants to put their hands up if at this point they are pleased that they did not volunteer to give loving thoughts. Most raise their hands. It is suggested that we are more practised at listing 'depressed' and 'anxious' thoughts than at listing positive things that we have done.

We ask the volunteer shamelessly to list three things they have done about which they are proud, for example, to list things they have done as a parent, or as a son or daughter. We then ask the volunteer, 'Given that you have done these loving things for others during the last year, what special treat would you like to give yourself on your birthday?' We point out that while the actions of people who think depressed, anxious, or angry thoughts are boringly predictable, the performances of people who think calmly or lovingly are quite unpredictable. The volunteer might say, 'I will take the morning off' or 'I will take a long bath with scented oil' or 'I will go out and get my hair done/have a massage/buy some new clothes for myself'. We then ask the volunteer to name some people who have done nice things for them during the last year. The volunteer is then asked to list people, describe some things the person has done during the year which they have appreciated and then to describe how they can communicate this appreciation to the person today. Many people have great difficulty describing loving thoughts and feelings for themselves and others. This form of prompting helps them to express the thoughts simply and in performance terms on which they can easily act. It helps them to list ways in which they can easily express love, towards themselves or towards others, today or on any other day. For example, they can telephone, send cards, cuddle, make food for, invite out, perform chores for, send flowers. Participants are helped to see that there is no harm from the expression of loving thoughts either to oneself or to others. This active loving, which is healthy, is carefully distinguished from unhealthy demands that others express love to us. We are able to control our own thoughts and performances, but we are not able to control those of others. Therefore, if we believe that our 'worth' as humans depends on the expression of love to us by other fallible human beings, we are likely seriously to upset ourselves. On the other hand, we may healthily want or prefer others to express love toward us, and healthily feel disappointed, sad or annoyed when they do not do so. Participants are helped to see that it is particularly helpful to be able to express loving thoughts about people about whom we also have angry thoughts. This is contrasted with the belief that if we do so it would prove that we are wimps, two-faced, insincere or worthless shits.

We then draw some conclusions from the birthday exercise. We suggest that we all have the ability to think both healthy and unhealthy negative and positive thoughts about any event occurring in our lives. We can begin to use this ability in relation to the sorts of events that occur in our lives by asking participants to think in these styles about some home and work situations. Examples from home include, 'We were burgled last night', 'My son passed his driving test', 'The baby didn't sleep, the car won't start, the washing machine has broken down and the Inland Revenue want £500'. Examples from work include, 'My supervisor gives me no feedback', 'My client has kicked me on the shin for the seventh time this morning', 'My client hits her head on the wall very hard'. We also draw the conclusion that without special help we will all continue to respond to events in the same way we, and everyone else, always have. We hope this will be accepted as a very human, fallible tendency. We can make our healthy emotional pain even worse by thinking depressed, panicky or anxious thoughts about the fact that we have this pain, we can even label ourselves 'abnormal' for doing this. However, this is not compulsory! We hope that being aware of our ability to think in a variety of ways will help us to work creatively with our healthy negative thoughts through focusing on what is not working and through celebrating things that are working. Through a goal planning and prioritization process we can describe in detail what needs to be done if things are to work in a situation that has become problematic. If review shows they are now working then this can be celebrated, if it is not working then this can be accompanied by healthy negative feelings and set the occasion for trying another way.

CONCLUSIONS

The approach described here is best seen as the beginning of a process of continuing personal development. As in other forms of personal development staff, carer and client skills will accelerate with more precision if it takes place in the context of individual or group supervision. We note that without special help and attention we are all likely, intuitively, to respond to events in ways that we have practised and are now good at. It is valuable to accept this fallible tendency of all humans with full creative awareness. The first author has at least seven years of experience applying these approaches alongside staff and carers whose clients have severe, moderate, mild and no learning disabilities. Many of these clients have presented severely aggressive behaviour to staff and clients or have damaged themselves seriously. Even when challenges continue over a long period, carers supported in this model may value learning to become aware of and to accept their own feelings and beliefs about their clients when they (the carers) get things wrong. They can also learn how to avoid escalating the challenges, respond better to the early communications, how to design and get clients' agreements in practising new and more effective ways of communicating their feelings, 'wants' and 'not wants', and how they can create more positive opportunities for high quality living for the client and themselves, despite the expression of severe challenging behaviour some of the time.

Learning new approaches is always uncomfortable. Like clients who present challenges, professionals also feel more comfortable using ineffective but well-practised approaches. Like clients, they feel comfortable with new approaches only when they begin to get better results from using them than from their current approaches. In the early stages of applying new approaches staff, carers and clients may experience 'cognitive dissonance' (Festinger, 1957): That is they may believe new approaches are right, but feel uncomfortable about applying them. This is likely to continue until the results they get from applying the new approaches work better for them and their clients than do the old approaches. A key aim for individual and group supervision is, therefore, to support new learners through this phase and to help them to avoid giving up too early. The key indicators that things are working will arise from well-kept data on what is effective for the individual concerned and whether it is being attained better with the new methods.

There are a number of ways forward with this work. Training and support with care staff working with people with learning disabilities and challenging behaviour often focuses on the non-verbal behaviour of the client and carers. However, staff values, beliefs and ideologies have been acknowledged as important issues to be addressed by service (Emerson *et al.*, 1994b). The training described here addresses these issues, in relation to staff, carers and clients from a coherent and well-established theoretical base. There is a need for properly documented and systematic evaluation of the effect of introducing a cognitive-behavioural component into such training. The first author has applied these approaches with carers and clients who have psychiatric and medical problems as well as challenging behaviour. They have potential for use with carers and clients with a range of ages, disabilities and challenges.

This chapter has described a comprehensive and innovative approach that introduces into training in constructional behavioural methods a consideration of our own and our clients' responses to events at a cognitive-behavioural level. The approach offers an overall direction within which to view our lives and work with people with learning disabilities and challenging behaviour. The implications of this approach are important. Much of our current service and research practice views disabled people as 'abnormal' and as presenting unique 'problems' or 'burdens' to the 'normal' carers, family members and professionals. This frequently leads to 'solutions' involving mainly changing the behaviour of the disabled person to make it less stressful to the carer. However, in supporting carers and celebrating their emotional and cognitive responses to their work we can create services where we can enjoy supporting our own development in designing effective environments which enable people with a wide range of different behaviours to live together creatively and safely. In this way we can work with people with learning disabilities and challenging behaviour whilst working towards high quality lives for them and for ourselves. This is a demanding but worthwhile goal.

REFERENCES

Aiello, J.R., and Thompson, D.E. (1980) Personal space, crowding and spatial behaviour in a cultural context. In I. Atman, A. Rapoport and J.F. Wohlwill (eds), *Human Behavior and Environment*. New York: Plenum Press.

Bijou, S.W., Peterson, R.F. and Ault, M.H. (1968) A method to integrate descriptive and experimental field studies at the level of data and empirical concepts. *Journal of Applied Behavior Analysis*, 1, 175–91.

Bijou, S. and Baer, D.M. (1961) *Child Development*, Vol. 1. A Systematic and Empirical Theory. New York: Appleton-Century-Crofts.

Boe, R.B. (1977) Ecological procedures for the reduction of aggression in a residential setting. *Mental Retardation*, **15**, 25–8.

Carr, E.G. (1988) Functional equivalence as a mechanism of response generalisation. In R.H. Horner, G. Dunlap and R.L. Koegel (eds), *Generalization and Maintenance: Lifestyle Changes in Applied Settings*. Baltimore: Paul H. Brookes.

Carr, E.G. and Durand, V.M. (1985) Reducing behavior problems through functional communication training. *Journal of Applied Behavior Analysis*, **18**, 111–26.

Dagnan, D., Trower, P. and Smith, R. (1996) Staff responses to challenging behaviour. Paper presented at the Division of Clinical Psychology Annual Conference, Brighton.

Dagnan, D.J., Look, R., Ruddick, L. and Jones, J. (1995) Changes in the quality of life of people with learning disabilities who moved from hospital to live in community-based homes. *International Journal of Rehabilitation Research*, **18**, 115–22.

Egan, G. (1986) *The Skilled Helper: A Systematic Approach to Effective Helping*. Pacific Grove, NY: Brookes/Coles.

Ellis, A. (1962) *Reason and Emotion in Psychotherapy*. Secaucus, NJ: Citadel Press (rev. edn 1994, Carol Publishing Group).

Ellis, A. and Harper, R.A. (1975) *A New Guide to Rational Living*. Hollywood: Wiltshire.

Emerson, E. (1992) Self-injurious behaviour: an overview of recent trends in epidemiological and behavioural research. *Mental Handicap Research*, **5**, 49–77.

Emerson, E., Barret, S., Cummings, R., Hughes, H., McCool, C., Toogood, A. and Mansell, J. (1987) *The Special Development Team: Developing Services for People with Severe Learning Disabilities and Challenging Behaviours*. Canterbury: Institute of Social and Applied Psychology, University of Kent at Canterbury.

Emerson, E., McGill, P. and Mansell, J. (eds) (1994a) *Severe Disabilities and Challenging Behaviours*. London: Chapman & Hall.

Emerson, E., Hastings, R. and McGill, P. (1994b) Values, attitudes and service ideology. In E. Emerson, P. McGill and J. Mansell (eds), *Severe Disabilities and Challenging Behaviours*. London: Chapman & Hall.

Felce, D. and Perry, J. (1995) Quality of life: its definition and measurement. *Research in Developmental Disabilities*, **16**, 51–74.

Ferster, C.B. and Skinner, B.F. (1957) *Schedules of Reinforcement*. New York: Appleton-Century-Crofts.

Festinger, L. (1957) *A Theory of Cognitive Dissonance*. Palo Alto, CA: Stanford University Press.

Goldiamond, I. (1970) A new social imperative: positive approaches to behavior control. In M. Wertheimer (ed.), *Confrontation: Psychology and the Problems of Today*. Glenview, IL: Scott Foresman.

Goldiamond, I. (1974) Toward a constructional approach to social problems. *Behaviorism*, **2**, 1–84.

Hall, S. and Oliver, C. (1992) Differential effects of severe self-injurious behaviour on the behaviour of others. *Behavioural Psychotherapy*, **20**, 355–66.

Hastings, R. and Remington, B. (1994a) Staff behaviour and its implications for people with learning disabilities and challenging behaviours. *British Journal of Clinical Psychology*, **33**, 4423–38.

Hastings, R. and Remington, B. (1994b) Rules of engagement: towards an analysis of staff responses to challenging behaviour. *Research in Developmental Disabilities*, **15**, 279–98.

Horner, R.H., Dunlap, G., Koegel, R.L., Carr, E.G., Sailor, W., Anderson, L., Albin, R.W. and O'Neill, R.E. (1990) Towards a technology of 'non-aversive' behavioral support. *Journal of the Association for People with Severe Handicaps*, **15**, 125–32.

Jones, R.S.P. and Eayres, C.B. (eds) (1993) *Challenging Behaviour and Intellectual Disability: A Psychological Perspective*. Clevedon: BILD Publications.

Koegel, R.L., Russo, D.C. and Rincover, A. (1977) Assessing and training teachers in the generalised use of behavior modification with autistic children. *Journal of Applied Behavior Analysis*, **10**, 197–205.

Kushlick, A. (1975) Some ways of setting, monitoring and attaining objectives for services for disabled people. *British Journal of Mental Subnormality*, **21**, 84–102.

Kushlick, A. (1988) Role-play steps: part of a workshop 'Enjoying working with people who have severe challenging behaviours'. Unpublished workshop papers.

Kushlick, A., Felce, D. and Lunt, B. (1983) Monitoring the effectiveness of services for severely handicapped people: implication for managerial and professional accountability. In R. Jackson (ed.), *Wessex Studies in Special Education*, **3**, 51–92. Winchester: King Alfred's College.

La Vigna, G. and Donnellan, A. (1986) *Alternatives to Punishment: Solving Behavior Problems with Non-Aversive Strategies*. New York: Irvington.

Rago, W., Parker, R.M. and Cleland, C.C. (1978) Effect of increased space on the social behavior of institutionalized profoundly retarded male adults. *American Journal of Mental Deficiency*, **82**, 554–8.

Schalock, R.L., Keith, K.D., Hoffman, K. and Karen, O.C. (1989) Quality of life: its measurement and use. *Mental Retardation*, **27**, 25–31.

Skinner, B.F. (1953) *Science and Human Behavior*. London: Collier-Macmillan Limited.

Weiner, B. (1980) A cognitive (attribution)-emotion-action model of helping behaviour: an analysis of judgements of help giving. *Journal of Personality and Social Psychology*, **39**, 1142–62.

Weiner, B. (1985) An attributional theory of achievement motivation and emotion. *Psychological Review*, **2**, 543–71.

Willis, T.J. and La Vigna, G.W. (1989) *Problem Behavior Inventory*. California: Institute for Applied Behavior Analysis.

10 Sustaining a cognitive psychology for people with learning disabilities

John Clements

INTRODUCTION

An interest in cognitive functioning has always marked the field of learning disabilities (hardly surprising when a major requirement for admission to the diagnostic category is performance on standardised cognitive assessments). The focus of this interest has varied. Some work has targeted discovery of the underlying cognitive processes that might explain poor performance on intelligence tests; for example, short-term memory capacity, attentional processes, general processing speed. Other work has had a more remedial perspective and has sought ways to enhance learning, problem-solving and conceptual understanding; for example, enhancing the learning of discriminations, boosting the understanding of moral concepts, acquiring self-directed problem-solving strategies (see Clements 1987, Chapters 3 and 10 for a brief overview of earlier cognitive work). The background to these earlier endeavours has been general experimental and developmental psychology. Most recently the cognitive approaches for people experiencing a range of emotional and behavioural difficulties have begun to be applied to assist people with learning disabilities who experience similar problems.

Historically, the salience of cognitive perspectives in the field of pervasive learning disabilities has tended to wax and wane. It has proved difficult to define the difficulties underlying poor performance on intelligence tests as studies have generated a maze of conflicting results, and it has proved difficult to effect generalised change in cognitive functioning (Clements, 1987). Cognitive perspectives have also attracted controversy. Intelligence testing in particular was fiercely rejected as discriminating against people from non-white cultural backgrounds, as offering no help to people with learning disabilities and as limiting expectations (see, for example, Mercer, 1973). Cognitive work has tended to become identified with positions that emphasise the biological determinants of behaviour (particularly genetic) and that downplay the role of the environment. The nature–nurture debate is a recurring and often bitter controversy with a major political dimension, a point to which I will return later.

Now, with a change in psychology fashion, both experimental and applied, there is a revived interest in the cognitive functioning of people with learning disabilities and cognitive interventions to enhance that functioning. From a general psychological perspective this is as it should be. Cognitive functioning is of relevance to understanding human behaviour when set alongside other perspectives (for example, social, developmental, behavioural, neuro-psychological).

The most challenging issue is to effect cognitive change in people with learning disabilities. Yet one of the fundamentals of psychology is that past behaviour is a good guide to future behaviour. It would follow that the current rush of enthusiasm for cognitive approaches may falter in the face of the real difficulties in effecting cognitive change; and that the loss of interest in this vital area would probably be hastened by a controversy about the political implications of the 'GO COGNITIVE!' imperative.

This chapter will try to identify a number of factors that might influence the likelihood of cognitive perspectives achieving a more sustained place in both experimental and applied work for people with learning disabilities. Five issues will be considered.

THE NEED FOR A MORE COMPREHENSIVE VIEW OF COGNITION

First thoughts

Information enters the processing system through a number of channels – auditory, visual, olfactory, tactile, kinesthetic. It may be processed to a number of levels – raw experience (it feels . . .), basic categorisation (it's like . . .), extraction of symbolic meaning to a range of conceptual levels. Individuals may vary in what they attend to, how it is experienced (some people will experience colour with music, for example), the level and medium of abstraction, memory and recall, future utilisation. For example, music may be heard, responded to emotionally, similarities and repetitions noted, individual notes, chords and themes recognised, the total architecture and symbolism understood, the experience used to guide shopping or mood management behaviour (this example is chosen as most of us are disabled when it comes to extracting higher order information from musical input, although most of us hear and enjoy some forms of it and make use of our experience in everyday life. It also exemplifies a layered system where higher order analysis is not based upon verbal language). The processing of information will also vary on dimensions such as speed and degree of consciousness. There is no doubt that the cognitive functioning of human beings is dazzlingly diverse and correspondingly complex (in other words, we do not understand it very well).

Yet cognitive work in the field of learning disabilities has been extremely limited in the approaches taken to cognitive analysis and intervention. It has been heavily dominated by verbal representation of information. This is as true for experimental work as it is for intervention work and is a theme that cuts across the psychological background from which the particular cognitive approach is derived. Areas such as memory, problem-solving, self-control and cognitive therapy have all tended to focus upon verbally mediated aspects of cognition. Applied cognitive psychology has also been concerned with higher order levels of analysis (conceptual organisation, general problem-solving strategies, general interpretive strategies). It has neglected other ways of experiencing and representing the world, other ways in which information may be handled, beliefs and expectations formed and other levels of analysis. Cognitive-behaviour therapy, including many forms of self-control training, also lay strong emphasis upon consciousness as a determinant of functioning and as a vehicle for change. Finally, intervention has focused almost exclusively upon the goal of remediation, of implanting 'normal' functioning for missing or defective functioning. There has been a relative neglect of compensation or prosthesis, of finding ways around a functional difficulty which may be different from the 'normal' way but may achieve the desired outcome. If the area under consideration was motor disability, normal walking would not be the only focus of concern, mobility aids would be seen as having an important role to play.

This overselectivity in applied cognitive psychology sets limits upon how problems are defined and what constitutes intervention at the cognitive level. It produces a near guarantee of negative outcomes for many people with learning disabilities. Many will not be seen as suited at all for cognitive training or cognitive-behaviour therapy because they lack the verbal skills and understanding. Even those with reasonable language will find it hard to work in this way and if they can manage it, it may need longer for benefit to accrue (this last point is an important one, given the increasing emphasis in health care purchasing upon brief psychological interventions). Such overselectivity also neglects ways in which the cognitive functioning of people with learning disabilities is extremely sophisticated. Examples include the complex analysis of social encounters revealed by conversational analysis (Rapley and Antaki, in press), the stunning capacities of people with special mathematical, artistic or musical skills; and the pioneering work of psychotherapists such as Valerie Sinason (1992) and Nigel Beail (1995) with people who have severe/profound learning disability.

The implications of this overselectivity are twofold. The difficulties of incorporating narrowly defined cognitive approaches into helping endeavours for a large number of people with learning disabilities may create a more generalised pessimism about cognitive intervention. The exclusion of people with learning disabilities from such a mainstream perspective will add to the burden of stigma that they already bear. It will emphasise failure and draw attention to the gulf between them and 'normal people' (if by normal is meant the verbally articulate middle-class people who write and talk about cognition!).

It therefore is important, for the field of learning disabilities at least, that a broad-based conceptualisation of cognitive functioning and cognitive intervention is adopted. This allows a more generalised interest in how information is attended to and processed and the impact of a range of mediations upon feelings and behaviour. It allows a wider spectrum of interventions to be considered. It enfranchises everyone as well as more adequately representing the true complexity of human cognitive functioning. A broader base will add to the likelihood that cognitive perspectives will achieve a more sustained role in both experimental and applied work for people with learning disabilities.

Implications

One of the most profound implications of 'going cognitive' has been to reinstate the significance of people's inner worlds; how events are experienced and the sense that is made of them at whatever level. It complements the tenets of behavioural analysis: that an individual's behaviour makes sense because it achieves important personal outcomes. It adds that the behaviour also reflects a response to events which may be different from the response of others but that is none the less valid for that person.

Once the view of cognition and cognitive intervention is expanded it becomes possible to acknowledge a range of ways in which events are processed and experienced and a number of possible routes to influencing the experience of events. Whilst this book is full of examples of how to use verbally mediated cognitive interventions, there are many other possibilities. By expanding the model of cognition the possibilities of learning about people's inner worlds through non-verbal media such as art and music can be explored. These traditional therapies are commonly present in services for people with learning disabilities and commonly absent from research and mainstream psychological practice for people with learning disabilities. They emphasise that the media for experience and articulation can vary and perhaps greater dialogue would enable further exploration of their potential from both assessment and intervention perspectives. The sooner we see the brain as a whole and not just a left hemisphere the better!

A recognition of alternative processing channels and an acknowledgement of the role of compensation open up the field of adapting environmental input so that personal experience is altered. By definition people with intellectual impairment may have difficulty 'accessing' information, not just interpreting it. To take an extreme example, people with multi-sensory impairments may be unable to process information in the visual and auditory channels so that it becomes necessary to deliver information down tactile channels via a direct medium (feedback from a walking cane, for example) and a symbolic medium (for example, finger spelling). Such interventions will profoundly alter the cognitive functioning, personal experience and overt behaviour of the individual. 'Maps' can be built, sense made, expectations influenced, anxiety reduced and allocation of attention altered. In this example the long-term effect of intervention may be to alter the priorities in information processing away from internal input in favour of external input. This in turn may enhance learning and decrease self-stimulation. Of course research would be needed to demonstrate this. What is emphasised here is that an intervention that may have immediate behavioural effects may also have longer term cognitive effects of profound significance.

An additional example which relates more directly to learning (as opposed to sensory) difficulties is the TEACCH system in the field of autism (Mesibov *et al.*, 1988). Early research showed that, on psychometric testing, people with autism tend to do better on performance tasks than they do on verbal tasks (Lockyer and Rutter, 1970). Theories of autism have emphasised the verbal language and communication difficulties of people with autism whilst practitioners have noticed their eye for visual detail and profound difficulty in grasping concepts of time and time lapse. More recent research has identified a specific difficulty in extracting social meaning from incoming stimuli (Baron-Cohen, 1989). This clearly makes it very difficult to function in a world guided by social rules. The autobiographies of people with autism have confirmed these observations and illustrate graphically how differently the world can be experienced when the cognitive system operates in the way that outsiders call autistic (Grandin and Scariano, 1986; Williams, 1992) .

The TEACCH system grew out of some of this basic knowledge. There are many components to the total TEACCH service delivery model. However, one key element is the long-term use of visually based systems to convey information about the sequence of events in time and behavioural requirements in a variety of social situations (for example, formal teaching sessions, leisure time, employment). The visual format used is adapted to the processing capabilities of the individual (pictures, symbols, objects of reference, written words), time is represented as a concrete dimension (left to right, top to bottom) and the time span conveyed adapted to individual need (next 5 minutes, the session, this morning, today, this week, this month). To give examples, a morning's events may be represented as a sequence of pictures which are reviewed initially. At each transition point between activities the schedule is referred to again – attention is gained, the representation of the completed activity removed, turned around or ticked off and the next symbol in the sequence attended to. More detailed picture sequences may be used to guide the individual through specific task sequences. Concepts of start and finish are encouraged in school settings by having start and finish work boxes on the left and right respectively with tasks removed from the start box, completed and placed to the right in the finish box. This vehicle of communication is used throughout the day and is maintained over time (the details of application may vary over time but not the general approach). It becomes a long-term part of the living environment for the person with autism.

From a practitioner's perspective this is a powerful tool for enhancing understanding, reducing frustration and anxiety and increasing self-directed functioning. It makes it possible to set accurate expectations so that the person knows where he or she is going when getting on the bus, for instance. If this is not done fears can overwhelm (belief that the trip will involve an aversive experience) or disappointment set in (belief that the trip will incorporate a favourite hobby which does not then occur). With this system it becomes possible to manage better sudden changes in routine (for example, the bus breaks down so that swimming is no longer possible), changes that often generate tremendous anger or anxiety for people with autism. With such a system it becomes possible to communicate about an important personal issue, such as the number of sleeps before next going home. This approach also makes it easier for the individual to guide his or her own behaviour without personal prompting and facilitates the often difficult issue of making choices (that is, it assists self-management, an important goal in many cognitive-behavioural interventions).

The emphasis upon visual media reflects the understanding that people with autism are often better able to analyse information presented in the visual medium than information presented in spoken language. Visual media can also be permanently present and this reduces the speed requirements on information processing as the information can be handled at a pace controlled by the individual (in marked contrast to the situation where information comes from the speech of another). Such an approach reduces the social input which can be distracting for people with autism. The very concrete nature of the system reflects our understanding that people with autism have difficulty deriving abstract concepts and need more direct information to assist social functioning. Overall the system compensates for a number of processing difficulties for which there is no remedy at the present time. The TEACCH approach affects general understanding, beliefs and expectations. It is a cognitive approach but not cognitive-behavioural therapy 'as we know it'. It does not cure autism, it does not work for everyone who has this label, and it can take a long time for some people to grasp the system. But it does illustrate a way of intervening in the cognitive system that falls outside the traditional psychological approaches, although one which is very prominent in everyday life (timetables, to-do lists, DIY manuals, advent calendars, universal road and airport signs).

Once the field of cognition is opened up in this way many intriguing possibilities emerge. For example, could music or olfactory inputs be used to build understanding and memory? Could photographs and videos provide memories of pleasurable experiences to assist those people whose cognitive biases mean that they are prone to recall only aversive experiences, with consequent impact upon their emotional well-being and behavioural functioning? A recent parental report illustrated the use of video to effect change in communicative competence that appeared otherwise stuck (Zihni and Zihni, 1995). Are there ways of building understanding of higher order concepts by more systematic associations with non-linguistic input? In a recent discussion, a parent described how he had systematically responded to being pinched by his non-speaking autistic son with a sharp intake of breath which was also used when the son hurt himself (non-verbal equivalent of an explanation?). This caused laughter for 18 months followed by the first clear evidence of self-control: the son hesitated before pinching and reduced the intensity and persistence of the pinches. Of course, some of these phenomena are well known and there are always any number of explanations for anecdotal findings. The examples given also illustrate behavioural change with no independent evidence of cognitive change.

However, the point at issue here is that once cognitive processing is put in a broader context many possibilities are opened up for accessing personal worlds and for influencing cognitive functioning. Whether such possibilities are realised only time and research will show. But if the field of cognition in learning disabilities is to survive it may be important for it to be broadly based. It will also be important to develop improved assessment techniques so that interventions can be tailored better to need.

THE NEED FOR IMPROVED ASSESSMENT TECHNIQUES

Cognitive intervention practice has tended to run ahead of assessment. Innovative practitioners find ways of influencing cognitive functioning without detailed assessment methodologies and rational intervention decisions. As in any pioneering phase, the initial excitement comes from people trying things out and finding that some of them work for some people some of the time; and occasionally something quite spectacular happens. To consolidate development it will be important for the area of assessment to catch up with the field of intervention, a point explicitly recognised in the organisation of this book.

The history of behavioural work is informative in this respect. The 'suck it and see' world of behaviour modification by contingency management stalled in the mid-1970s. Behavioural work has flowered again after renewed interest in functional analysis which has led to the development of assessment methodologies and to newer forms of environmental intervention (see, for example, Carr and Durand 1985; O'Neill *et al.*, 1990; Oliver, 1991, 1995). Of interest also is that this revival has included an expansion of the basic behavioural model to a broader conceptualisation of environmental influence. It has moved beyond Antecedent-Behaviour-Consequence formulations to incorporate ecological conditions (e.g. Donnellan *et al.*,1988; Zarkowska and Clements, 1994). The parallel with cognitive work is striking and suggests that to move beyond the pioneering phase there is a need not only to expand the concept of cognition but also to develop more informative assessment techniques.

Until recently little has really been achieved in terms of assessing individual cognitive processes that may be relevant to understanding individual behaviour. This situation is now beginning to change. Cognitive-behaviour therapy has made important advances in both identifying cognitive phenomena relevant to understanding human functioning and in developing approaches to assessing the relevant cognitions of individuals (see other chapters in this volume and Hawton *et al.*,1989). There have been tremendous advances in understanding developmental aspects of social and emotional cognition and some of the specific processing blocks that people with autism can experience (Dunn, 1988; Baron-Cohen, 1989; Frith, 1989; Happe, 1994). The pioneering work on 'theory of mind' has not only highlighted the presence of specific cognitive difficulties that some people may experience but has also offered some methodologies for assessing the nature and extent of these difficulties. Other developmental research has generated methodologies that facilitate people with learning disabilities reporting on their emotional state, and has begun to clarify the processes involved in the development of that which we call self-control (see, for example, Chapter 5).

However, assessment issues are both exciting and daunting. Daunting because of the lack of a clear model of human information processing in all its individual facets, one that incorporates both developmental and social-cultural influences. Exciting because, as this book illustrates, clearer ideas of relevant issues and ways in which even our limited understanding can be articulated into assessment and intervention strategies are emerging.

It is worth recalling that for all its faults and limitations the child development model has proved enormously useful in stimulating understanding and practical help for people with learning disabilities (and many others). Research on early human development has generated assessment and intervention strategies in many areas (for example, sensorimotor, perceptual, communication, social and self-care skills). Many of the most influential models of early intervention such as Portage have been built around developmental checklists that are used to generate teaching targets (Shearer and Shearer, 1972). Language intervention programmes likewise have been strongly influenced by developmental assessment and intervention strategies (Bricker, 1972; Miller and Yoder, 1974). There has also been an interesting stream of work drawing upon developmental research into relationship formation (e.g. Nind and Hewett, 1988). Whilst many of these assessment and intervention programmes are strongly behavioural, it is also clear that both cognitive and affective outcomes can and do occur.

The whole field of early intervention provides interesting examples of links between assessment and intervention, the interplay between cognitive and behavioural outcomes and the politics of applied psychology. The expressed targets of the many 'head start' programmes for children at all levels of ability were initially cognitive: to eliminate or to reduce intellectual impairment (boost IQ). Many programmes reported success in terms of accelerated rates of development. Such acceleration often proved short lived. However, long-term follow-up provides evidence of significant efficacy at both behavioural and cognitive levels, the exact mix depending upon the particular follow-up period and measures used. Significant impacts (compared to controls) are reported for variables such as school achievement and behaviour, school motivation and expectations for the self, employment and likelihood of offending (Schweinhart and Weikart, 1980; Consortium for Longitudinal

Studies, 1983; Berrueta-Clement *et al.*, 1984). Developmental assessment and intervention in early life seems to have been effective in generating long-term behavioural and cognitive changes although not the cognitive changes that were initially expected. However, the stunning achievements of some early intervention programmes were not sufficient to protect them against major cutbacks when the political and ideological climate swung sharply against social intervention.

With the advancing knowledge of developmental cognition it becomes possible to see how developmental skill checklists may be supplemented by more process-focused assessment. For example, the experimental methodologies used to explore children's social cognition (theory of mind) might be adapted to guide intervention strategies with those who have major difficulty making sense of social information. The outcome of such work remains uncertain in terms of effecting cognitive change although anecdotal information provides some encouragement. A recent paper that failed to find significant differences between autistic and non-autistic children on theory of mind tasks found that the lack of significance was due to superior performance of one half of the autistic sample. The children who attended a school whose curriculum laid strong emphasis upon interpersonal relating performed better than those who attended a school with a 'more standard' curriculum (Tager-Flusberg and Sullivan, 1994). This suggests that an environmental difference impacted at the cognitive level, although caution in interpretation is necessary given the anecdotal nature of the finding.

Another example of cognitively-focused work that closely links assessment and intervention is the pioneering work of Reuven Feuerstein (Feuerstein, 1979a, 1979b). He developed both an assessment package and a linked long-term educational strategy for general problem-solving skills in young people with learning disabilities. Although the generalised impact of Feuerstein's programme remains the subject of research, it illustrates techniques for trying to get at the underlying cognitive processes and for targeting intervention at that level, with assessment and intervention intimately linked (see also Chapter 6).

Feuerstein's work is also a reminder that, for all their limitations, traditional cognitive assessments such as developmental or intelligence tests contain elements which may help to pinpoint ways in which information is processed and judgments made (his assessment programme draws heavily upon traditional psychometric material but uses it in a more constructive way). Such assessments permit crude judgments about the relative strengths of the information-processing system in the visual and verbal domains and detailed analysis may show the level of processing in particular areas.

Whilst traditional cognitive testing and other 'static' assessment methodologies will still have a valued place, increasingly sophisticated analyses of functioning under more natural conditions also promise much. For example, the computerised analysis of event sequences to explore functional linkages between events (Repp *et al.*,1991) may not just enrich behavioural analysis but may also enable insights into areas such as ways in which attention is allocated (which stimuli get through and to what effect, for example). Techniques such as conversational analysis may access the ways in which an individual is analysing a social encounter and guiding her or his behaviour according to rules which the person could not themselves articulate (Rapley and Antaki, in press). This last example highlights the usefulness of qualitative approaches to data-gathering alongside the more traditional quantitative methods.

Thus the long-term viability of cognitive work in the field of learning disabilities requires an expanded conceptualisation of cognition, attention to compensation as well as remediation, and the development of more sophisticated assessments of cognitive functioning.

However, there are other conditions that it will be important to meet: one of which relates to the integration of cognitive approaches with other branches of psychology to provide a more holistic approach to understanding individual needs.

THE NEED FOR A MORE INTEGRATED VIEW OF PSYCHOLOGICAL FUNCTIONING

The sheer volume of information and the contingencies of academic life lead to the fragmentation of psychological knowledge into discrete branches. It seems important for applied psychology to avoid mirroring these divisions. To understand the needs of any individual it is necessary to combine sociological, social, developmental, cognitive, behavioural and neurobiological perspectives. A useful applied psychology cannot afford to be split into discrete camps, be they friendly or at war. Elsewhere it has been argued that applied psychologists need problem-solving models and job aids that help to bring together diverse perspectives and data sources (Clements, 1992; McGill, 1993). This point is reemphasised here. Cognitive contributions need to be integrated with other perspectives, to be seen as an addition to, not a replacement for, other approaches. This has implications for how applied psychologists are trained, the writing of textbooks, the design and funding of applied research and intervention programmes. Unless applied psychology can find a way of organising itself along these lines it will continue to mirror traditional academic divisions, individuals will continue to be either behavioural or cognitive or social or developmental in prominent orientation; precious time and resources will be frittered away as camps battle for turf, keeping up with developments will require taking and processing journals and textbooks by the lorry-load; no one will really know what they are going to get when they call for a psychologist; and individuals in need will receive unnecessarily limited help (to highlight but a few of the arguments!).

This point also links with the need to be clear about the concept of intervention, as this too may affect the likelihood of a sustained contribution from cognitive perspectives to applied work.

THE NEED FOR A MORE ECOLOGICAL APPROACH TO INTERVENTION

Cognitive perspectives focus upon processes and outcomes that occur internal to the individual. They have often focused upon influencing those processes and outcomes that are likewise part of the individual, things that are intrinsic and not directly related to the environment; for example, IQ, developmental level, recurrent thinking patterns applied to disparate situations. This fosters the notion that intervention at the cognitive level requires getting inside the person and 'fixing' things. The focus is the individual and the internal world, not the external environment.

Cognitive-behaviour therapy illustrates some of the tensions of this perspective. It often seeks to address in traditional one-to-one treatment formats beliefs about the self and the world which were apparently developed via social interactions in the natural environment ('upbringing'). The intervention is in an unnatural environment and focuses exclusively upon a single player. Cognitions are unearthed, challenged, adjusted and changed so that the individual can now better cope with how the world is. Intervening at the individual cognitive level becomes in some way like an immunisation, an inoculation against whatever pathogens lie out there in the environment. Such conceptualisations are often comfortable in that they offer clear solutions without troubling the social system.

However, such approaches can have very limited impact on serious human problems. Inoculations against childhood diseases may be of little value without attention to nutrition and water supply. High-yield crops will not impact upon starvation without attention to land distribution, water and energy distribution, transportation and storage systems. To put it more bluntly, what use is cognitive-behaviour therapy for a man who is violent towards women, who grew up in a home where his father beat up his mother and who himself sits in a hierarchically organised institution where men have the high-status, managerial, 'powerful' jobs and women have the low-status, caring, 'powerless' jobs? It seems vital to the long-term survival of cognitive-behavioural work in the field of learning disabilities that more ecological perspectives are taken both in relation to the origins of cognitive difficulties and in relation to the delivery of interventions. This is not to argue against individual work carried out in traditional ways: there will always be a need for this. However, as the primary vehicle for help it is inadequate and there is an urgent need to bring applied cognitive work into everyday living situations.

There are four lines to this overall argument. The first two reflect ideas about the determinants of cognitive functioning. It is clear that cognitive functioning should not be seen as something located just within the individual but as located within a broader social-cultural domain. The worlds that we live in are constructed from the dynamic interplay of forces outside the individual and the information processing of the individual. What we notice, think, feel and believe cannot be isolated from the messages pouring in via our personal histories, our social relationships, media and culture in general. Take, for example, self-esteem. Self-esteem is not something that an individual possesses but is something that an individual experiences under certain social-cultural conditions. You cannot give someone self-esteem by giving them some positive self-talk/self-evaluation skills unless that person exists within a network of relationships and activities that are valued and valuing. Positive thinking is helpful but it plays only a small part in a much bigger picture. Likewise attitudes and beliefs are commonly seen as reflecting predominant messages sustained over time and delivered by a range of media. Thus, media messages about ideal body shapes are seen as implicated in the minor anxieties that many people face about their weight and the major eating disorders such as anorexia and bulimia. Denigratory portrayal of women in pornography is attacked for maintaining general discriminatory practices by men against women and supporting more serious violent behaviours directed by men towards women. Newspapers and television have a profound effect upon the information available to people and the attitudes that they hold. In terms of assessing and intervening cognitively, it therefore becomes important to look to the environment, the messages that it conveys, the ways that it conveys them and the duration that it conveys them for.

The second line of argument for environmental intervention is derived from the more specific area of developmental psychology. There is increasing evidence that the extent to which children learn to understand their own and other people's feelings and learn to internalise rules of social behaviour is in part determined by specific aspects of parenting, including factors such as amount of warmth, discussion of feelings, willingness to compromise, use of explanations, firm and consistent boundaries, modelling of concern for others (e.g. Harris, 1994; Hay, 1994). These sustained environmental inputs, embedded within close relationships, effect changes at both the cognitive and behavioural levels. The example given here is deliberately chosen as central to many of the concerns of practitioners in the field of learning disabilities. The importance of this is emphasised by data on the relationship style with children who have disabilities where research suggests much greater likelihood of control-oriented relating which may effect short-term behavioural control but inhibit longer-term cognitive development (e.g. Beveridge and Berry, 1977; Beveridge *et al.*, 1978; Beveridge and Hurrell, 1980) .

The third line of argument for looking to the natural environment as an important arena for assessment and intervention is derived from a more historical consideration of how psychological concepts gain in applied significance. This can happen when approaches move out of the therapy room or training area and into the systems and interactions that go to make up everyday life. This classic process is exemplified in many ways. The most obvious is in applied behavioural work. Early behavioural work in the field of learning disabilities was conducted in traditional formats – individual sessions with specialist practitioners. However, once the data validated the approaches there was a rapid growth in terms of training staff and parents to use these approaches and indeed designing complete environments along behavioural lines (see Clements, 1987, Chapters 6 to 8 for brief reviews of this area). The development brought great benefits to the lives of those with disabilities and to those who live and work with them; it brought psychological principles into everyday life and thus enabled progress that is impossible under normal delivery conditions of psychological help. It also of course empowers those involved in the everyday lives of people with learning disabilities and retains their ownership of shared but often uncomfortable issues.

A similar process has been evidenced in other areas. For example, developmental psychology findings have been used to devise early intervention programmes which carry the relevant knowledge and skills into the home and day-care environments. Even in the more traditional area of psychotherapy one could argue that a major contribution of Rogerian approaches has been to identify a number of skills which appear to benefit those on the receiving end but are easily taught to a wide range of people (e.g. Egan, 1986). Approaches such as active listening and reflecting can be incorporated into more everyday social encounters thus meaning in effect that more people get help more often.

The fourth line of argument is derived from the finding that, in the field of learning disabilities, any change tends to take a long time and has a habit of not generalising across times and situations (e.g. Stokes and Baer, 1977). This also impels the drive to get interventions into everyday situations and real-world contexts.

Thus whether the argument is derived from data exploring the natural influences on cognitive functioning, the history of psychological interventions which gain social significance or the particular needs of people with long-term and pervasive disabilities, the implications are the same. Serious efficacy is only likely when cognitive assessment incorporates assessment of living environments and when cognitive intervention is implemented in a sustained way over time in the natural environment, delivered by those people who constitute the natural environment; primarily family members and paid carers. Intervention may involve consideration of general styles of relating and the incorporation of the some of the very specific techniques developed in more controlled situations. It means a transformation from problem-solving training to the problem-solving environment, from Socratic dialogue in therapy to skilled questioning in real-world problem situations, from control-oriented relationships to growth-oriented relationships. There are plenty of examples to encourage optimism about the feasibility of such an enterprise: Division TEACCH, Head Start programming, Reuven Feuerstein, the overtly cognitive work of Jordan and Powell to promote self-awareness and problem-solving in children with autism (Jordan and Powell, 1995), delinquency prevention programmes (e.g. Farrington, 1995) or general education. Whilst all such examples have a strong behavioural component, they also have cognitive components and this book, and the research literature on which it draws, illustrates many additional cognitive approaches which might be particularly relevant to the needs of people with learning disabilities (see, for example, Kushlick *et al.*'s description of cognitive-behavioural training workshops for carers in Chapter 9). In so far as cognitive approaches focus upon the individual and neglect the context, they will remain weak and variable in their impact and likely to fade in prominence. If cognitive approaches are integrated with broader spectrum social environmental interventions then a powerful synergy may be created.

Such a reconfiguration of the cognitive enterprise goes some way to meeting the charge that cognitive approaches are inherently conservative, in that they tend to emphasise intra-individual variables. However, it is a fact that vitriolic controversies regularly engulf applied psychology and can lead to the exclusion of approaches on the grounds of attributed moral rather than empirical defects (such phenomena can be seen in relation to behavioural and cognitive work in the field of learning disabilities). Conversely, approaches can be included on grounds of moral preference rather than empirical support. Thus, for an approach to be better assured of long-term survival something more than data on its constructive contribution is required. It should also be embedded within a clearly articulated value base that makes the needs of those who are the 'end users' of applied psychology a central concern. Such core values will serve to unite the helping enterprise no matter what specific form it takes. This may enable a broad-based psychology to survive without the specific approaches going to war with each other.

APPLIED PSYCHOLOGY AND THE POLITICS OF CARE

The dilemmas that this section seeks to address arise from a number of propositions:

- that the prominence of any one particular approach to psychology varies from time to time;
- that different approaches tend to battle with each other in terms of claims for significance;
- that the social acceptability of approaches to applied psychology varies in relation to factors other than just the strength of the supportive data;
- that any approach to applied psychology can be used to oppress or to liberate those to whom it is applied; and
- that human behaviour is multiply determined.

The concern is therefore to sustain a broad-based applied psychology that does not oppress those on the receiving end.

Given the emphasis in this book on cognition, I will use as a starting point some of the vulnerabilities of the cognitive movement to moral and political engulfment. As mentioned earlier 'cognitive' has often been associated with an emphasis upon individual characteristics as the source of individual variation. It focuses away from environmental issues and by implication downplays the significance of broad social and environmental intervention. Such a view will always be popular with those who disagree with any form of social spending and who would wish to exclude from participation in society all those who are not 'people like us'. Despite the warm overtones of 'therapy', the facts that cognitive-behaviour therapy emphasises verbal thinking, uses terms such as 'Socratic dialogue' and has a strong base in the headlands of white, Anglo-Saxon, Protestant academia, delivers an implicit message. This is, that to resolve human problems all that is needed is to talk things over in a civilised fashion, to learn to think a bit differently and be a little more moderate and constructive in response. Such an emphasis downplays the real dilemmas and oppressions experienced by many human beings who find themselves officially labelled as pathological in some way (Smail, 1993). It invalidates alternative perceptions of 'reality'. It offers a way out that misses some very important points and is difficult for those whose communications may not be in the preferred medium (and who will not therefore pass the selection criteria which define 'suitability for treatment').

Cognitive interventions also suggest a notion of the ideal human being: the autonomous archetype. There is a strong emphasis upon promoting some ill-defined notion of self-direction and regulation. The 'final outcome' sought appears to be the autonomous, self-contained individual living without need for others. The value systems underpinning such outcomes seem to regard dependency and supportive interrelating as defects. They sit well with the (male) philosophy of rugged individualism (Brown and Smith, 1989; Burns, 1993; Clements, Clare and Ezelle, 1995). The merging of an area of psychology with such value systems leads to a misrepresentation of human experience and of the determinants of cognitive functioning. It acts to obscure the real-world oppressions and difficulties that people face and may indeed exacerbate those feelings of alienation, oppression and failure. An emphasis upon 'change the individual not the status quo' may be comfortable politically but it is self-defeating psychologically.

This is of course not to suggest that those who work cognitively subscribe to these beliefs. It illustrates a vulnerability of cognitive psychology to a particular alignment of values and politics. It is equivalent to the vulnerability of behavioural approaches to alignment with forces of social control, of psychoanalysis to alignment with patriarchal power. There is always an interplay between psychology, social values and politics. To assure the longevity of cognitive perspectives, and indeed of any particular perspective in psychology, psychology must do more than collect the data: it must also articulate its value base and political stance and look for common cause at this level.

The question is how a broad-based, empirical, non-oppressive psychology can survive in a wicked world. The real world of human behaviour in many societies is one of oppression and exploitation. People seek for personal advantage either alone or as members of an elite, worth is judged in terms of how much one is able to control and a few personal attributes that are thought to confer advantage in the climb (things such as intelligence and good looks). This ignores the fact that most advantage is gained by chance (accidents of birth, strokes of good fortune) or gross discrimination and only rarely by individual acts of competence. People often deal with each other in violent and abusive ways, and discrimination and prejudice are rife. This social world is hierarchical and the people at the top are 'better' than the people at the bottom although in a benign form there will be platitudes about 'safety nets' and 'equal opportunities', but with little real action in this area. This is not a party political stance as the complexion of the government in power makes little difference to the social fundamentals to which I am alluding.

The values underpinning care work stand in marked contrast to those which appear to operate in mainstream society. We talk of partnership between those who use and those who provide, of according respect and value to individuals irrespective of their power and competence, and we speak of rights, of empathy and of empowerment. These things may be hard to live up to but nevertheless remain important aspirations.

The contrast is presented in gross terms to suggest that offering care to the disadvantaged and disenfranchised is not about normalisation but about creating a counter-culture; albeit on a sometimes very small scale. It aspires to offer opportunities and experiences not available in mainstream society. It is potentially revolutionary and must be recognised as having an overt political dimension. Counter-cultures may be tolerated in pluralistic societies but when those societies are under pressure, or when counter-cultures themselves become too intrusive, the dominant value system will seek to eliminate the counter-culture, whether it concerns 'new age' travellers or hero innovators (Georgiades and Phillimore, 1975).

It is when this political dimension goes unrecognised that danger accrues. It is when those engaged in caring absorb the dominant value system (with or without realisation) that things go seriously astray. This is when psychotherapists bed their patients, behaviour modification becomes assault and humiliation, cognitive psychology supports elitism and apartheid, and carers abuse the cared for. Undoubtedly this is an oversimplification but it is a way of trying to say that moral worth does not reside in any particular approach to psychology. However, in a wicked world whose ideology is essentially elitist and oppressive, unless there is a clear and sustained articulation of an alternative set of values any approach to psychology may be subverted. If subverted, its contribution may come to be wholly rejected by those seeking to help, irrespective of the data supporting its significance.

There is a need to state clearly the values that inform our work, to recognise the likelihood that these will from time to time bring us into conflict with the dominant culture and to be prepared for that. We should do this primarily by forging alliances with those who share such values, even if their interest in psychology differs from our own. There may be others who provide or who use services. Applied psychological work with the disenfranchised and disadvantaged must take an anti-establishment stance if it is not to fragment. The implications of this go beyond just a stance; there are implications for teaching, research and the organisation of those who apply psychological knowledge.

Although this argument is presented in a rather dramatic form it does seem important to look at all the conditions that will sustain a pluralist psychology, in this particular case one that includes a cognitive focus. A philosophy that sustains care defined in terms of equal opportunities, respect and enhancement will sustain a pluralist psychology but the social pressures against inclusion will always remain strong and the potential for subversion will always remain significant. Exclusion is an ever present possibility whether it is of a client or of a branch of psychology. Values must be articulated and debated and many areas of applied psychology must adopt an adversarial stance towards mainstream society and its organisations. Without this stance subversion is likely and this presents serious risks to those whom psychology seeks to assist and to psychological knowledge itself.

CONCLUSIONS

The field of cognitive-behavioural psychology has been an exciting and fashionable one of late. There are many promising avenues that can enrich our capacity to assist people with learning disabilities. These avenues are additional to those that have been opened up already by social, behavioural and developmental psychology. It has been the argument of this chapter that if this promise is to be fulfilled a number of conditions need to be met. There needs to be:

- a broader definition of the cognitive domain;
- an emphasis upon compensation as well as remediation;
- improvements in assessment techniques;
- the integration of cognitive psychology with other perspectives;
- a clearer articulation of the social-environmental influences over cognition;
- the development of longitudinal programmes in everyday environments;
- a clear articulation of the value base from which applied psychology operates;
- an adversarial stance towards mainstream social values and organisations.

Although the issues are complex many important foundations are in place and, as this book illustrates, cognitive psychology is at last beginning to realise its potential for meeting some of the needs of people with learning disabilities.

REFERENCES

Baron-Cohen, S. (1989) The autistic child's theory of mind: a case of specific developmental delay. *Journal of Child Psychology and Psychiatry*, **30**, 285–97.

Beail, N. (1995) Outcome of psychoanalysis, psychoanalytic and psychodynamic psychotherapy with people with intellectual disabilities: a review. *Changes*, **13**, 186–91.

Berrueta-Clement, J.R., Schweinhart, L.J., Barnett, W.S., Epstein, A.S. and Weikart, D.P. (1984) *Changed Lives*. Ypsilanti, MI: High/Scope.

Beveridge, M.C. and Berry, R. (1977) Observing interactions in severely mentally handicapped children. *Research in Education*, **17**, 13–22.

Beveridge, M.C. and Hurrell, P. (1980) Teachers' responses to severely mentally handicapped children's initiations in the classroom. *Journal of Child Psychology and Psychiatry*, **21**, 175–81.

Beveridge, M.C., Spencer, J. and Mittler, P. (1978) Language and social behaviour in severely educationally subnormal children. *British Journal of Social and Clinical Psychology*, **17**, 75–83.

Bricker, W.A. (1972) A systematic approach to language training. In R.L. Schiefelbusch (ed.), *Language of the Mentally Retarded*. Baltimore: University Park Press.

Brown, H. and Smith, H. (1989) Whose 'ordinary life' is it anyway? *Disability, Handicap and Society*, **4**, 105–19.

Burns, J. (1993) Invisible women – women who have learning disabilities. *The Psychologist*, **6**, 102–5.

Carr, E.G. and Durand, V.M. (1985) The social-communicative basis of severe behavior problems. In S. Reiss and R. Bootzin (eds), *Theoretical Issues in Behavior Therapy*. New York: Academic Press.

Clements, J. (1987) *Severe Learning Disability and Psychological Handicap*. Chichester: John Wiley.

Clements, J. (1992) I can't explain . . . 'challenging behaviour': towards a shared conceptual framework. *Clinical Psychology Forum*, **39**, 29–37.

Clements, J., Clare, I. and Ezelle, L. (1995) Real men, real women, real lives? Gender issues in learning disabilities and challenging behaviour. *Disability, Handicap and Society*, **10**, 425–35.

Consortium for Longitudinal Studies (1983) *As The Twig Is Bent . . . Lasting Effects of Preschool Programmes*. Hillsdale, NJ: Laurence Erlbaum.

Donnellan, A.M., La Vigna, G.W., Negri-Shoultz, N. and Sassbender, L.L. (1988) *Progress Without Punishment: Effective Approaches for Learners with Behavior Problems*. New York: Teachers College Press.

Dunn, J. (1988) *The Beginnings of Social Understanding*. Oxford: Basil Blackwell.

Egan, G. (1986) *The Skilled Helper: A Systematic Approach to Effective Helping*. Pacific Grove, NY: Brookes-Coles.

Farrington, D.P. (1995) The Twelfth Jack Tizard Memorial Lecture. The development of offending and antisocial behaviour from childhood: key findings from the Cambridge Study in Delinquent Development. *Journal of Child Psychology and Psychiatry*, **36**, 929–64.

Feuerstein, R. (1979a) *The Dynamic Assessment of Retarded Performers: The Learning Potential Assessment Device*. Baltimore: University Park Press.

Feuerstein, R. (1979b) *Instrumental Enrichment: Redevelopment of Cognitive Functions of Retarded Performers*. Baltimore: University Park Press.

Frith, U. (1989) *Autism: Explaining the Enigma*. Oxford: Basil Blackwell.

Georgiades, N.J. and Phillimore, L. (1975) The myth of the hero innovator and alternative strategies for organisational change. In C.C. Kiernan and E.P. Woodford (eds), *Behaviour Modification with the Severely Retarded*. Oxford: Elsevier: Associated Scientific Publishers.

Grandin, T. and Scariano, M. (1986). *Emergence Labelled Autistic*. Tunbridge Wells: Costello.

Happe, F. (1994) *Autism. An Introduction to Psychological Theory*. London: UCL Press.

Harris, P.L. (1994) The child's understanding of emotion: developmental change and the family environment. *Journal of Child Psychology and Psychiatry*, **35**, 3–28.

Hawton, K., Salkovskis, P.M., Kirk, J. and Clark, D.M. (eds) (1989) *Cognitive Behaviour Therapy for Psychiatric Problems: A Practical Guide*. Oxford: Oxford University Press.

Hay, D.F. (1994) Prosocial development. *Journal of Child Psychology and Psychiatry*, **35**, 29–72.

Jordan, R. and Powell, S. (1995) *Understanding and Teaching Children with Autism*. Chichester: John Wiley.

Lockyer, L. and Rutter, M. (1970) A five to fifteen year follow up of infantile psychosis: IV Patterns of cognitive ability. *British Journal of Social and Clinical Psychology*, **9**, 152–63.

McGill, P. (1993) Challenging behaviour, challenging environments and challenging needs. *Clinical Psychology Forum*, June, 14–18.

Mercer, J. (1973) *Labelling the Mentally Retarded: Clinical and Social Systems Perspectives on Mental Retardation*. Berkeley: University of California Press.

Mesibov, G.B., Schopler, E. and Hearsey, K. (1988) Structured Teaching. In E. Schopler and G.B. Mesibov (eds), *Assessment and Treatment of Behavior Problems in Autism*. New York: Plenum Press.

Miller, J. and Yoder, D. (1974) An ontogenetic language teaching for retarded children. In R.L. Schiefelbusch and L. Lloyd (eds), *Language Perspectives: Acquisition, Retardation and Intervention*. Baltimore: University Park Press.

Nind, M. and Hewett, D. (1988) Interaction as curriculum. *British Journal of Special Education*, **15**, 55–7.

Oliver, C. (1991) The application of analogue methodology to the functional analysis of challenging behaviour. In R. Remington (ed), *The Challenge of Severe Mental Handicap*. Chichester: John Wiley.

Oliver, C. (1995) Annotation: self-injurious behaviour in children with learning disabilities. Recent advances in assessment and intervention. *Journal of Child Psychology and Psychiatry*, **35**, 909–27.

O'Neill, R.E., Horner, R.H., Albin, R.W., Storey, K. and Sprague, J.R. (1990) *Functional Analysis: A Practical Assessment Guide*. Sycamore, IL: Sycamore Publishing Company.

Rapley, M. and Antaki, A. (in press) A conversation analysis of the 'acquiescence' of people with learning disabilities. *Journal of Community and Applied Social Psychology*.

Repp, A.C., Felce, D. and Karsh, K.G. (1991) The use of a portable microcomputer in the functional analysis of maladaptive behaviour. In R. Remington (ed.), *The Challenge of Severe Mental Handicap*. Chichester: John Wiley.

Schweinhart, L.J. and Weikart, D.P. (1980) *Young Children Grow Up*. Ypsilanti, MI: High/Scope.

Shearer, M.S. and Shearer, D.E. (1972) The Portage Project: a model for early childhood education. *Exceptional Children*, **39**, 210–17.

Sinason, V. (1992) *Mental Handicap and the Human Condition*. London: Free Association Books.

Smail, D. (1993) *The Origins of Unhappiness: A New Understanding of Personal Distress*. London: HarperCollins.

Stokes, T.F. and Baer, D.M. (1977) An implicit technology of generalisation. *Journal of Applied Behavior Analysis*, **10**, 349–67.

Tager-Flusberg, H., and Sullivan, K. (1994) Predicting and explaining behaviour: a comparison of autistic, mentally retarded and normal children. *Journal of Child Psychology and Psychiatry*, **35**, 1059–76.

Williams, D. (1992) *Nobody Nowhere*. New York: Doubleday.

Zarkowska, E. and Clements, J. (1994) *Problem Behaviour and People with Severe Learning Disabilities*. London: Chapman & Hall.

Zihni, F. and Zihni, F. (1995) The AZ method. *Communication*, Summer, 13–14.

Author index

Subject index